Taylor's Guides to Gardening

A Chanticleer Press Edition

Taylor's Guide to Perennials

Houghton Mifflin Company Boston

Contributors

Gordon P. DeWolf, Jr., Ph.D.
Coordinator of the Horticultural Program at Massachusetts Bay Community College in Wellesley Hills, Massachusetts, Gordon P. DeWolf revised and edited the fifth edition of *Taylor's Encyclopedia of Gardening,* upon which this guide is based. DeWolf previously served as Horticulturalist at the Arnold Arboretum at Harvard University.

Pamela Harper
General consultant for this book and its principal photographer, Pamela Harper is the coauthor of *Perennials: How to Select, Grow, and Enjoy* published by HPBooks. A well-known horticultural writer, photographer, and lecturer, her articles have appeared in such magazines as *Flower and Garden, Horticulture,* and *Pacific Horticulture.* Harper has also taken more than 80,000 photographs of plants and gardens.

Mary Ann McGourty
Author of the essay on buying perennials, Mary Ann McGourty is the proprietor of Hillside Gardens, a nursery in Norfolk, Connecticut, that specializes in uncommon perennials and perennial-garden design. She and her husband, Fred, grow some 700 kinds of perennials in their garden.

David Scheid
Editor of the gardening essays, David Scheid is the Executive Director of the United States Botanic Gardens in Washington, D.C. Previously he was Vice President for Horticulture at the New York Botanical Garden. Scheid has published articles in *Popular Mechanics* and *Garden* magazines.

Steven M. Still
The editor of the flower descriptions, Steven M. Still holds a Ph.D. in Horticulture from the University of Illinois. He is a Professor at The Ohio State University in Columbus. Still's work has appeared in *American Nurseryman, HortScience,* and other periodicals, and he is the author of the book *Herbaceous Ornamental Plants.*

Katharine Widin
Author of the essay on pests and diseases, Katharine D. Widin holds an M.S. and Ph.D. in plant pathology. Currently Widin operates a private consulting firm, Plant Health Associates, in Stillwater, Minnesota.

Based on Taylor's Encyclopedia of Gardening. Fourth Edition, copyright © 1961 by Norman Taylor, revised and edited by Gordon P. DeWolf, Jr.

Library of Congress Cataloging-in-Publication Data
Taylor's guide to perennials,
(Taylor's guides to gardening)
Based on: Taylor's encyclopedia of gardening. 4th edition. 1961.
Includes index.
1. Perennials. I. Taylor's encyclopedia of gardening. II. Title: Guide to perennials. III. Series.
SB434.T38 1986 635.9'32 85-30495
ISBN: 0-395-40448-7 (pbk.)

Prepared and produced by Chanticleer Press, Inc., New York
Cover Photograph: *Paeonia* hybrid 'Felix Crousse' by Pamela Harper
Designed by Massimo Vignelli
Color reproductions by Reprocolor International, s.r.l., Milan, Italy
Printed by Dai Nippon, Hong Kong
Typeset by American-Stratford Graphic Services, Inc.

First Edition.

DNP 15 14 13

Contents

Preface

Of all the plants that gardeners grow, perennials are the most beloved. These long-lived plants form the backbone of all gardens in temperate climates and are the encouragement of the beginning gardener and the mainstay of the advanced one. Perennials make low-maintenance flower gardens a reality, yet they offer unlimited opportunities for the gardener who wants to spend time at a hobby. Most important, the majority of our most beautiful and dependable flowers are perennials.

Experienced gardeners in England, Europe, and America have always admired and grown perennials. What has created the enormous boom in perennial-growing among all gardeners is the relatively recent introduction of container-grown plants. Where previously only a few nurseries sold perennials in any significant number, today you can find all sorts of common and unusual varieties. Moreover, since the plants are potted up and growing in containers, they are very likely to survive, without so much as a wilted leaf, when they are transplanted. With extra care, container-grown plants can even be transplanted successfully in the summer.

New gardeners, especially, should feel comfortable growing perennials. Most of these plants are hardy and good-natured—if you don't like where you put a plant, you can easily move it to a new location. More experienced growers will enjoy expanding their collection to include the many new and often improved cultivars available, and they will delight in using perennials in unusual and special ways.

All gardens have areas that are perfect for perennials—the traditional border is not their only use. Large sweeps of *Hosta* or *Hemerocallis* are handsome under trees or along walks. These low-maintenance plants serve as ground covers; at the same time, their bold foliage accentuates tall tree trunks and serves as a barrier to pedestrian traffic.

Certain plants work well as accents. A small bed of *Cyclamen* near the entrance to a house adds a cheerful touch in late fall when most other plants have stopped blooming. A clump of ornamental grass planted next to a pool or a small group of irises grown near a stone wall can add interest to an area that might otherwise seem dull. Use trial and error as you experiment with these versatile plants. After all, if you don't like the results, you can always change what you have done.

Whether you are interested in border plantings, cutting gardens, ground covers, rock gardens, bog gardens, container plantings, or gardens for sun or gardens for shade, this book will introduce you to a wonderful family of garden plants and show you how to grow them.

Acknowledgments

Steven M. Still, the editor of the flower descriptions, gratefully acknowledges the support and patience of his wife, Carolyn

McKenzie Still, and his children, Steven McKenzie, Shannon Michael, Stephanie Michelle, and Sara Maria. His thanks also go to his parents, Christina and Virgil (Mike), for nurturing his early interest in horticulture.

David Scheid, the editor of the gardening essays, extends his thanks to Thomas H. Everett for his guidance and assistance.

Robin A. Jess and Aija Sears executed the plant drawings that appear next to the color plates and the flower descriptions. Alan D. Singer provided the drawings that accompany the gardening essays. The title page illustration was contributed by Sarah Pletts, and the zone map by Paul Singer.

How to Use

Perennials are, in many ways, the most rewarding flowers. Once planted, they bloom year after year, repaying you richly for all the time and effort invested in planning and planting your garden. There is no mystery to growing perennials—all that you need to know can be found in this guide. Designed to answer the needs of both amateurs and seasoned gardeners, this book makes it easy to cultivate a garden that suits your individual tastes and needs. It can also help you identify plants that you see when you visit gardens and nurseries.

If you have never planted a garden before, you will find practical tips that will get you started and keep you going. If you have been growing perennials for years, you will discover new plants and fresh ways to use old favorites.

How This Book Is Organized

This guide contains three types of material: color plates, flower descriptions, and expert articles that guide you through every aspect of growing perennials.

Color Plates

More than 380 of the most popular and interesting perennials in cultivation today are illustrated in the color plates. Each plate is accompanied by a drawing; together, they clearly illustrate the plant's flowers and its overall shape. The plates are arranged according to color, and within each color group, by shape. Plants that are grown primarily for their foliage appear together in a separate section.

If you are a novice, browse through the color plates looking for plants that appeal to you. Even if you are unfamiliar with their common and scientific names, you will no doubt encounter many that you have seen before. To find out more about these familiar perennials, turn to the page numbers provided in the captions.

Color Key

A color key introduces the color plates and explains the variations in hue that occur within each group. For example, the group white flowers includes some flowers that appear white but may, in fact, be cream colored, pale yellow, or pale blue.

Flower Chart

The chart that begins on page 52 makes it simple to select plants that are right for you. The chart presents the most important characteristics of each flower: its hardiness zone, height, soil and light requirements, when it blooms, and its suitability as a cut flower or as a foliage plant.

Like the color plates, the flower chart is divided into six groups; within each group, the plants are arranged alphabetically by scientific name.

This Guide

Captions
The captions that accompany the color plates provide essential information at a glance: the kind of soil a plant needs, how much sunlight it can tolerate, and when it blooms. The captions also give the scientific name of the plant, its height, and the length or width of individual flowers or flower clusters. Finally, a page reference directs you to the description of your plant in the *Encyclopedia of Perennials.*

Encyclopedia of Perennials
Here you will find a full description of each flower featured in the color plates. These flower descriptions are based on the authoritative *Taylor's Encyclopedia of Gardening,* revised and updated for this guide. The descriptions are arranged alphabetically by genus and cross-referenced by page number to the color plates. If you are unfamiliar with scientific names, turn to the index on page 468 and look for your plant's common name.
Each description begins with a heading indicating the genus name, followed by the common and scientific family names. Pronunciation of the scientific name precedes a brief overview of the genus.

Genus
This section presents the general characteristics of the garden plants in the genus; the How to Grow section outlines broad growing requirements for the genus.

Species and Hybrids
After the genus description, you will find detailed information on the flowers included in the color plates and additional information about popular cultivars. Each species description includes the plant's country of origin and the zone to which it is hardy. Next to the species description, you will find a black-and-white illustration depicting the mature plant.

Gardening Articles
Written by experts, these articles explain every aspect of gardening with perennials—how to prepare the soil, when to plant, and other important cultivation information, as well as tips on designing your garden. The zone map on page 24 tells you the zone in which you live; it is important to know your zone so you can select perennials that are hardy in your particular location.
In the section on botany, beginners will learn how plants reproduce and how to identify the parts of a flower. They will discover, too, the importance of scientific names. The article on keeping records offers practical advice on keeping track of what you plant, when you plant it, and seasonal weather variations. Tips on working with cut flowers will help you become an expert in flower arranging.
The gardening calendar provides a practical schedule for monthly

maintenance activities geared to the area in which you live. Should you run into difficulty, the pest and disease chart will help you identify your problem, then cure it. Common-sense advice on buying perennials includes a list of major nurseries and seed suppliers. Finally, all the technical terms you may encounter are defined in the glossary.

Using the Color Chart
Using the chart is simple. If, for example, you live in Maryland you are in zone 7. You want to add a border of red flowers to a hedge of shrubs that grows in front of your house. The plants can't be too tall—no more than 12 inches—or they will spoil the effect made by the shrubs. You also want flowers that will bloom in summer. Turn to the section of the chart that deals with red to orange flowers. Scan the chart looking for plants that are hardy to zone 7 and summer-blooming, then find those under 12 inches in height.
Four plants may suit your needs: *Helianthemum nummularium* 'Fire Dragon', *Sedum* 'Ruby Glow', *Sedum spurium,* and *Verbena peruviana.* Since your site is in shade for part of the day, you can eliminate the helianthemum and the verbena because they require full sun. Now turn to the color plates of the two remaining plants, and read their descriptions, then choose the one that most appeals to you.

Using the Color Plates to Plan Your Garden
Perennials come in a wide array of colors, and today it is almost impossible to learn about every new cultivar that is introduced. In this guide, typical color varieties are illustrated. As you plan your garden, you can narrow your choices by referring to these typical garden plants. First, decide what colors you want in your garden and how tall the plants should be. You may, for example, design an island bed composed chiefly of warm hues—reds, yellows, and oranges. Turn to the plates that feature red to orange flowers (pages 134–151) and choose those that appeal to you and that are the right height. Follow the same procedure in selecting your yellow flowers. Once you have made your selection, turn to the corresponding flower descriptions and make sure that the plants you have chosen are hardy in your zone.
If you are unable to find exactly what you are looking for, or want a broader range of choices, turn to the other color sections and look for shapes that you like. Check the appropriate flower descriptions, which will tell you if these flowers come in the warm tones that you want for your garden.

Basic Botany

Herbaceous garden plants are divided into three groups: annuals, biennials, and perennials. These groups are based on the length of time it takes for a plant to flower and die.

Annuals
An annual completes its life cycle in one growing season. The seed, usually planted in the spring, germinates quickly. The plant blooms the same year. Just before it dies in the fall, it sets seed, which is either sown naturally (self-seeded), or collected by the gardener to be sown the following year.

Biennials
A biennial requires two years to complete its life cycle. During the first growing season, the seed is sown and germinates. The plant grows, but produces only foliage. During the second growing season, the plant flowers, and by the fall of that year it sets seed and dies. Some biennials flower sparsely the first year, with the main bloom occurring the second year. Others can be forced to bloom in a year if they are started indoors well before the last spring frost.

Perennials
Plants that bloom for more than one year are called perennials. They may last for a few years or for generations. Woody perennials include trees and shrubs. Herbaceous perennials, the ones considered in this book, include flowers and grasses, most of which die back to the ground in the winter. Although the tops of these plants are dead, their roots remain alive throughout the winter. It is through these persistent rootstocks that the plants renew themselves the following growing season.

Setting Seed
Perennials reproduce naturally both by setting seeds and by vegetative means. These methods can be used by both home gardeners and professionals to increase their stocks of perennials. Seeds can be purchased, collected from flowering plants, or exchanged with other gardeners.
In nature, the seeds of many perennials are sown naturally in the fall, and remain dormant until the spring, when they germinate. The gardener who collects seeds from flowering plants may find that some of them will not germinate in the fall while others will. In some plant species the seeds must go through a freezing cycle before they will germinate. This protective adaptation prevents the seedlings from dying when they are exposed to harsh winter conditions. If seeds that require a freezing cycle are kept cold during the winter, on the ground or in a plastic bag in the refrigerator, they will usually germinate the following spring.

Vegetative Reproduction

In nature many perennials reproduce through vegetative means—by division or layering or through the production of bulbils or offsets. You can use these same means to increase your stock of perennials. As many plants grow, they form a new crown—that part of the plant between the root and the stem, usually at soil level. To increase your stock by division, carefully dig up the plant and divide the crown.

In nature, branches of many perennials touch the ground, then become covered with soil. The branches then take root and form a new plant. The process by which the gardener imitates this form of propagation is called layering.

Bulbils are black, seedlike projections that occur at the junction of the leaves and the stem; some lilies produce bulbils. The projections are not really seeds, but miniature bulbs. When they fall to the ground, they produce new plants. If you collect bulbils late in the summer and plant them, you can increase your stock of lilies.

Offsets are short, lateral shoots that arise at or near the base of a plant. They sometimes root and form a new plant, which you can then cut away and transplant.

Scientific Names

Common names may vary from region to region or country to country, but scientific names are the same worldwide. Although some plants have common names that have been derived from their scientific names (*Iris* is one example), many, like balloon flower (*Platycodon*), do not. Scientific names are governed by an international set of rules that maintains uniformity.

The scientific name of a plant has two parts. The first part is the generic name, which tells us the genus to which the plant belongs. Within each of these groups, or genera, there are many members.

The second part of the scientific name is the specific epithet; it indicates one member, or species, within the genus. The generic name is always capitalized, while the specific epithet is rarely capitalized. They are both underlined or printed in italics.

Subspecies, Varieties, and Forms

In nature, plants of a given species frequently vary in color, size, or form. If the variation is geographical, the different populations are called subspecies; some botanists call these subspecies varieties. In some species, variations occur that are not geographical. The two variants occur together and are called forms. These designations should not be confused with the common use of the word variety, which refers to those plants that are the result of selection or breeding.

Cultivated Varieties

Plant breeders can select or breed plants for any of a wide range of characteristics such as flower size, fragrance, number of petals, leaf shape, leaf color, or plant height. Plants that are the result of selection or controlled breeding are referred to as cultivated varieties, or cultivars.

A cultivar is a race of plants that have identical characteristics (flower color, size, growth habit, and so forth) and are propagated vegetatively or from seed to maintain those characteristics. The cultivar name is indicated after the species name by single quotation marks; for example, *Achillea tomentosa* 'Nana'. This cultivar name assures you that the plant you receive will be identical to the one you chose. Cultivars are the most common types of garden perennials. If the perennial is listed as a form or variety and not as a cultivar, it is part of a naturally occurring variant and is not a cultivated garden variety.

Hybrids

Many garden plants are hybrids—crosses between species, subspecies, or even plants of different genera. These hybrids are often more resistant to disease than the original parents, or have a fragrance lost long ago in cultivation. In a scientific name, the symbol × indicates that the plant is a hybrid.

The Parts of a Flower

A typical flower is composed of four groups of parts. The outermost, the calyx, is usually green; its individual parts are called sepals. Within the calyx is the corolla, which is composed of petals and is usually colorful. Together, the calyx and corolla are termed the perianth. In some plants, the sepals and petals look alike; in others, the petals may be absent and only the sepals visible. Sometimes the sepals are colorful and resemble petals. The petals may be separate, or united to form a tube. The sepals may also be separate or joined in a tube.

Within the corolla are the stamens, the male reproductive organs. Each stamen consists of a thin filament bearing a sac-like anther that contains pollen. Inside the pollen grains are the germ cells. At the center of the flower are one or more pistils, the female reproductive organs. Each pistil consists of an ovary, a style, and a stigma. The ovary contains ovules; after pollen reaches the stigma, the ovules develop into seeds as the ovary swells and ripens into the fruit.

Symmetry

In most flowers, the petals are alike and radiate like the spokes of a wheel from a central point; such flowers are said to be radially symmetrical or regular. In some plant families, the flowers are not radially symmetrical. Instead, the flower is divisible into two equal

These drawings show the most common anatomical parts of flowers.

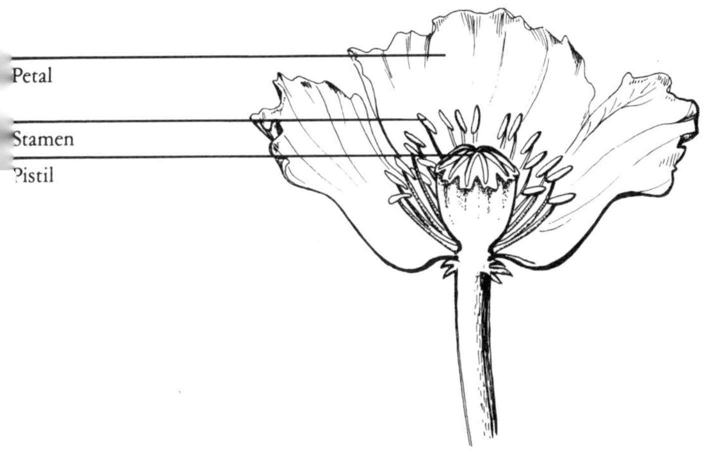

Stamen
Pistil
Corolla lobe
Throat
Corolla tube
Calyx

Involucre
Disk flowers
Ray flowers

halves along a single plane that passes through the center of the flower. Such flowers are bilaterally symmetrical or irregular.

Ray Flowers
In the daisy family (Compositae), the individual flowers are very small, and are gathered into heads that superficially resemble single flowers. Usually there are two kinds of flowers in such a composite head. At the center are disk flowers, with very rudimentary petals, while around the edges of the disk are showy ray flowers, each bearing a straplike "ray."

Flower Clusters
While many flowers are borne singly, clusters of various forms are common in some families. The most common clusters are umbels, corymbs, cymes, panicles, racemes, and spikes.

Leaves
The arrangement and form of leaves can be important in identification. If each leaf is attached at a different level along the stem, the leaves are called alternate. If they occur in pairs along the stem, they are considered opposite. If more than two are attached at the same level on the stem, they are termed whorled.

Leaves may be simple, consisting of a single blade, or compound, composed of many small leaflets, each with its own blade. If the leaflets radiate from a single point, so that they resemble fingers, the leaf is said to be palmately compound; if the leaflets are arranged along a central axis, the leaf is termed pinnately compound.

The edges, or margins, of leaves and leaflets may be lobed, toothed, or entire (that is, without lobes or teeth). The upper and lower surfaces of leaves may be smooth to hairy.

Clusters

Umbel	A flower cluster in which the individual flower stalks grow from the same point	
Corymb	A flattened cluster in which stalks grow from the axis at different points and flowers bloom from the edges toward the center	
Cyme	A branching cluster in which the flowers bloom from the center toward the edges, and in which the tip of the axis always bears a flower	
Panicle	An open flower cluster, blooming from bottom to top, and never ending in a flower	
Raceme	A long, tall cluster in which individual flowers are borne on short stalks	

Leaves

Alternate

Arranged singly along a twig or shoot, and not in whorls or opposite pairs

Opposite

Arranged along a twig or shoot in pairs, with one on each side

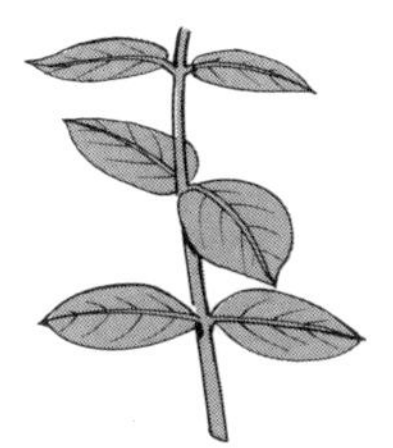

Whorled

Arranged along a twig or shoot in groups of three or more at each node

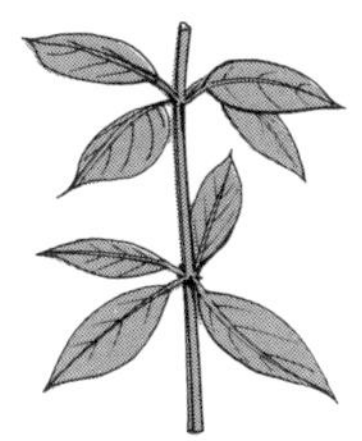

Pinnate

Having leaflets arranged in two rows along an axis

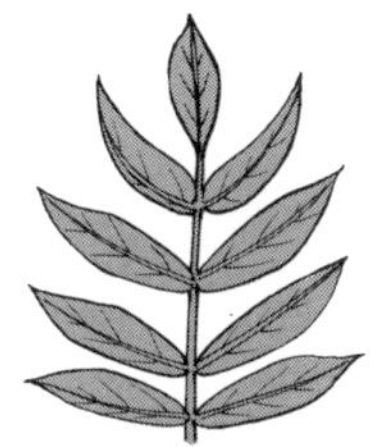

Palmate

Having leaflets arranged like the fingers on a hand, arising from a single point

Getting Started

No other plants are as versatile and offer so much variety to the gardener as perennials. No matter where you garden, in the country or the city, on a small terrace or an acre of land, in sun or in shade, a great many perennials will grow and flourish there. The key to success is to choose the right plants for your environment.

Where Does Your Garden Grow

The perennials that you plant must be able to survive in your garden, be it hot or cold, dry or wet. Some perennials are so hardy that they can survive almost anywhere; others can only live within certain temperature or humidity ranges.

Plant hardiness is based on three factors: temperature, availability of water, and soil conditions. Of these, temperature is by far the most important.

The United States Department of Agriculture has devised a map that divides the country into ten zones based on average minimum temperatures. (Refer to the map on page 24.)

These zones run from north to south and indicate the best time to plant outdoors. Zone 1 begins in northern Canada, where the average minimum temperature is −50° F. Zone 10, the southernmost zone, ends at the tip of Florida, where the average minimum temperature is 30° to 40° F. Knowing the zone in which you live is particularly useful when you buy a plant you have never grown before. If the description in this book or in a nursery catalogue contains the notation "zone 4," it means that the plant is hardy as far north as the northernmost areas of zone 4. If the note says "zones 4 to 7," it means that the plant will not grow north of zone 4 or south of zone 7.

Microclimates

Within each zone, conditions can fluctuate because of variations in temperature, rainfall, or soil type. These microclimates can occur within states, cities, or even on a small plot of land. Successful gardening is based, in part, on understanding how these variations affect your garden.

On the north side of your house, the temperature may be colder than it is elsewhere. Similarly, colder-than-normal temperatures often occur at the bottom of hills or on ground that is exposed to wind. Areas that receive plenty of sun are usually warmer than those that do not; so are areas that are protected from the wind and those that get reflected heat in the winter.

By learning to recognize the microclimates on your land, you will be able to grow a wider variety of plants than if you based all your plant choices on zone alone. At first, stick to plants that are known to be hardy in your zone. As you become accustomed to temperature variations, begin to experiment. If you live in zone 4, you may find that some plants hardy only to zone 5 survive in a warm, protected area near your house. Use common sense, too, as you select perennials. Windy sites aren't suitable for tall plants unless you stake them or provide a windbreak. Shorter, bushier plants will be easier to grow and will require less maintenance.

Sun and Shade

Unlike vegetables or annuals, which almost always need full sun, many perennials thrive in shade or partial shade. Even when perennials are said to require full sun, they usually don't need sun for the entire day. In the heat of summer, most plants require some shade to protect them from intense sunlight. In the South, this protection is especially important. If a plant gets morning sun, and then receives some shade from the shadow of a building, fence, hedge, or tree in the afternoon, it will flourish. Sun-loving plants will also thrive if they get shade during the most intense part of the day, and then late afternoon sun. They will also survive if they get filtered light throughout the day.

When you are determining how much sun a plant requires, keep latitude in mind. In the Deep South midsummer days are relatively short and the nights are long. In the far North, midsummer days are very long. This extra light can make plants grow rapidly in the North, while those in the South may grow more slowly.

Although some perennials actually prefer shade and grow beautifully in it, no plant can flower in deep shade beneath dense tree canopies or in areas where they are shadowed by buildings all day long. Either grow your plants somewhere else, or be content with ferns, or perennials such as hostas that have handsome foliage. If shade is caused by a tree, you can "limb up the tree"—cut off the lower branches and remove some of the inner branches to allow light to reach the plant. If that doesn't let enough light in, you may have to remove the tree altogether, or grow other plants.

Soil

Most perennials prefer soils that are loamy, well-drained, and high in organic matter. Many of those that do well in poor soil will grow even better in richer soil.

Soil is made up of three main components: sand, silt, and clay. These components all consist of particles; sand particles are the largest, clay the smallest. If the soil is too sandy, water will pass between the large sand particles and the soil will become dry rapidly. If the soil has too much clay, the small clay particles will trap the water, and the soil will remain wet and sticky. The ideal soil contains some sand, some clay, and some silt.

The Role of Organic Matter

Good soil also contains organic matter—humus, rotted leaves or plants, or composted material. This organic matter acts like a sponge to help the soil retain water and nutrients, yet allows adequate air to pass to the roots of the plants. Organic matter also activates

Hardiness Zone Map

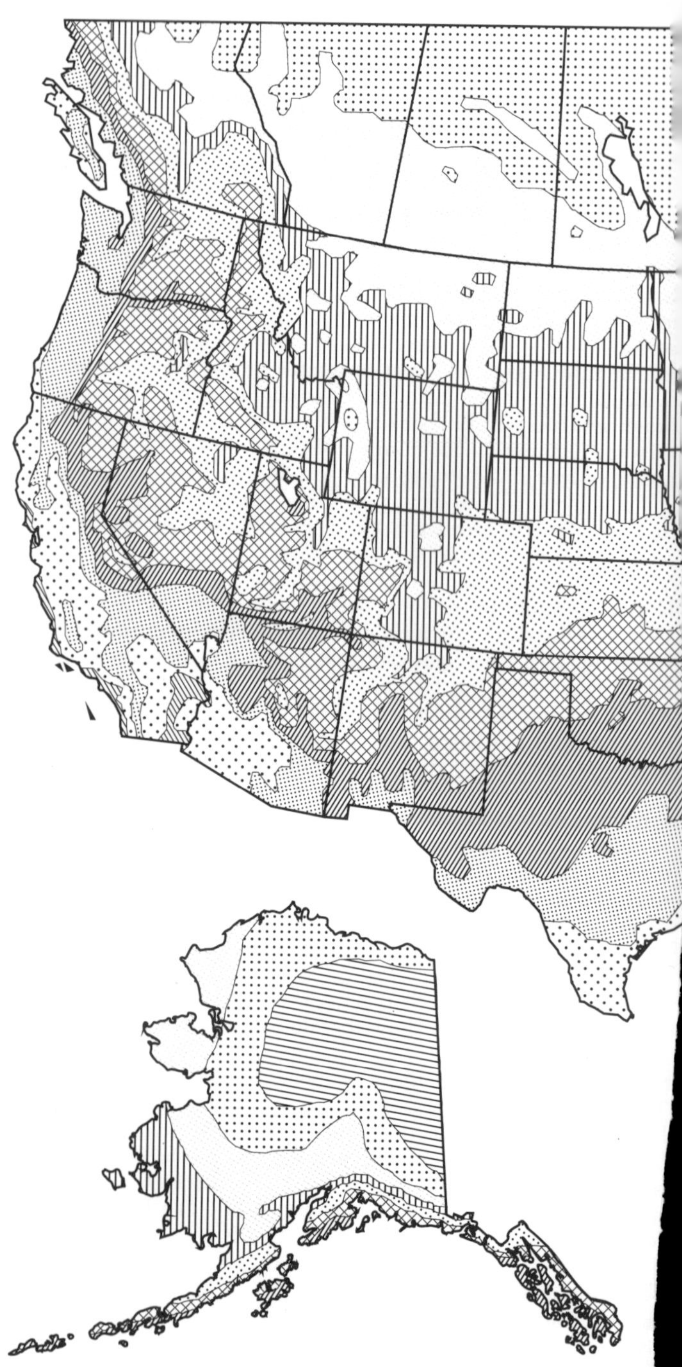

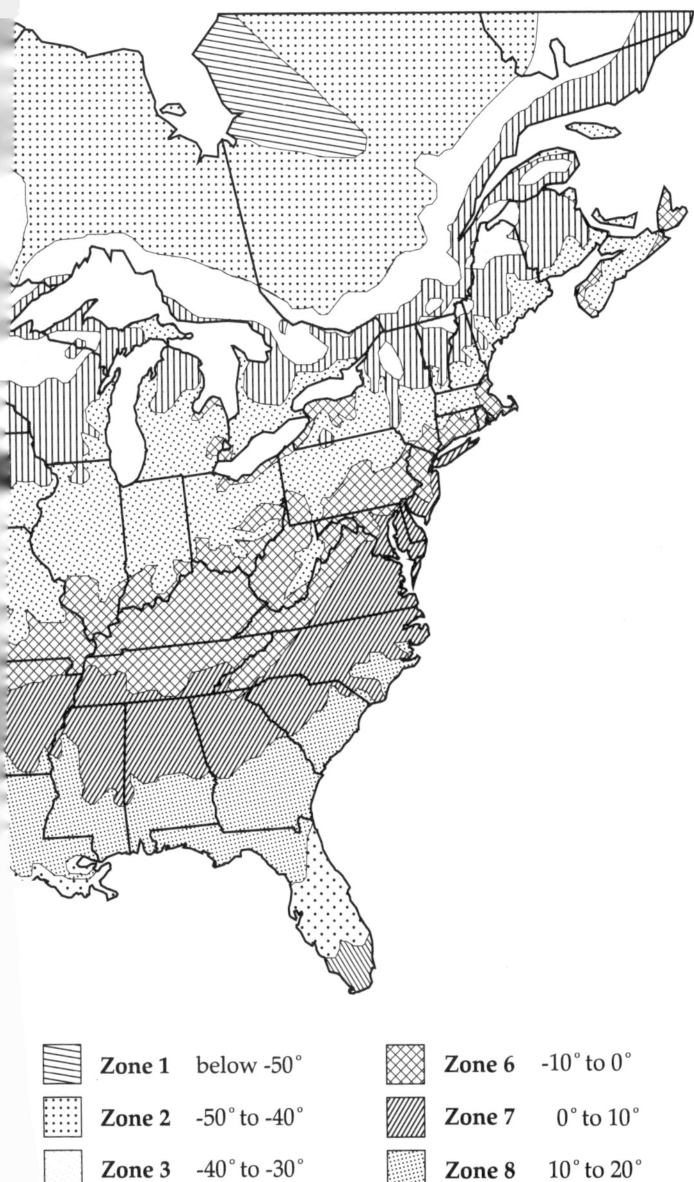
Zone 1 below -50°
Zone 2 -50° to -40°
Zone 3 -40° to -30°
Zone 4 -30° to -20°
Zone 5 -20° to -10°
Zone 6 -10° to 0°
Zone 7 0° to 10°
Zone 8 10° to 20°
Zone 9 20° to 30°
Zone 10 30° to 40°
Zone 11 above 40°

organisms in the soil that break down soil particles and fertilizers to release plant nutrients. It is easy to add organic matter to soil. Peat moss, which is actually the decomposed remains of various mosses, is most commonly used. Avoid using very fine peat moss, however, because it decomposes rapidly. Rotted leaves and composted garden wastes are also good sources of organic matter.

pH Levels

A soil's pH level measures its level of acidity or alkalinity, factors that influence the uptake of secondary and micro-nutrients such as iron, calcium, manganese, zinc, and copper. pH is rated on a scale from 1 to 14, with 7 representing a neutral level, the level of pure water. The lower numbers indicate acidity, the higher ones alkalinity.

Although perennials are not overly fussy, most prefer a slightly acidic to neutral soil (a pH level of 5.5 to 7.5). Where you live can help determine the pH level of your soil. If you live in the East and have oak trees, azaleas, and rhododendrons on your property, you have acidic soil and probably should add lime to it. If you live in an area that has a good deal of limestone, such as much of the Midwest, your soil is alkaline. Use the agricultural grade of sulfur to make your soil more acid. Adding a generous amount of sphagnum moss to the soil will also make it slighty more acidic.

To discover the pH level of your soil, either buy a simple soil test kit or send a soil sample to a local soil test lab. Most of these labs are associated with land-grant universities or with the Cooperative Extension Service. The test lab will analyze your soil and tell you what additives you need to grow the plants you want to grow.

Fertilizer

A complete fertilizer contains nitrogen, phosphorus, and potassium. The amounts of each of these elements is described by the three numbers on the package; they may be 5-10-5, 10-10-10, 10-6-4, or some other formula. The first number refers to the percentage of nitrogen the fertilizer contains, the second to its phosphate, and the third to its potash.

Most perennials grown for their flowers prefer a fertilizer that is relatively low in nitrogen, because too much nitrogen encourages the growth of foliage at the cost of flowers. Fertilizer can be applied in a granular form the first time the bed is prepared, as a liquid after planting, or in time-release pellets in the spring.

Testing for Moisture

Before you begin to work the soil, you must determine how wet it is. Take a handful and squeeze it tightly. If it contains too much moisture, the soil will break into large clods, and many years will pass before the plant roots and weather action can transform the clods into a workable soil. Similarly, if it is too dry, the soil will turn to dust as you squeeze it. If you find the soil too wet to work, wait for three or four days, then test it again. If the soil is extremely dry, soak it deeply then wait for three or four days, or wait for a heavy rainfall.

Preparing the Soil

Because perennials live for many years in the same spot, it is worth the effort to prepare the soil well before you plant them. This allows plants to establish good root systems. Even if you choose to move the plants, well-prepared soil will make it easier to lift them and divide them.

To prepare a new bed, first turn the soil over to a depth of one spade (about 18 to 20 inches). Next, spread a layer of compost, peat moss, or other organic material over the soil surface. The amount of granular fertilizer you add depends upon the amount of organic matter already in the soil. If your soil is very acid you may want to add lime, again following the recommendations on the package. Since most soils in the United States are low in phosphorus, gardeners customarily add five pounds of superphosphate (0-46-0) per 100 square feet of bed. Mix the phosphorus in thoroughly, since it tends to stay where it is placed.

Incorporate the organic material, fertilizer, lime, and phosphorus into the soil by turning them in with a spade or by rototilling. Place a sprinkler on the bed for a few hours to settle the soil. Finally, rake the ground and tamp it lightly by walking across it in short steps, wearing heavy work boots or shoes.

Planting the Perennials

If you are planting a new bed, lay the plants in their pots out on the ground according to your design and move them around until you are satisfied with the arrangement. If the bed is too deep to reach across without stepping into the freshly prepared soil, place a wide board across the bed and use it as a bridge. Dig a hole for each plant using a hand trowel. Remove the plant from its pot by turning it over and hitting the bottom to loosen it—never pull it out by the stem—and set it in the hole. Firm the soil around the plant using your fingers. The plant should be one-half inch above the soil level; as it settles in, it will sink.

If you are working with an existing bed, set the plants in their pots out in the bed. Once you are satisfied with the position, mark the location, remove the plants, and dig the holes. Add organic matter and other amendments to the soil removed from the hole and incorporate your additions thoroughly. Plant as directed above.

Once the plants are in the ground, water them well with either a watering can or a hose with a water breaker. Carefully soak each plant at the base, and avoid wetting the foliage. Be sure the plants are soaked thoroughly and deeply. If the weather is hot or especially

Mulches	
Buckwheat hulls	Clean, lightweight, and easy to apply, but can blow about in areas with high winds.
Shredded hardwood bark	Easy to apply, lightweight, and resistant to wind. However, some bark may be acidic, and the size of the pieces varies.
Corncobs	Ground into small pieces, corncobs are a serviceable mulch, but not terribly attractive. This mulch is easy to apply but requires extra nitrogen as it decomposes.
Leaves	Leaves are an excellent natural mulch if they are ground up, slightly composted, and come from several different types of trees. Oak leaves tend to be acidic, maple leaves alkaline. Unshredded, the leaves will mat.
Redwood bark	An extremely rot-resistant mulch. Good looking, but expensive and often overly coarse.
Pine needles	Pine needles are attractive, but too acidic for most flowering plants. In periods of heat or drought, they are also a fire hazard.
Peat moss	An attractive mulch, but not recommended because it becomes a waterproof cover when it dries.
Sawdust	Easy to apply, but a potential fire hazard. It may also blow in the wind, and it ties up nitrogen as it decomposes.
Grass clippings	Easily available, but clippings break down rapidly. They tie up nitrogen and may burn plant crowns if applied too thickly.
Hay	Easy to apply, but susceptible to fire and wind. Hay can be mixed with leaves or similar materials to provide a better mulch.
Wood chips	Chips can vary in coarseness and they require extra nitrogen as they decompose.
Rotted manure or half-rotted compost	Both are excellent mulches that also provide food for the plants.

dry, water the plants regularly until they are established and new growth begins.

Mulching

Mulch helps plants by conserving soil moisture, suppressing weeds, and keeping the root zone cooler than the air temperature. Mulching also saves work by reducing the need for manual cultivation. Apply the mulch thickly—it will mat down—but keep it away from plant crowns where it may encourage damage from diseases and slugs.

When you are choosing the kind of mulch you will use, consider several factors: availability, cost, appearance, and durability. Also determine the acidity of the mulch, which will affect the soil, and whether or not it is a potential fire hazard. Finally, make sure it is free of weeds and diseases. Organic materials are preferable to those that are inorganic because they benefit the soil.

Maintaining the Perennial Bed

Weeding is a chore no gardener can avoid. You can make the job less time-consuming, however, if you catch weeds when they are young. Left alone to grow, flower, and set seed, weeds will become worse with each passing year. Adding a layer of mulch to the perennial bed also helps to keep weeds in check.

Most plants appreciate an application of fertilizer when they are in bud. Use one that has a low nitrogen content (the first number of the three on the bag) to avoid the production of excess foliage, which can limit the number of flower buds that will blossom.

Water

In the heat of the summer, and through periods of drought, water your plants regularly. Soak them to a reasonable depth, taking care to avoid getting the foliage wet. Light waterings, no matter how frequent, are of little value and may do more harm than good by causing the feeder roots to grow near the surface. Recently transplanted seedlings may require watering three or more times a day when the weather is dry and windy.

Staking

Some perennials produce many small stems that tend to flop over if they aren't staked. These include *Achillea* and *Coreopsis.* Other perennials, such as *Delphinium* and *Digitalis,* are very tall and need support to protect them from the wind. Those with small stems are easily supported by the use of "pea stakes," twiggy branches two to three feet long. You can cut these in the winter from trees on your property. As the plant begins to grow in the spring, insert the stakes in the ground around the plant, taking care not to damage the crown. As the plant grows, the twigginess of the stakes will support the growth and the bushiness of the plant will hide the stakes. The result is a plant that appears to support itself naturally.

For plants that need support because they grow tall, use bamboo stakes or similar wooden poles. Insert these into the ground to a depth of one foot and tie the plant to the stake using a natural twine or twist ties. Be very sure the tie is loose; if it is placed too tight it will impede the flow of water and nutrients up the stem and seriously injure the plant.

Pinching and Disbudding

The removal of a small amount of a plant's growing tip to encourage branching or to modify flowering is known as pinching. Pinch the plants with your fingers. Plants like *Phlox* and *Chrysanthemum,* and others with many stems, require pinching to encourage branching. Pinch them once or twice in the spring, usually before the first of July so they will have time to form flower buds. Plants that are pinched are usually shorter and sturdier and produce more flowers than plants that are not. However, the flowers on plants that have been pinched are generally smaller and bloom later.

Perennials such as *Delphinium* that have many stems may produce small flowers. To achieve blooms that are larger, pinch all but one stem.

Disbudding is another method used to grow larger flowers. Simply removing some of the flower buds on a plant will benefit those that are left to grow. With plants such as peonies, *Delphinium,* and *Digitalis,* secondary side buds form around the main bud. Removal of these buds encourages the remaining buds to produce larger, showier blooms. In plants like *Chrysanthemum,* you can remove the central bud instead of the side buds to produce a spray of smaller flowers.

Throughout the gardening season, faded flowers and flowering stalks should be removed. This not only improves the appearance of the garden, but helps to conserve a plant's strength as well, since seed production requires the greatest expenditure of a plant's resources. The constant removal of dead blossoms can extend the growing season of some plants. In others, cutting plants back severely will induce a second, although smaller and less vigorous, bloom. *Delphinium, Helenium,* and other early-blooming members of the Daisy family profit from this treatment. Some plants (Hollyhocks, for example) respond to a hard cutting back after flowering by producing more blooms the following year.

Fall Cleanup

In the autumn, before the first killing frost, clean flower beds of all dead foliage to reduce disease and eliminate areas where insects can overwinter. Don't cut back ornamental grasses, though; they will be beautiful for most of the winter.

Pinching encourages side growth. Remove a small portion of the plant's tip. As a result, your plants will be bushier and produce more flowers.

Disbudding changes the way a plant flowers. Remove side shoots for larger flowers (illustrated), or remove the main shoot for smaller, but more profuse, blooms.

After the ground has frozen, protect newly planted perennials. They are endangered not by the cold, but from alternate periods of freezing and thawing in the early spring, which can heave the plants from the ground, destroying their crowns. The best protection is a layer of evergreen boughs—old Christmas tree branches are excellent. These branches form a framework on which you can place leaves. The branches keep the plants dry and the leaves act as insulation, keeping the ground frozen during fluctuations in temperature. Place a few branches on top of the leaves to keep the leaves from blowing in the wind. Once the weather begins to warm in the spring, remove the covering.

Buying Plants

Gardeners are generous people, and perennials, which grow and multiply, help foster these generous instincts. The plants that you receive as gifts from neighboring gardeners are likely to grow well for you because they were successful in your area. They also add a sentimental dimension to your garden because you associate them with the person who gave them to you.

In the beginning, however, you'll probably buy plants and seeds, and only later learn to increase your stock by propagating your own plants. Most garden centers and nurseries carry some perennials, but you would do well to patronize a dealer who has a wide selection. Plants are also available through mail-order catalogues. If you don't know the company, judge it by the descriptions and the other information the catalogue gives on plants, not by the color photographs. These descriptions should always include the botanical name of the plant as well as its hardiness zone, and soil, sun, or shade requirements.

Examine plants that you buy at a nursery carefully to be sure they are healthy and growing. Look for signs of insects and disease, discolored foliage, misshapen flowers and distorted growth. Dormant plants are safe only if you know both the plant and the supplier; a dormant plant in June may be permanently dormant. For additional information on buying perennials, refer to the essay on page 450.

Although perennials can almost always be planted in either spring or fall, spring is best if you are buying them, because that is when the garden centers have their healthiest stock. Buy plants as early in the season as you can to give them as much time as possible to become established.

Get the plants into the ground as soon as you can. If you have to leave them in their pots, be sure to water them well. Unpack mail-order plants immediately and plant them if possible; if you cannot, pot them and put them in a cold frame or in a cool, sheltered place.

Cold Frames

If you are going to grow plants from seed or do any form of plant propagation yourself, a cold frame is a useful and versatile device. It seals out cold and admits sunlight.

Basically a cold frame is nothing more than a bottomless box with a top made of a transparent material like glass, polyethylene plastic, or fiberglass, that can be opened or removed. Cold frames are unheated and vary in size; most are 3 feet by 6 feet. Old storm windows or window sashes are often used for the top of the frame. Sheets of fiberglass or plastic film can be substituted, but the sash will have to be anchored to prevent it from blowing away in high winds. Make sure that the cover props open securely, too.

Frames can be portable or permanent. Portable frames, usually made of wood, are placed over plants in the garden or put up for use during the winter and taken down in the spring. If a permanent frame is made of wood, it should be pressure-treated lumber to prevent rot; other good materials are concrete block or brick. The back of a 3-foot by 6-foot frame is 3 feet wide and usually 20 inches high; the front is 10 inches high; and the sides are diagonally cut to connect the back and front. Because the cover is pitched at an angle, it easily sheds rain. The sash or top is hinged to the top of the back piece, and lifts from the front.

Where to Place a Cold Frame

For maximum use a frame should slope to the south to allow it to trap as much sun as possible early in the year. It should be on ground that is high enough to prevent surface water from seeping in under normal conditions. Since wind will lower the temperature inside the frame, try to place it in a protected area near a fence, a hedge, or a wall.

If you plan to grow seeds directly in the cold frame, the soil must be well drained and should have a quantity of leaf-mold or similar organic matter incorporated into it. If the plants are to be grown in pots, then line the bottom of the frame with builder's sand, fine gravel, or coal ash.

Where winters are severe, provide extra protection for the overwintering plants in the frame. Bank soil or leaves outside the frame to keep out the frost, and mulch the plants inside after the ground has frozen to prevent heaving from alternate freezing and thawing. Place reed mats, old burlap bags or blankets, or wood shutters over the sash during extreme cold to help reduce heat loss.

Ventilating the Cold Frame

As the weather begins to warm in the spring, control excess heat and humidity by admitting fresh air to the frame without creating a draft. Open the sash gradually, using a notched block or a brick set on its side under the corner of the sash. As the weather warms, slowly increase the opening. On very warm days, you can remove the sash for most of the day. The interior mulch should be removed as soon as growth begins.

The lid of a cold frame should prop open securely to three positions: slightly open, half-open, and fully open. Sink the frame into the ground or build a bank of soil part way up the sides.

Many cold frames also have rubber insulation around the inner rim.

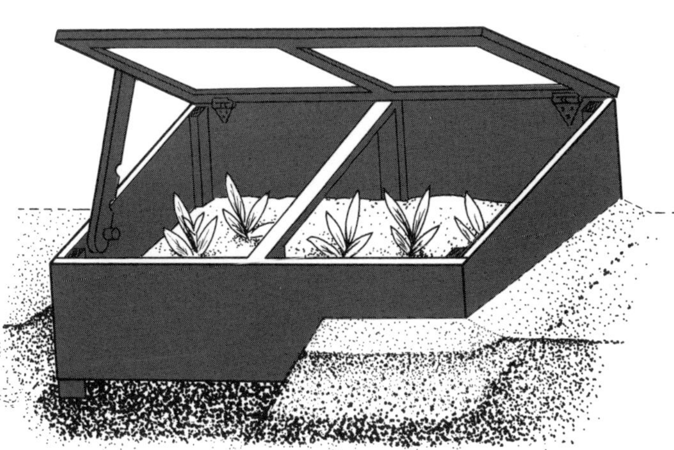

As you ventilate the frame, water the plants. Before the frame is totally opened, water the plants in the morning, just enough to keep the soil evenly moist. Once the frame is uncovered, this is not as critical.

Cold frames are also available as prefabricated units in a wide range of sizes and materials. Many of the commercial prefabricated frames have temperature-sensitive devices that open the sash automatically. These frames vary in cost. Evaluate the materials used, the quality of construction, the type of sash, and the ease of installation and use. Avoid frames that are made of thin sheet metal or similar materials that may afford little protection in the winter, or those that are very shallow.

Seeds

Raising perennials from seed for one's own garden is simple. Outdoors you can sow seeds directly into the bed or the cold frame; inside you can start them in pots or flats, then transport them to the frame or garden when the weather becomes warm. Each packet of seeds contains valuable information. On the back, it lists the proper depth at which to plant the seeds, how far apart to space them, and when to plant them, as well as any special treatment or conditions required for germination. The date on the package tells you if the seed is fresh. If the seeds are more than a year old, the percentage that germinate may be greatly reduced.

Seeds need moisture, light, and either warm or cool conditions to germinate. Those that need cool conditions can be germinated on a windowsill; those that need warmth will germinate on the top of a refrigerator. For warmth-loving plants, you can also buy special heating coils and place them in a flat of sand under the pots.

Sowing Seeds Outdoors

If you plan to sow seeds directly into a bed or cold frame, the soil should be adequately prepared. Make sure it is well drained and that it contains the proper amount of organic matter. Add sand if the drainage is not adequate, and try to choose a location with partial shade. Sow the seeds thinly and uniformly in blocks or rows and cover them with a layer of fine soil to a depth of about three times the thickness of the seed. Firm the soil lightly over the seeds and water them with a fine mist. Keep the seeds moist and remove competing weeds after the seeds have germinated, but be careful not to disturb the roots of the seedlings. Transplant the seedlings to their permanent place in the garden after they are well established. For summer-sown seeds, transplant them the following spring. If your climate is mild, they can be transplanted in the early autumn.

Starting Seeds Indoors

Indoors, sow seeds in a flat or a pot. Fill the container with a light mix of one half peat moss and one half horticultural grade perlite or vermiculite. You can substitute coarse, sharp sand for the perlite or you can buy a seed-starting mixture. Whatever you use, be sure it has been sterilized to prevent damping-off, the fungus that kills the seedlings before or shortly after they emerge.

Starting Seeds Under Fluorescent Lights

To control the light that seeds and seedlings receive, consider starting them under fluorescent lights. Under a two-tube fluorescent light fixture, consisting of 40 watts per tube, you can fit 12 six-inch pots. You should rotate the pots occasionally because the end position receives less intense light than the center. When the tiny seedlings have sprouted, transplant them.

Two 40-watt daylight-type tubes in a reflecting fixture will cast the equivalent of strong sunlight on an area of 12 by 40 inches. To use these lights properly, hang them in a cool spot, 50° to 65° F. protected from cold and drafts. Rooms that are warmer, 65° to 75° F. or more, may result in tall, spindly plants. Hang the lights so they can be lowered to within two inches of the top of seeded pots. The slight warmth and strong light from the tubes will make seedlings grow in a hurry. When the seedlings are the size of a dime, raise the lights so that they hang about six inches above the seedlings. If you start some containers late, you can still use the same light set-up by setting the new containers on empty pots. If the seedlings start to stretch and appear spindly, lower the lights and, if possible, the room temperature as well.

Hardening Off Seedlings

Tender seedlings must be acclimatized before they are set outside. They need to adjust to drying winds, cool temperatures, and sunlight.

Hardening off is simple. A week before you wish to transplant the seedlings, find a corner in an area that is protected from wind, yet open to sunlight and fluctuations in temperature. Move the transplants there. Water them twice a day if they seem to dry out rapidly. After they have been outside for three or four days, place them in a fully exposed outdoor location. Beware of cold night temperatures; if the thermometer is supposed to plunge, move them indoors.

Cold frames are ideal locations for hardening off seedlings, since their covers can be opened gradually to accustom the plants to their new environment.

Storing Leftover Seeds

Put leftover seeds in a cool, dry place. Fruit jars that have a rubber seal are ideal. Drop desiccant capsules into the jar, then add a wad of paper, then the seed packets with their tops folded over and taped down. Seal the jar and place it in a refrigerator.

Getting Started

When you start seeds under fluorescent lights, lower the chains so the light tubes are within two inches of the top of the seeded pots. Raise the lights to six inches as soon as seedlings sprout. If seedlings start to stretch, lower the lights again.

Transplanting Seedlings

Once the seeds have germinated, watch for the development of the first set of true leaves. This is the time for the young seedlings to be transplanted from the seed flat or pot to a new pot or an outdoor bed. Carefully loosen the soil around the roots of the seedlings with a small pointed stick, then lift the young seedling out of the flat or pot using the stick. If you must touch a seedling, hold it by a leaf, not the stem. Transplant the seedling to its new location and firm the soil around the roots to close up any air pockets. Water it very carefully after transplanting. Be sure to allow plenty of space between the plants as they will now begin to grow rapidly. Another method of transplanting seedlings consists of digging holes for the tiny plants, then filling the holes with water. After the water has soaked in thoroughly, add still more water. Let the water drain, then gently place the plants in the holes. This method ensures that the seedlings will have a reservoir of soil moisture when they are placed in the ground. It is especially helpful if you are working with soil that tends to shed water.

Division

In addition to sowing seeds, you can increase your stock by dividing the plants you have or by taking cuttings from them. Although herbaceous perennials vary in their root formation, the majority spread by the development of growth buds, or eyes. Each bud, although attached to the parent plant, grows independently the following season.

Propagation by division involves the separation of these growth buds to increase the number of plants. Most perennials can be divided—it is usually the simplest and quickest method of propagation for the gardener.

Plants like peonies and *Hemerocallis* have fleshy rootstocks. When you dig them out, you'll notice that the roots intertwine and that there are several growth buds on each root. Pull these roots apart gently or cut them with a knife to get several independent pieces, each with one or more growth buds. Plant the pieces in a prepared bed.

In tuberous rooted plants such as irises, the stem branches out at or below the surface of the ground. At each underground node on the stem you will find a bud and one or more roots. If the clump is large, pull the stems apart, making sure that each stem has one or more growth buds. If the clump has only one stem, cut the individual growth buds apart, making sure that each bud has one or more roots.

Perennials like *Heuchera* and *Ajuga* develop many crowns. Dig up the plant and carefully pull the crowns apart. Plants like *Physostegia* and *Aster,* which have numerous stems (each with growth buds) can also be dug up and pulled or cut apart.

To divide a clump of tangled roots, first dig the roots up, then pry them apart with two cultivating forks. Continue dividing the smaller clusters until you have the number of divisions that you want.

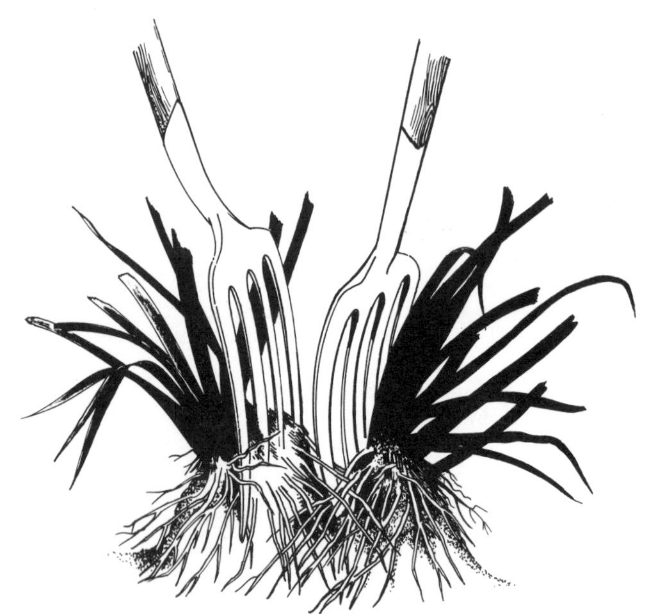

Use a sharp knife to divide tough, tuberous roots. Each clump that you separate should have one or more growth buds. When you plant the root divisions, make sure that the growth buds are one to two inches below ground.

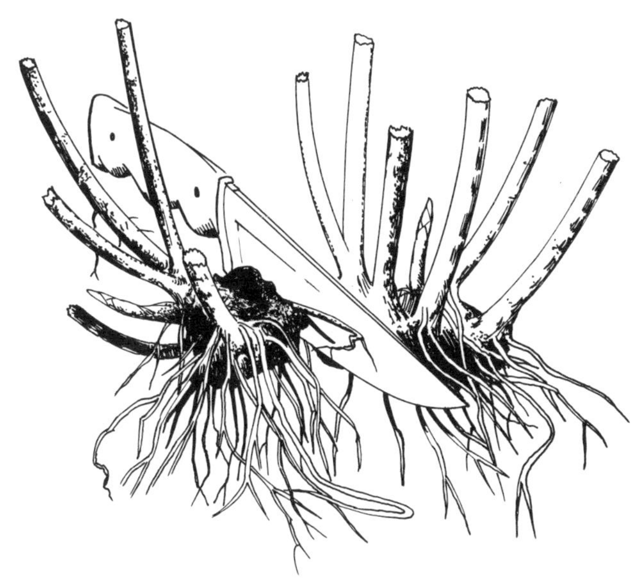

Dividing perennials not only increases the number of plants, it also rejuvenates older plants that may show signs of straggling or loss of bloom.

When to Divide Perennials

In colder areas it is better to divide plants in the spring before the foliage is two inches high. In milder climates, divide the perennials in early fall after they have finished blooming. If you are dealing with plants that are very overgrown, first cut the plant back to the ground and lift the entire clump. To separate a large clump, insert two digging forks back to back into the center and push them apart. You can also cut the plant apart with a sharp spade or an axe, or pull small clumps apart with your fingers.

After the plants are divided, treat any cut surfaces with a fungicide. Replant the divisions, taking care to place the crowns at the proper depth, and then water them. Give plants divided in the fall adequate winter protection.

Cuttings

Another method of propagating perennials is by taking stem cuttings. Plants like chrysanthemums, *Aster, Helenium,* and some others are easy to increase using this method. The plant must be in the middle of its growth cycle at the time the cuttings are made. Choose a shoot that is healthy and bears the characteristics of the parent plant. Don't take the most vigorous shoots, however, since they don't make the best cuttings. Instead, use side shoots or the less vigorous longer shoots. Your cuttings will be more successful if they have a minimum of three leaf joints. With a razor blade or sharp knife, cut the shoot one-quarter to one-half inch below a leaf or pair of leaves. The new roots will come out below the node where the stem buds are located in the axils of the leaves.

Caring for Cuttings

To keep the cuttings moist and prevent them from wilting, immediately place them in a damp towel or in a plastic bag. Fill a pot or flat with the same medium recommended below for root cuttings. Smooth the surface of the soil, taking care not to firm it, and moisten it with a fine mist of water. Insert the cuttings in rows, spacing them so their leaves barely touch. Remove the lowest leaves of the cutting and push the stem gently down; this prevents the development of air spaces around the cutting. After you have inserted all the cuttings, water them to make the planting medium firm.

After the pot or flat is filled, cover it with plastic film, using a wire frame or wooden stakes to keep the bag from touching the cuttings. Place the container in indirect light, never in sunlight. Watch for signs of discoloration or disease, and remove any plants with these symptoms. After the plants are rooted, remove the bag. You will

To propagate new perennials from stem cuttings, cut off the uppermost part of the stem just below a leaf joint, then remove the leaves at the base.

Plant the stem cuttings upright in individual pots or a bed.

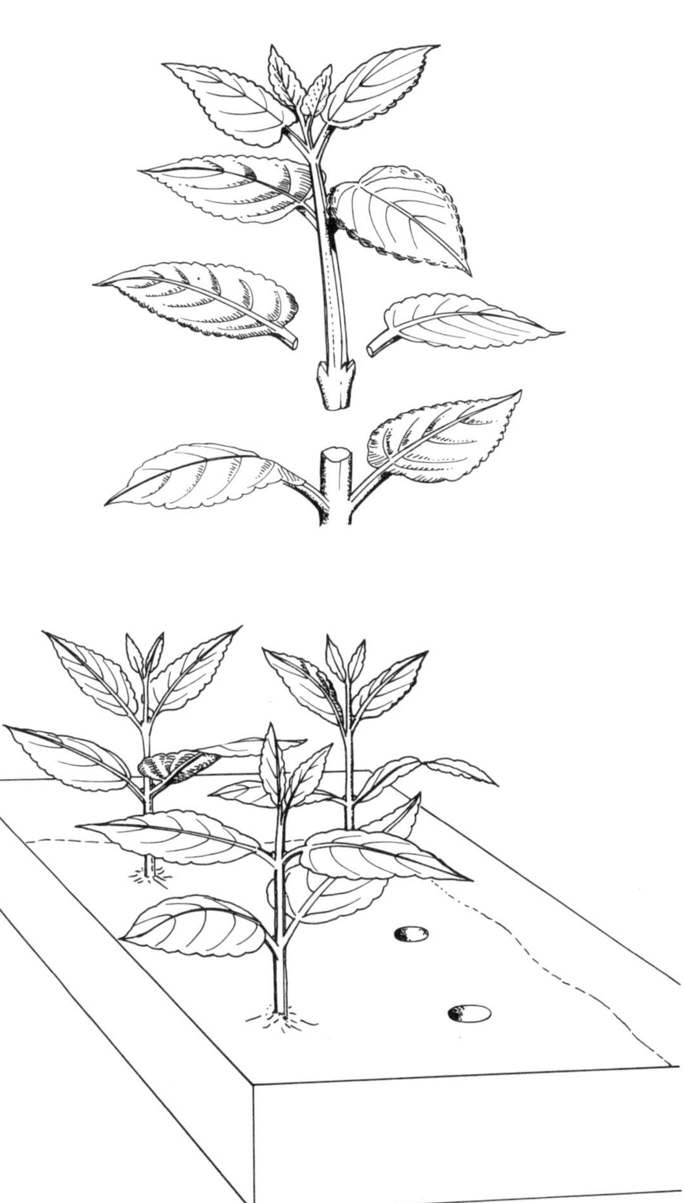

To propagate new plants from root cuttings, separate long roots from the parent plant, clean them, then cut off both ends of each root.

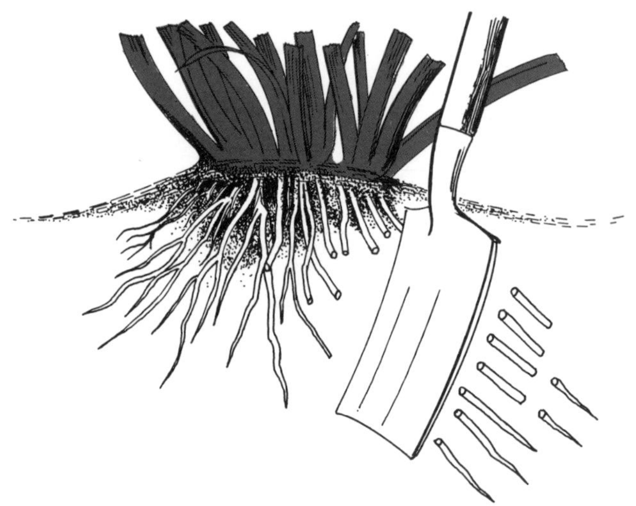

The remaining piece should be one to two inches long. If the roots are thin, place them on their side in a bed of soil, then cover them with a light application of sand or soil. Plant thicker root cuttings upright in individual pots or a bed.

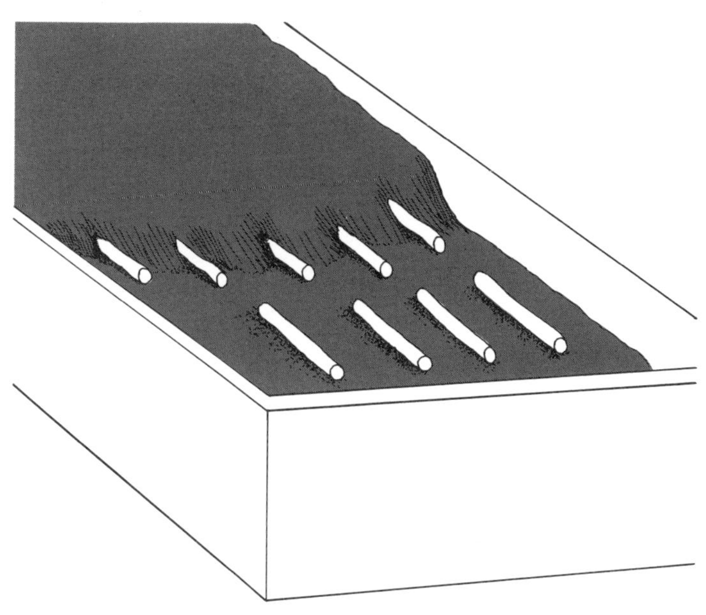

know that roots have formed when you see new growth and when the cuttings resist a gentle tug.

Root Cuttings
Poppies, anemones, and phlox can be propagated from root cuttings. Dig up the roots after the plants have finished their period of active growth (usually in midsummer) or in the fall after they have lost their foliage. Prepare a box or flat by filling it with moist sand. With a sharp knife, cut the roots into one- to two-inch pieces. Place the cuttings into the sand and put the flat or box into a cold frame or cool area. Keep the growing medium moist but not wet and check the cuttings periodically for rot. You can also line the root cuttings directly in the cold frame, spacing them far enough apart to allow adequate room for the developing plants.
Transplant the rooted cuttings into separate pots or larger containers, handling them very gently. Leave the transplanted cuttings in a shaded spot or cold frame for at least a week before putting them in the garden; in cold regions, leave the pots in a closed cold frame until all danger of frost is past. After the cuttings are in the garden, pinching out the tips will encourage strong root development.

Gardening Tools
Cheap tools can break or bend the first time you use them. Ask your dealer for the grade of tools sold to professional landscapers; they will last for years. Clean your tools regularly and store them in a safe place.

Starter Tools

Spade	Do not confuse this tool with a round-point shovel. A spade has a straight blade and a D-shaped handle. It is essential for bed preparation.
Steel rake	Use this tool for leveling the soil.
Cultivating fork	This three-pronged implement is suited for weed control and bed cultivation.
Hand trowel	An essential tool for planting. It should have a solid shaft.
Pump sprayer	Depending on your strength, either a one- or two-pound plastic sprayer.
Long-necked watering can	Use this to water individual plants and those in the cold frame.
Hose	Make sure the hose you buy is long enough to reach all parts of your garden. When you are watering seedlings or mature plants, use a water breaker.

The plates on the following pages are divided into six groups: foliage plants; yellow flowers; red to orange flowers; pink flowers; blue to purple flowers; and white flowers. Preceding the color plates, there is a Color Key, which shows the range of hues included in each color group. To help you select the right flower for the right place, the Flower Chart indicates important characteristics of each plant.

Color Key

Everyone sees color somewhat differently; what appears cream-colored to one gardener may seem pale yellow to another. Even pink and blue tones can seem quite similar, especially if viewed at different times of the day. The Color Key presents the variations in intensity and tone included in each color group.

When you purchase seeds or seedlings, be aware that the color indicated in the catalogue or on the package and identification tag may differ from the way you interpret that color. For example, nurseries and horticulturalists use the term "blue" to describe colors ranging from lavender to blue to dark purple or even magenta.

Flower Chart

The Flower Chart is divided into six groups. Within each group, the scientific names of the flowers are listed in alphabetical order, and the names are followed by the page numbers of the color plates and text descriptions. The flowers are evaluated in seven ways: zone; suitability for cut flowers; interesting foliage; the season when the flowers bloom; soil requirements; light requirements; and plant height.

Color Key

Yellow Flowers

Red to Orange Flowers

Pink Flowers

Blue to Purple Flowers

White Flowers

This chart shows the range of hues in each group of color plates.

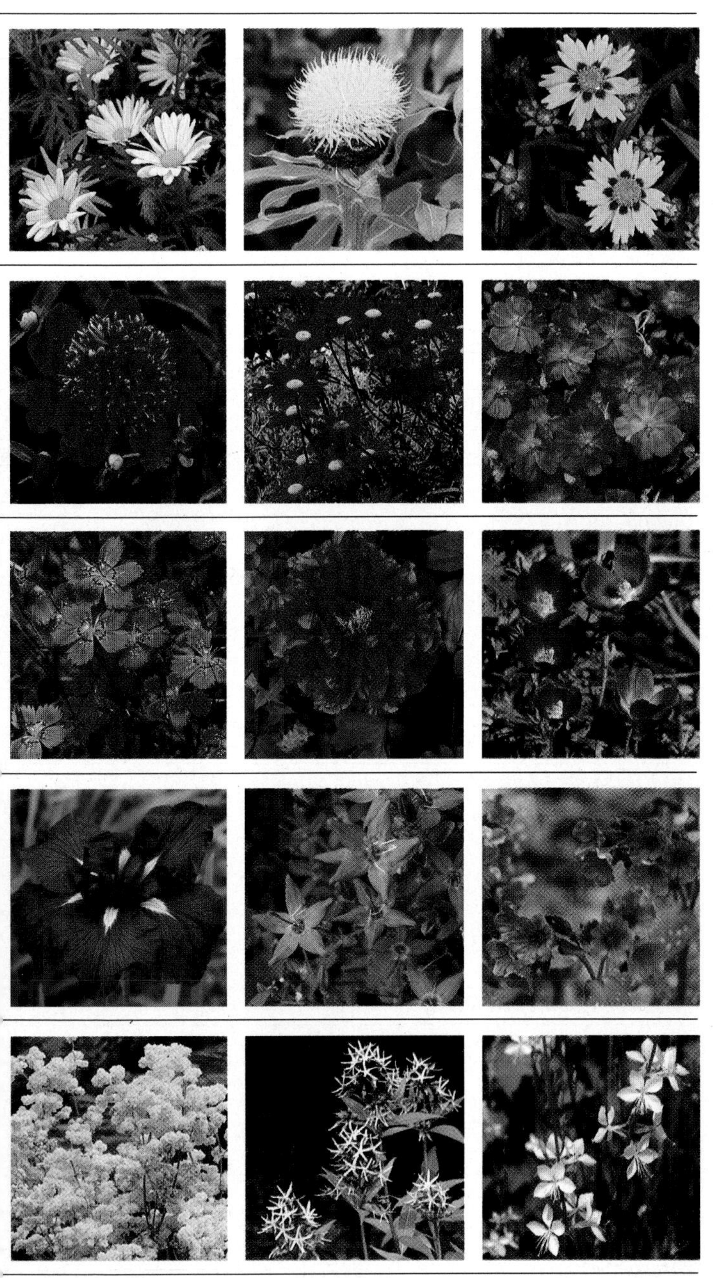

Flower Chart

	Page Numbers	*Zone*
Foliage Plants		
Acanthus mollis 'Latifolius'	76, 274	8
Aegopodium podagraria 'Variegatum'	84, 279	4
Ajuga reptans 'Burgundy Glow'	85, 280	3
Alchemilla conjuncta	77, 281	4
Artemisia absinthium 'Lambrook Silver'	90, 291	4
Artemisia canescens	88, 291	4
Artemisia ludoviciana	89, 292	5
Artemisia schmidtiana 'Silver Mound'	89, 292	4
Artemisia stellerana	91, 292	3–4
Arum italicum 'Pictum'	81, 293	5–6
Asarum canadense	82, 294	4
Asarum europaeum	81, 294	5
Baptisia perfoliata	87, 298	8
Foeniculum vulgare	88, 334	4
Hosta fortunei 'Aureo-marginata'	79, 351	4
Hosta 'Krossa Regal'	78, 351	4
Hosta sieboldiana	77, 78, 351	4
Hosta undulata	80, 351	4
Houttuynia cordata 'Variegata'	84, 352	5
Iris pallida var. *dalmatica* 'Variegata'	92, 355	6
Lamiastrum galeobdolon 'Herman's Pride'	83, 357	4
Ligularia dentata	83, 361	4
Ligularia tussilaginea 'Aureo-maculata'	80, 361	6–7
Liriope muscari 'John Birch'	91, 364	6
Marrubium incanum	82, 369	4
Origanum vulgare 'Aureum'	86, 375	4
Pachysandra procumbens	86, 376	5
Pachysandra terminalis	87, 376	5
Phormium tenax 'Variegatum'	93, 383	9
Salvia argentea	76, 396	5
Salvia officinalis 'Icterina'	85, 396	5
Stachys byzantina	90, 406	5
Veratrum viride	79, 414	5–6

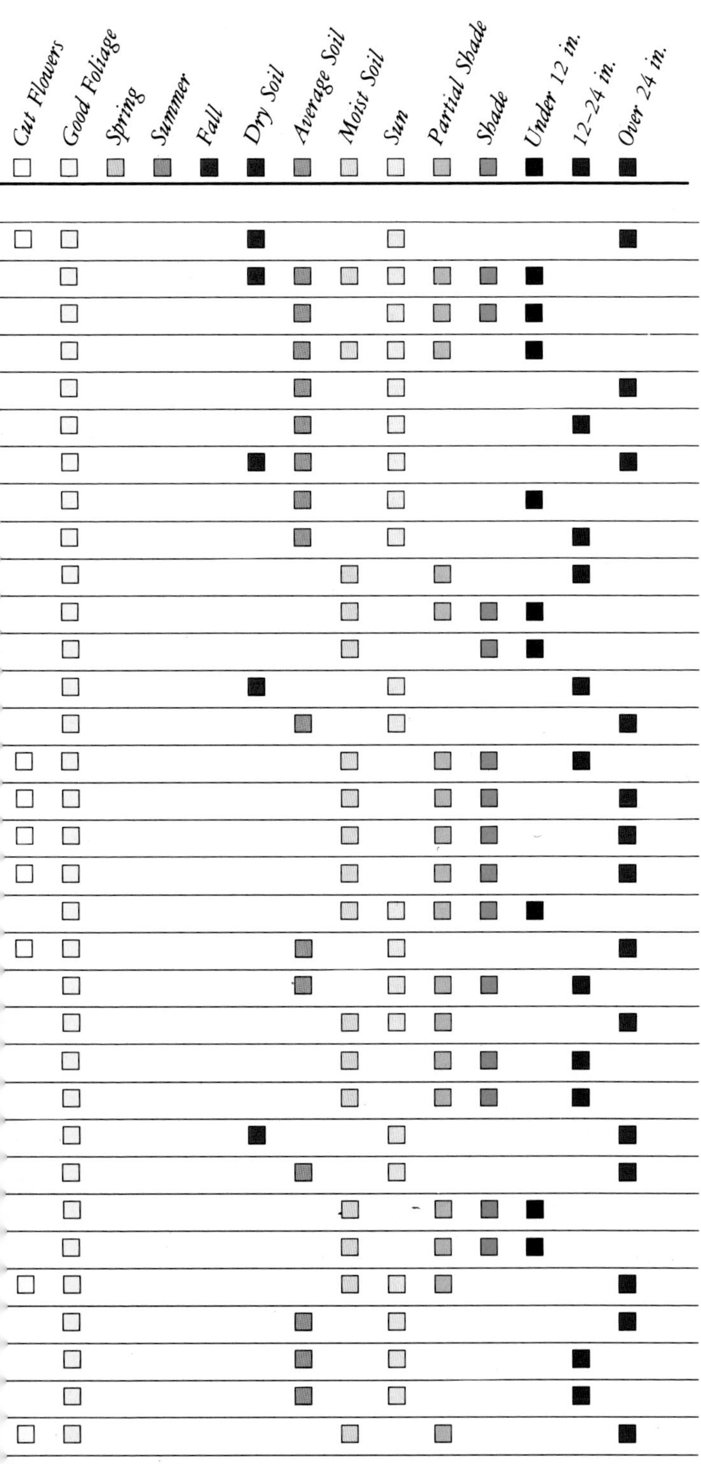

Cut Flowers	Good Foliage	Spring	Summer	Fall	Dry Soil	Average Soil	Moist Soil	Sun	Partial Shade	Shade	Under 12 in.	12–24 in.	Over 24 in.
■	■				■			■					■
	■				■	■	■	■	■	■	■		
	■					■		■	■	■	■		
	■					■	■	■	■		■		
	■					■		■					■
	■					■		■				■	
	■				■	■		■					■
	■					■		■			■		
	■					■		■				■	
	■						■		■			■	
	■						■		■	■	■		
	■						■			■	■		
	■				■			■				■	
	■					■		■					■
■	■						■		■	■		■	
■	■						■		■	■			■
■	■						■		■	■			■
■	■						■		■	■			■
	■						■	■	■	■	■		
■	■					■		■					■
	■					■		■	■	■		■	
	■						■	■	■				■
	■						■		■	■		■	
	■						■		■	■		■	
	■				■			■					■
	■					■		■					■
	■						■		■	■	■		
	■						■		■	■	■		
■	■						■	■	■				■
	■					■		■					■
	■					■		■				■	
	■					■		■				■	
■	■						■		■				■

	Page Numbers	Zone
Foliage Plants continued		
Yucca filamentosa 'Variegata'	92, 418	5
Yucca glauca	93, 419	5
Yellow Flowers		
Achillea 'Moonshine'	102, 275	4
Achillea filipendulina	103, 275	4
Adonis amurensis	118, 278	4
Alchemilla mollis	100, 281	4
Anthemis sancti-johannis	129, 286	4
Anthemis tinctoria 'Moonlight'	127, 286	4
Arcotheca calendula	128, 289	9
Asphodeline lutea	108, 295	6
Aurinia saxitilis 'Citrina'	116, 298	4
Buphthalum salicifolium	128, 302	4
Calceolaria 'John Innes'	115, 302	7
Caltha palustris	113, 303	4
Centaurea macrocephala	105, 306	3–4
Chelidonium majus	121, 308	5
Chrysanthemum frutescens	127, 310	9
Chrysogonum virginianum	118, 311	5–6
Chrysopsis mariana	131, 312	5
Coreopsis auriculata 'Nana'	124, 314	4
Coreopsis lanceolata 'Baby Sun'	125, 315	4
Coreopsis verticillata 'Golden Shower'	125, 126, 315	4
Corydalis lutea	112, 316	5
Digitalis grandiflora	110, 322	4
Disporum flavum	111, 323	4
Doronicum cordatum	130, 324	4
Draba densiflora	116, 325	4
Duchesnea indica	120, 325	4
Eriophyllum lanatum	126, 330	5
Euphorbia characias 'Wulfenii'	97, 332	8
Euphorbia cyparissias	117, 332	4
Euphorbia epithymoides	105, 332	5

Cut Flowers	Good Foliage	Spring	Summer	Fall	Dry Soil	Average Soil	Moist Soil	Sun	Partial Shade	Shade	Under 12 in.	12–24 in.	Over 24 in.
■	■						■	■					■
■	■						■	■					■
■	■		■			■		■				■	
■			■			■		■					■
		■				■		■	■		■		
■		■	■			■		■	■			■	
■			■			■		■					■
■			■			■		■					■
■		■				■		■			■		
■			■			■			■	■			■
		■			■			■			■		
■			■				■	■	■			■	
			■				■		■		■		
		■					■	■	■			■	
■			■		■			■					■
			■			■		■					■
■			■			■		■					■
		■	■			■		■	■		■		
■			■			■		■	■				■
■			■				■	■	■			■	
■			■		■			■					■
■			■		■			■	■				■
■			■			■		■	■		■		
■			■				■	■	■				■
■		■			■				■	■			■
■		■					■	■	■				■
		■				■		■	■		■		
	■		■			■		■	■		■		
			■		■			■				■	
■	■	■			■			■					■
	■	■			■			■			■		
	■	■			■			■	■		■		

	Page Numbers	Zone
Yellow Flowers continued		
Euphorbia myrsinites	96, 332	5
Helenium autumnale	132, 343	4
Helianthus angustifolius	132, 345	6–7
Helianthus × *multiflorus*	129, 345	5
Helichrysum 'Sulfur Light'	104, 345	5
Heliopsis helianthoides scabra	130, 346	4–5
Helleborus foetidus	97, 346	6–7
Helleborus lividus	96, 347	8
Hemerocallis 'Bonanza'	107, 348	4
Inula ensifolia	131, 354	4
Iris 'Louisiana'	95, 355	5
Iris pseudacorus 'Variegata'	94, 355	5–6
Kirengeshoma palmata	110, 356	5
Ligularia × *przewalskii* 'The Rocket'	108, 361	4
Linum flavum	119, 363	5
Lysimachia punctata	109, 366	5
Meconopsis cambrica	122, 369	6
Mimulus guttatus	114, 370	9
Oenothera missourensis	107, 373	5
Oenothera tetragona	106, 373	5
Opuntia humifusa	115, 375	5–6
Paeonia lactiflora 'Honey Gold'	95, 377	6
Phlomis russelliana	101, 381	6
Potentilla recta 'Macrantha'	123, 387	4
Potentilla tabernaemontana	119, 388	5
Potentilla × *tonguei*	124, 388	5
Primula helodoxa	100, 389	6
Primula veris	113, 389	5–6
Primula vulgaris	112, 389	5
Ranunculus repens 'Pleniflorus'	122, 391	4
Rodgersia podophylla	101, 392	5–6
Rudbeckia fulgida	133, 394	4
Rudbeckia nitida 'Herbstsonne'	133, 394	4

Cut Flowers	Good Foliage	Spring	Summer	Fall	Dry Soil	Average Soil	Moist Soil	Sun	Partial Shade	Shade	Under 12 in.	12–24 in.	Over 24 in.
■	■	■	■	■	■	■	■	■	■	■	■	■	■
	■	■			■			■			■		
■			■	■			■	■					■
■				■			■	■					■
■			■				■	■					■
■			■		■			■				■	
■			■			■		■	■				■
■	■	■					■		■	■		■	■
■	■	■					■		■	■		■	
		■				■	■	■				■	
■			■			■	■	■			■		
■		■					■	■	■				■
■	■	■	■				■	■					■
	■		■	■			■		■				■
	■		■				■	■	■				■
			■			■		■				■	
■		■	■				■	■	■				■
		■	■				■		■			■	
			■	■			■	■				■	
			■		■			■			■		
			■		■	■	■	■				■	
	■		■		■			■			■		
■		■					■	■	■				■
■			■			■		■					■
			■		■			■				■	
			■		■			■			■		
		■	■		■			■			■		
■			■				■		■				■
■		■					■		■		■		
		■					■		■		■		
■		■	■				■	■	■			■	
	■		■				■	■	■				■
■			■	■		■		■					■
■			■			■	■	■					■

	Page Numbers	*Zone*
Yellow Flowers continued		
Ruta graveolens	99, 395	5
Santolina chamaecyparissus	99, 398	6
Santolina virens	98, 398	6
Sedum aizoon	104, 401	4
Sedum kamtschaticum	114, 401	4
Sisyrinchium striatum	94, 404	7–8
Solidago 'Gold Dwarf'	117, 405	4
Stylophorum diphyllum	120, 407	6
Tanacetum vulgare var. *crispum*	98, 408	4
Thalictrum speciosissimum	102, 410	5–6
Thermopsis caroliniana	109, 410	4
Trollius europaeus	123, 413	5–6
Trollius ledebourii 'Golden Queen'	106, 413	5–6
Uvularia grandiflora	111, 413	5
Waldsteinia ternata	121, 418	4
Red to Orange Flowers		
Actaea rubra	141, 264, 277	4
Alcea rosea	136, 280	4
Alstroemeria ligtu	137, 282	8
Anigozanthos flavidus	140, 285	9
Aquilegia canadensis	146, 288	4
Asclepias tuberosa	139, 294	4
Astilbe × *arendsii* 'Faral'	144, 296	5
Belamcanda chinensis	138, 299	5
Chrysanthemum coccineum 'Brenda'	134, 310	4
Crocosmia masoniorum	139, 317	6
Epimedium × *warleyense*	147, 328	5
Eremurus stenophyllus	142, 329	7
Euphorbia griffithii 'Fire Glow'	140, 332	5
Gaillardia × *grandiflora*	134, 335	4
Geum quellyon 'Mrs. Bradshaw'	148, 341	5–6
Geum reptans	147, 341	5–6
Helianthemum nummularium 'Fire Dragon'	150, 344	6

Cut Flowers	Good Foliage	Spring	Summer	Fall	Dry Soil	Average Soil	Moist Soil	Sun	Partial Shade	Shade	Under 12 in.	12–24 in.	Over 24 in.
			■			■		■					■
	■		■			■		■				■	
	■		■			■		■				■	
			■			■		■				■	
	■		■			■		■	■		■		
	■		■			■		■				■	
■			■	■			■	■	■				■
		■					■		■			■	
			■	■		■		■	■				■
■	■		■				■	■	■				■
■		■	■			■		■					■
■		■					■	■	■			■	
■		■					■	■	■				■
■		■					■		■	■			■
	■	■				■		■	■		■		
		■					■		■	■		■	
			■				■	■					■
■			■			■		■	■			■	
■		■	■	■		■		■					■
■		■				■		■	■			■	
■			■		■	■		■					■
	■		■				■		■				■
■			■			■		■	■				■
■			■			■		■					■
■			■			■		■					■
	■	■					■		■	■	■		
■			■			■		■					■
■			■		■			■	■				■
■			■			■		■					■
■		■	■				■	■	■			■	
		■			■			■	■		■		
			■		■			■			■		

	Page Numbers	Zone
Red to Orange Flowers continued		
Hemerocallis 'Admiral Nelson'	138, 347	4
Heuchera sanguinea	145, 349	4
Kniphofia uvaria	143, 357	5
Lobelia cardinalis	143, 364	3
Lupinus 'Russell Hybrid'	142, 365	5
Lychnis × *arkwrightii*	149, 365	5
Lychnis chalcedonica	146, 366	4
Monarda didyma	135, 371	4
Paeonia lactiflora 'Ms. Wilder Bancroft'	136, 377	5
Paeonia tenuifolia	137, 377	5
Papaver orientale	135, 378	4
Penstemon barbatus	144, 379	4
Penstemon × *gloxinioides*	145, 379	9
Physalis alkekengi	141, 383	5
Potentilla atrosanguinea 'Gibson's Scarlet'	149, 387	5
Potentilla nepalensis 'Roxana'	148, 387	5
Sedum 'Ruby Glow'	151, 401	4
Sedum spurium	150, 401	4
Verbena peruviana	151, 415	5
Pink Flowers		
Achillea millefolium 'Fire King'	168, 275	3
Anemone × *hybrida*	161, 285	6
Anemone vitifolia 'Robustissima'	160, 285	5
Atennaria dioica var. *rosea*	152, 286	4–5
Aquilegia 'Dragon Fly'	179, 288	5
Armeria maritima	169, 291	4
Aster novae-angliae 'Alma Potschke'	196, 296	5
Astilbe chinensis 'Pumila'	191, 296	5
Astilbe tacquetii 'Superba'	186, 297	5
Aubrieta deltoidea	155, 297	5
Begonia grandis	160, 299	7
Bergenia cordifolia	182, 300	3
Bergenia 'Margery Fish'	177, 300	3

Cut Flowers	Good Foliage	Spring	Summer	Fall	Dry Soil	Average Soil	Moist Soil	Sun	Partial Shade	Shade	Under 12 in.	12–24 in.	Over 24 in.
		■	■			■	■	■					■
■	■		■				■	■	■			■	
■			■				■	■					■
■			■				■	■	■				■
■			■				■	■	■				■
■			■				■	■	■			■	
■			■				■	■	■				■
■			■			■	■	■	■				■
■		■					■	■	■				■
■		■				■		■	■			■	
			■			■		■					■
■			■			■		■					■
			■			■		■					■
		■				■		■	■			■	
			■			■		■				■	
			■		■			■				■	
	■		■			■		■			■		
	■		■		■			■	■		■		
			■			■		■			■		

Cut Flowers	Good Foliage	Spring	Summer	Fall	Dry Soil	Average Soil	Moist Soil	Sun	Partial Shade	Shade	Under 12 in.	12–24 in.	Over 24 in.
■			■			■		■				■	
			■	■			■	■	■				■
			■	■			■	■	■				■
			■		■			■			■		
■		■				■		■	■				■
		■			■			■			■		
			■	■		■	■	■					■
	■		■		■				■		■		
	■		■				■		■				■
		■				■		■	■		■		
	■		■	■			■		■	■		■	
■	■	■					■	■	■			■	
■		■					■	■	■			■	

	Page Numbers	Zone
Pink Flowers continued		
Callirhoe involucrata	164, 303	4
Centaurea hypoleuca 'John Coutts'	198, 306	4
Centaurea montana 'Violetta'	199, 306	3–4
Centranthus ruber	186, 307	5
Chelone lyonii	177, 309	4
Chrysanthemum × *morifolium*	197, 310	5
Chrysanthemum zawadskii 'Clara Curtis'	200, 311	5
Coronilla varia	182, 315	4
Dianthus × *allwoodii*	170, 319	4
Dianthus barbatus	169, 319	6
Dianthus deltoides	171, 319	4
Dianthus gratianopolitanus 'Tiny Rubies'	171, 320	5
Dianthus plumarius 'Agatha'	170, 320	4
Dicentra 'Luxuriant'	175, 321	4
Dicentra spectabilis	175, 321	3–4
Dictamnus albus 'Purpureus'	178, 321	3–4
Digitalis × *mertonensis*	174, 323	5
Echinacea purpurea	198, 326	4
Elsholtzia stauntonii	187, 327	7
Epimedium grandiflorum	158, 328	5
Epimedium × *rubrum*	159, 328	5
Erigeron 'Walther'	201, 329	5
Filipendula palmata	193, 333	4
Filipendula rubra	192, 333	3
Galega officinalis	183, 336	5
Geranium dalmaticum	166, 339	5
Geranium endressii 'A. T. Johnson'	167, 339	4
Geranium macrorrhizum	173, 340	4
Geranium maculatum	167, 340	5
Geranium psilostemon	165, 340	4
Geranium sanguineum var. *lancastriense*	166, 340	4
Goniolimon tataricum	158, 342	4
Gypsophila paniculata	156, 343	4

Cut Flowers	Good Foliage	Spring	Summer	Fall	Dry Soil	Average Soil	Moist Soil	Sun	Partial Shade	Shade	Under 12 in.	12–24 in.	Over 24 in.
			■		■			■			■		
■			■		■			■				■	
■		■	■			■		■				■	
■			■			■		■					■
			■				■		■				■
■				■			■	■					■
■			■			■		■				■	
			■		■			■				■	
■			■			■		■				■	
			■			■		■	■			■	
■	■	■				■		■			■		
		■				■		■			■		
■		■	■			■		■				■	
■		■	■	■			■		■			■	
■		■					■		■	■		■	
■			■				■	■					■
■			■				■		■				■
■			■			■		■	■				■
■				■		■		■					■
	■	■					■		■	■	■		
	■	■					■		■	■	■		
■			■			■		■				■	
	■		■				■		■				■
	■		■				■		■				■
■			■			■		■	■				■
		■	■		■	■	■	■	■		■		
		■	■				■	■	■			■	
	■	■	■			■		■	■			■	
		■	■			■		■	■			■	
			■				■	■	■			■	
	■	■	■			■		■	■			■	
■			■		■			■				■	
■			■			■		■					■

	Page Numbers	Zone
Pink Flowers continued		
Gypsophila repens 'Rosea'	157, 343	4
Helleborus orientalis	153, 347	5
Hesperis matronalis	181, 348	4
× *Heucherella tiarelloides* 'Bridget Bloom'	188, 349	4
Hibiscus coccineus	163, 350	6
Hibiscus moscheutos	162, 350	5
Incarvillea delavayi	174, 353	6
Indigofera incarnata	183, 353	8
Liatris spicata	187, 360	4
Limonium latifolium	157, 362	4
Linaria purpurea 'Canon Went'	191, 363	5
Lychnis coronaria	168, 366	4
Lychnis viscaria 'Splendens Plena'	178, 366	4
Lythrum salicaria	185, 367	4
Malva alcea	164, 368	4
Mimulus lewisii	180, 371	9
Monarda fistulosa	199, 371	4
Oenothera speciosa	165, 373	5
Paeonia officinalis 'Rubra Plena'	197, 377	5
Paeonia suffruticosa	196, 377	5
Petrorhagia saxifraga	156, 380	5
Phlox subulata 'Sampson'	154, 382	4
Physostegia virginiana	184, 384	4
Polygonum affine 'Superbum'	188, 386	4
Polygonum bistorta 'Superbum'	189, 386	4
Polygonum cuspidatum var. *compactum*	192, 387	4
Primula japonica	179, 389	6
Primula sieboldii	172, 389	5
Prunella grandiflora 'Rosea'	184, 390	5
Rhexia mariana	163, 392	6
Rhexia virginica	162, 392	6
Roscoea humeana	153, 394	7–8
Saponaria ocymoides	155, 398	4

Cut Flowers	Good Foliage	Spring	Summer	Fall	Dry Soil	Average Soil	Moist Soil	Sun	Partial Shade	Shade	Under 12 in.	12–24 in.	Over 24 in.
■			■				■	■			■		
■	■	■					■		■	■		■	
■			■				■	■	■				■
■	■	■	■				■	■	■			■	
			■				■	■					■
	■		■				■	■					■
■			■				■	■	■			■	
			■			■		■				■	
			■				■	■					■
■			■				■	■				■	
			■			■		■					■
■	■		■				■	■	■				■
		■	■				■	■				■	
■			■				■	■					■
■			■		■			■	■				■
			■				■	■	■				■
■			■		■	■	■	■	■				■
			■			■		■				■	
■		■					■	■	■				■
■		■				■		■	■				■
			■			■		■			■		
		■				■		■	■		■		
■			■				■	■	■				■
			■	■			■	■	■			■	
■			■				■		■	■			■
	■		■	■		■		■				■	
■		■					■		■			■	
■		■					■		■		■		
			■			■	■	■	■		■		
			■	■			■	■				■	
			■	■			■	■				■	
■			■			■		■	■		■		
		■	■			■		■			■		

	Page Numbers	Zone
Pink Flowers continued		
Saponaria officinalis	180, 398	4
Saxifraga × urbium	159, 399	7
Scabiosa caucasica 'David Wilkie'	200, 400	4
Sedum 'Autumn Joy'	194, 401	4
Sedum maximum 'Atropurpureum'	195, 401	4
Sedum sieboldii	154, 401	4
Sedum spectabile	195, 401	4
Shortia galacifolia	152, 402	5
Sidalcea malviflora 'Loveliness'	181, 403	5
Silene schafta	173	5–6
Stachys macrantha 'Robusta'	185, 406	4
Stokesia laevis	201, 406	5–6
Symphytum × rubrum	176, 408	5
Teucrium chamaedrys	189, 409	5–6
Thalictrum aquilegifolium	194, 409	5–6
Thalictrum rochebrunianum	161, 409	5–6
Tradescantia × andersoniana 'Pauline'	176, 411	5
Valeriana officinalis	193, 414	5
Veronica spicata	190, 416	4
Veronica virginica	190, 416	4
Viola cornuta	172, 417	5
Blue to Purple Flowers		
Aconitum × bicolor 'Bicolor'	230, 276	5
Aconitum carmichaelii	231, 277	3–4
Aconitum napellus	231, 277	5
Adenophora confusa	228, 278	4
Anchusa azurea	224, 284	4
Anemone pulsatilla	215, 285	5–6
Aquilegia caerulea	220, 288	4
Aster × frikartii	222, 296	6
Aster tataricus	223, 296	4
Baptisia australis	232, 298	4
Bearded Iris	219, 354	4

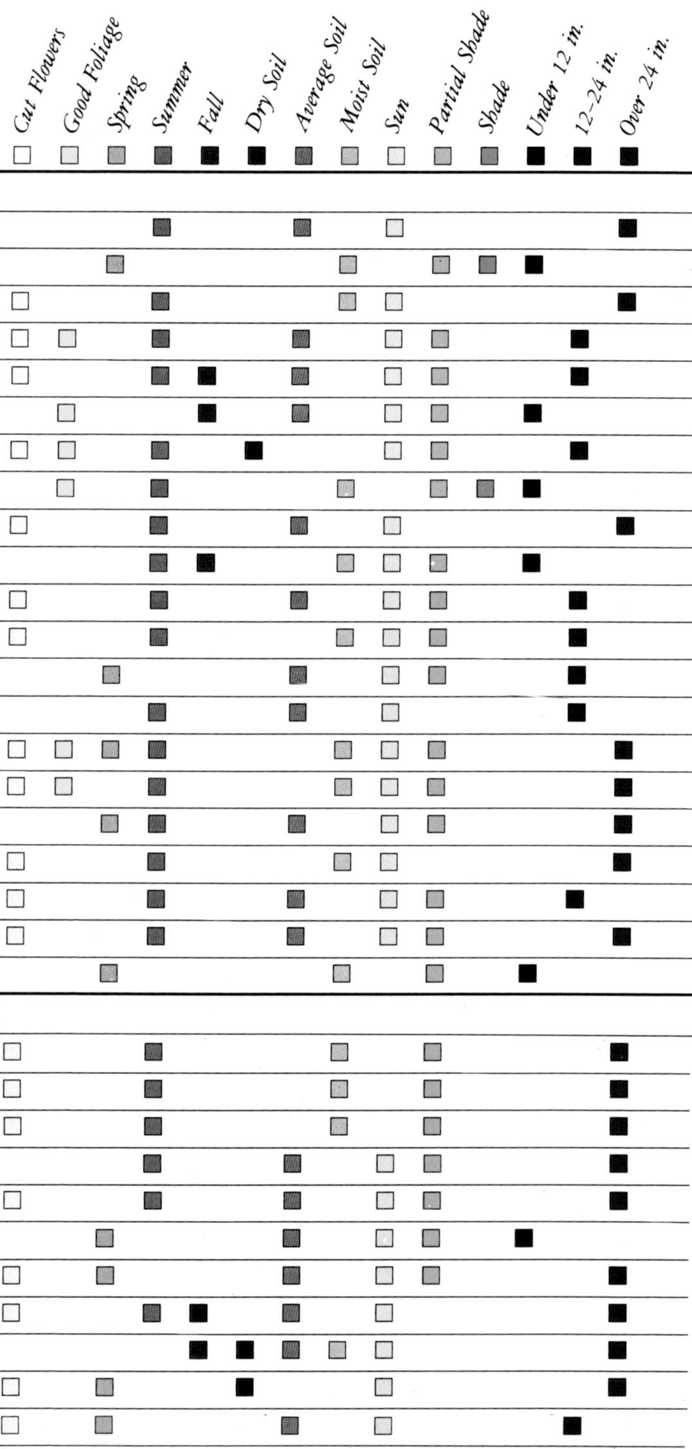
Cut Flowers
Good Foliage
Spring
Summer
Fall
Dry Soil
Average Soil
Moist Soil
Sun
Partial Shade
Shade
Under 12 in.
12–24 in.
Over 24 in.

	Page Numbers	Zone
Blue to Purple Flowers continued		
Brunnera macrophylla	206, 301	4
Campanula carpatica 'Isobel'	214, 304	4
Campanula garganica	202, 304	6
Campanula glomerata	213, 304	3–4
Campanula lactiflora	226, 304	4
Campanula latifolia	227, 304	4
Campanula portenschlagiana	203, 305	5
Campanula poscharskyana 'E. K. Toogood'	203, 305	4
Campanula rotundifolia	225, 305	3
Catanache caerulea	223, 305	5
Ceratostigma plumbaginoides	207, 308	6
Clematis heracleifolia var. *davidiana*	224, 313	4
Cynoglossum nervosum	205, 317	5
Delphinium elatum	230, 318	3
Echinops ritro 'Taplow Blue'	221, 327	4
Eryngium × *zabelii* 'Amethyst'	220, 331	5
Eupatorium coelestinum	222, 331	5
Gentiana asclepiadea	212, 339	6–7
Geranium himalayense	210, 340	4
Geranium 'Johnson's Blue'	209, 340	4
Hosta lancifolia	228, 351	4
Iris cristata	216, 354	4
Iris ensata 'Azure'	217, 355	5
Iris laevigata 'Variegata'	219, 355	5
Iris pumila	218, 356	4
Iris sibirica	218, 356	4
Iris tectorum	217, 356	5–6
Lavandula angustifolia	225, 359	5–6
Linum perenne	208, 363	5
Lobelia siphilitica	233, 364	5
Mertensia virginica	226, 370	4
Myosotis scorpioides var. *semperflorens*	206, 372	5
Nepeta mussinii	202, 373	4

Cut Flowers	Good Foliage	Spring	Summer	Fall	Dry Soil	Average Soil	Moist Soil	Sun	Partial Shade	Shade	Under 12 in.	12–24 in.	Over 24 in.
	■	■					■		■			■	
		■	■			■		■	■		■		
		■	■	■		■	■	■			■		
■			■		■	■	■	■	■				■
■			■				■	■	■				■
■			■				■	■	■				■
		■	■			■			■		■		
			■			■		■	■		■		
■			■			■		■				■	
■			■		■			■				■	
	■		■			■		■			■		
			■				■	■	■				■
			■			■		■				■	
■			■				■	■					■
■	■		■			■		■					■
■			■		■			■					■
■			■	■		■		■	■			■	
■			■				■		■			■	
		■				■		■	■			■	
		■	■			■	■	■	■		■		
■	■		■				■		■	■		■	
		■					■	■	■		■		
■			■				■	■	■				■
■			■				■	■					■
■		■				■		■			■		
■	■		■				■	■	■				■
■		■				■		■	■				■
			■		■			■					■
			■			■		■				■	
■			■				■	■	■				■
		■					■		■	■		■	
		■	■	■			■	■	■			■	
			■			■		■			■		

	Page Numbers	*Zone*
Blue to Purple Flowers continued		
Omphalodes cappadocica	204, 374	6
Omphalodes verna	205, 374	6
Penstemon hirsutus	229, 379	5
Perovskia atriplicifolia	235, 379	5–6
Phlox divaricata	208, 381	4
Phlox stolonifera 'Blue Ridge'	209, 382	4
Platycodon grandiflorus	215, 384	4
Polemonium caeruleum	214, 385	4
Polemonium foliosissimum	213, 385	4
Polemonium reptans	207, 385	4
Pulmonaria angustifolia	212, 390	4
Pulmonaria longifolia	211, 390	5
Pulmonaria saccharata	210, 391	4
Salvia azurea var. *grandiflora*	232, 396	6
Salvia farinacea 'Catima'	233, 396	8
Salvia pratensis	234, 396	6
Salvia × *superba* 'Mainacht'	234, 396	5
Symphytum × *uplandicum*	227, 304	5
Tradescantia hirsuticaulis	216, 411	6
Tricyrtis hirta	221, 411	6
Verbena rigida	211, 415	4
Veronica grandis var. *holophylla*	235, 416	5
Veronica latifolium 'Crater Lake Blue'	229, 416	4
Viola odorata 'Royal Robe'	204, 417	5
White Flowers		
Acanthus spinosus	258, 274	5–6
Achillea × *lewisii* 'King Edward'	242, 275	4
Achillea ptarmica 'The Pearl'	267, 275	4
Actaea rubra	264, 277	4
Amsonia tabernaemontana	241, 282	4
Anaphalis margaritacea	268, 283	4
Anaphalis triplinervis	269, 283	4
Anemone sylvestris 'Snowdrop'	246, 285	4

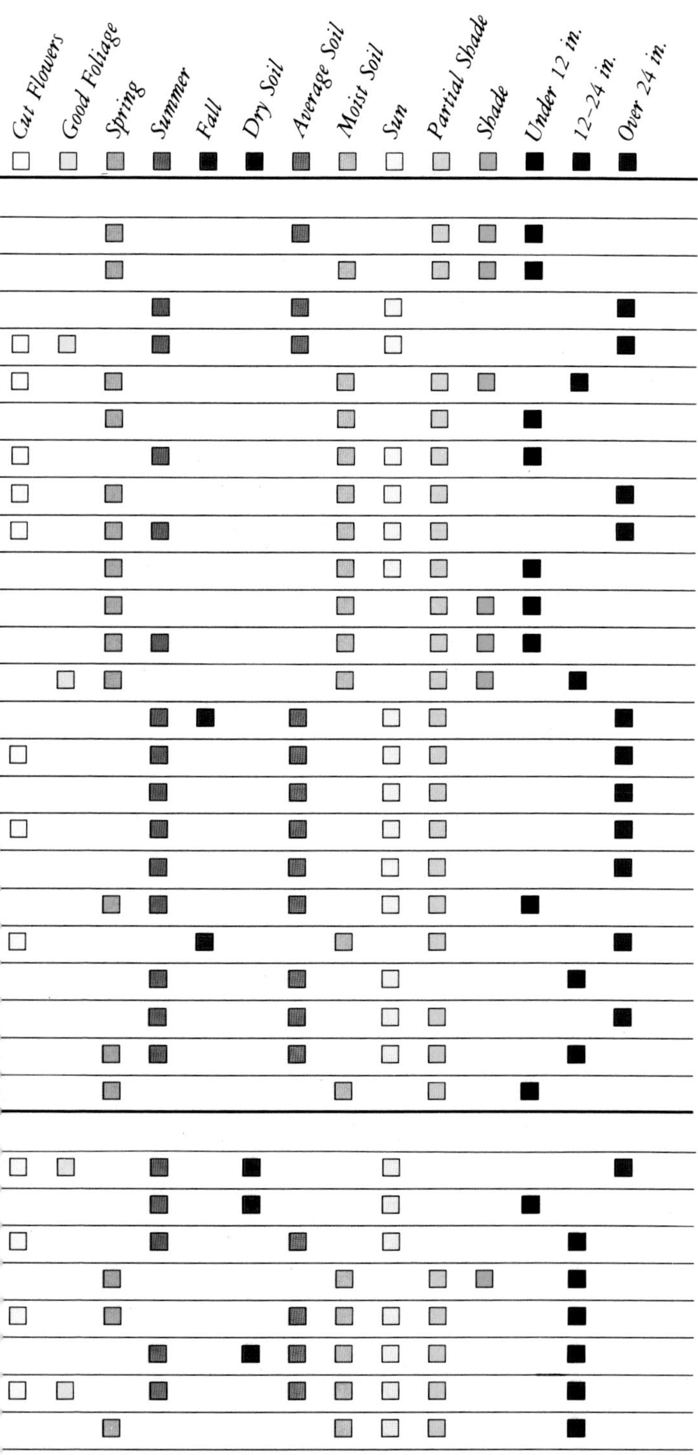

Cut Flowers	Good Foliage	Spring	Summer	Fall	Dry Soil	Average Soil	Moist Soil	Sun	Partial Shade	Shade	Under 12 in.	12–24 in.	Over 24 in.
		■				■			■	■	■		
		■					■		■	■	■		
			■			■		■					■
■	■		■			■		■					■
■		■					■		■	■		■	
		■					■		■		■		
■			■				■	■	■		■		
■		■					■	■	■				■
■		■	■				■	■	■				■
		■					■	■	■		■		
		■					■		■	■	■		
		■	■				■		■	■	■		
	■	■					■		■	■		■	
			■	■		■		■	■				■
■			■			■		■	■				■
			■			■		■	■				■
■			■			■		■	■				■
			■			■		■	■				■
		■	■			■		■	■		■		
■				■			■		■				■
			■			■		■				■	
			■			■		■	■				■
		■	■			■		■	■			■	
		■					■		■		■		
■	■		■		■			■					■
			■		■			■			■		
■			■			■		■				■	
		■					■		■	■		■	
■		■				■	■	■	■			■	
			■		■	■	■	■	■			■	
■	■		■			■	■	■	■			■	
		■					■	■	■			■	

	Page Numbers	Zone
White Flowers continued		
Anthericum liliago	256, 287	5
Arabis caucasica 'Snow Cap'	238, 288	4
Arabis procurrens	239, 289	5
Arenaria verna var. *caespitosa*	237, 290	5
Arisaema triphyllum	249, 290	4
Armeria pseudarmeria	266, 291	6–7
Artemisia lactiflora	262, 292	4
Aruncus dioicus	263, 293	4
Boltonia asteroides 'Snowbank'	244, 301	4
Campanula persicifolia var. *alba*	256, 304	4
Cerastium biebersteinii	241, 307	4
Cerastium tomentosum	240, 307	4
Chrysanthemum leucanthemum	242, 310	3
Chrysanthemum nipponicum	245, 310	5–6
Chrysanthemum parthenium	244, 310	4–5
Chrysanthemum × *superbum*	243, 311	4–5
Cimicifuga racemosa	261, 312	3–4
Cimicifuga simplex	260, 313	4
Clematis recta	265, 313	4
Convallaria majalis	252, 314	4
Crambe cordifolia	236, 316	6
Dicentra cucullaria	253, 320	4
Dictamnus albus	259, 321	3–4
Dietes vegeta	270, 322	8
Disporum sessile 'Variegatum'	252, 323	4
Dodocatheon meadia	254, 324	5
Epimedium × *versicolor* 'Sulphureum'	250, 328	5
Epimedium × *youngianum* 'Niveum'	251, 328	5
Eryngium bourgatii	269, 330	5
Euphorbia corollata	239, 332	4
Filipendula ulmaria 'Plena'	264, 333	4
Filipendula vulgaris 'Flore Pleno'	237, 333	4
Fragaria chiloensis	246, 335	5

Cut Flowers	Good Foliage	Spring	Summer	Fall	Dry Soil	Average Soil	Moist Soil	Sun	Partial Shade	Shade	Under 12 in.	12–24 in.	Over 24 in.
■			■				■	■					■
		■			■			■			■		
		■			■			■	■		■		
		■	■				■	■	■		■		
■		■	■				■		■	■			■
			■			■		■				■	
■			■				■	■	■				■
	■		■				■		■				■
■			■			■		■					■
■			■				■	■	■				■
	■		■			■		■			■		
	■	■				■		■			■		
■			■			■		■				■	
■	■			■		■		■				■	
■			■	■		■		■	■				■
■			■				■	■	■			■	
	■		■				■		■				■
	■		■	■			■		■				■
			■				■	■					■
■		■					■		■	■	■		
■	■		■			■		■					■
■		■					■		■	■	■		
■		■	■				■	■					■
■		■	■			■		■				■	
■	■	■			■				■	■		■	
		■				■			■			■	
	■	■					■		■	■	■		
	■	■					■		■	■	■		
■			■		■			■				■	
■	■		■		■			■					■
	■		■				■		■				■
	■		■		■	■			■	■			■
	■		■			■		■			■		

	Page Numbers	Zone
White Flowers continued		
Galax urceolata	260, 336	5
Galium odoratum	268, 337	5
Galtonia candicans	254, 337	5
Gaura lindheimeri	255, 338	6
Gillenia trifoliata	255, 342	5
Helleborus niger	247, 347	4
Iberis sempervirens	238, 352	4
Lamium maculatum 'White Nancy'	250, 358	4
Lathyrus latifolius	271, 359	4
Leontopodium alpinum	243, 360	4
Liatris aspera 'Alba'	261, 360	4
Lysimachia clethroides	259, 366	4
Macleaya cordata	262, 368	4
Malva moschata 'Alba'	257, 368	4
Pacific Coast Iris	271, 355	4–8
Paeonia mlokosewitschii	247, 377	6
Phlox carolina 'Miss Lingard'	258, 381	5
Phlox paniculata 'Mt. Fujiyama'	267, 382	4
Physostegia virginiana 'Summer Snow'	257, 384	4
Polygonatum odoratum var. *thunbergii*	253, 386	5
Potentilla tridentata	236, 388	5
Rodgersia aesculifolia	265, 392	5–6
Romneya coulteri	245, 393	7
Sanguisorba canadensis	263, 397	4
Saxifraga stolonifera	240, 399	6
Smilacina racemosa	266, 404	4
Symphytum grandiflorum	251, 407	5
Trillium grandiflorum	249, 412	5
Verbascum chaixii 'Album'	270, 415	5
Viola striata	248, 417	5
Zantedeschia aethiopica	248, 419	7

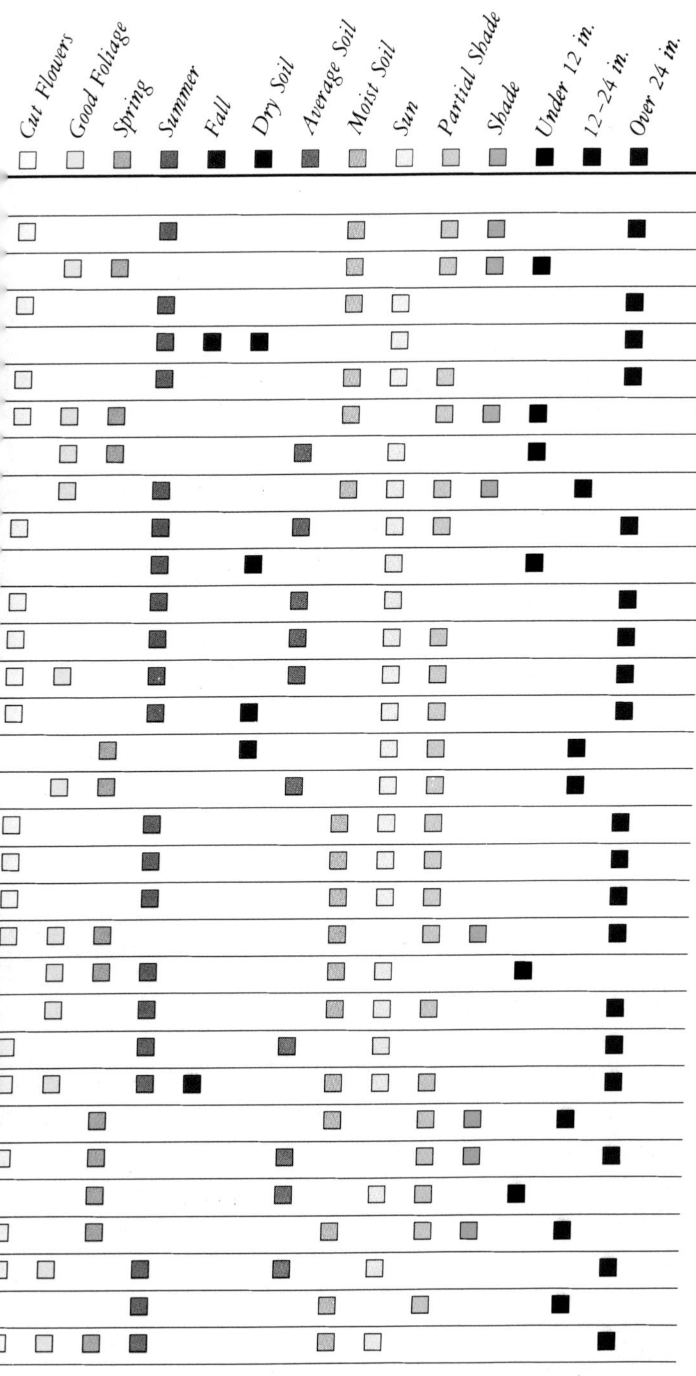

Cut Flowers	Good Foliage	Spring	Summer	Fall	Dry Soil	Average Soil	Moist Soil	Sun	Partial Shade	Shade	Under 12 in.	12–24 in.	Over 24 in.
■			■				■		■	■			■
	■	■					■		■	■	■		
■			■				■	■					■
			■	■	■			■					■
■			■				■	■	■				■
■	■	■					■		■	■	■		
	■	■				■		■			■		
	■		■				■	■	■	■		■	
■			■			■		■	■				■
			■		■			■			■		
■			■			■		■					■
■			■			■		■	■				■
■	■		■			■		■	■				■
■			■		■			■	■				■
		■			■			■	■			■	
	■	■				■		■	■			■	
■			■				■	■	■				■
■			■				■	■	■				■
■			■				■	■	■				■
■	■	■					■		■	■			■
	■	■	■				■	■			■		
	■		■				■	■	■				■
■			■			■		■					■
■	■		■	■			■	■	■				■
		■					■		■	■		■	
■		■				■			■	■			■
		■				■		■	■		■		
■		■					■		■	■		■	
■	■		■			■		■					■
			■				■		■			■	
■	■	■	■				■	■					■

Acanthus mollis 'Latifolius'

Plant height: 3–4 ft.
Full sun
Dry soil
Bear's-Breech
p. 274

Salvia argentea

Plant height: to 4 ft.
Full sun
Well-drained soil
Silver Sage
p. 396

Alchemilla conjuncta

Plant height: 4–6 in.
Sun to partial shade
Average to moist soil
p. 281

Hosta sieboldiana

Plant height: to 2½ ft.
Partial to full shade
Moist soil
Siebold Plantainlily
p. 351

Hosta 'Krossa Regal'

Plant height: to 3 ft.
Partial to full shade
Moist soil
Krossa Regal Plantainlily
p. 351

Hosta sieboldiana 'Frances Williams'

Plant height: to 2½ ft.
Partial to full shade
Moist soil
Siebold Plantainlily
p. 351

Veratrum viride

Plant height: 3–7 ft.
Partial shade
Moist soil
American White Hellebore
p. 414

Hosta fortunei 'Aureo-marginata'

Plant height: to 2 ft.
Partial to full shade
Moist soil
Fortune's Plantainlily
p. 351

Hosta undulata

Plant height: to 3 ft.
Partial to full shade
Moist soil
Wavyleaf
Plantainlily
p. 351

Ligularia tussilaginea
'Aureo-maculata'

Plant height: to 2 ft.
Partial to full shade
Moist soil
Leopard Plant
p. 361

Arum italicum
'Pictum'

Plant height: 12–16 in.
Partial shade
Moist soil
Italian Arum
p. 293

Asarum europaeum

Plant height: to 5 in.
Full shade
Moist soil
European Wild Ginger
p. 294

Asarum canadense

Plant height: 6–8 in.
Partial to full shade
Moist soil
Wild Ginger
p. 294

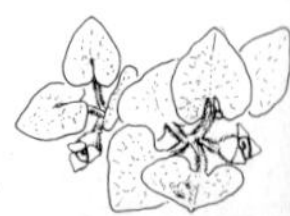

Marrubium incanum

Plant height: 2–3 ft.
Full sun
Dry soil
Silver Horehound
p. 369

Ligularia dentata

Plant height: to 4 ft.
Sun to partial shade
Moist soil
Bigleaf Goldenray
p. 361

Lamiastrum galeobdolon 'Herman's Pride'

Plant height: 1–2 ft.
Full sun to shade
Average soil
Yellow Archangel
p. 357

***Aegopodium podagraria* 'Variegatum'**

Plant height: to 12 in.
Full sun to shade
Dry to moist soil
Goutweed
p. 279

***Houttuynia cordata* 'Variegata'**

Plant height: to 12 in.
Full sun to shade
Moist soil
p. 352

Salvia officinalis 'Icterina'

Plant height: to 2 ft.
Full sun
Well-drained soil
Garden Sage
p. 396

Ajuga reptans 'Burgundy Glow'

Plant height: 3–6 in.
Full sun to shade
Well-drained soil
Bugleweed
p. 280

Pachysandra procumbens

Plant height: 8–10 in.
Partial to full shade
Moist soil
Allegheny Spurge
p. 376

Origanum vulgare 'Aureum'

Plant height: to 2½ ft.
Full sun
Well-drained soil
Pot Marjoram
p. 375

Pachysandra terminalis

Plant height: to 12 in.
Partial to full shade
Moist soil
Japanese Spurge
p. 376

Baptisia perfoliata

Plant height: to 2 ft.
Full sun
Dry soil
p. 298

Foeniculum vulgare

Plant height: 3–5 ft.
Full sun
Well-drained soil
Common Fennel
p. 334

Artemisia canescens

Plant height: 12–18 in.
Full sun
Well-drained soil
p. 291

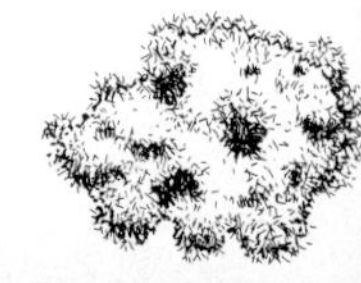

Artemisia ludoviciana

Plant height: to 3 ft.
Full sun
Average to dry soil
Silver King Artemisia
p. 292

Artemisia schmidtiana 'Silver Mound'

Plant height: 4–6 in.
Full sun
Well-drained soil
Silver Mound Artemisia
p. 292

***Artemisia absinthium* 'Lambrook Silver'**

Plant height: 2½–4 ft.
Full sun
Well-drained soil
Wormwood
p. 291

Stachys byzantina

Plant height: to 18 in.
Full sun
Well-drained soil
Lamb's-Ears
p. 406

Artemisia stellerana

Plant height: to 2 ft.
Full sun
Well-drained soil
Beach Wormwood
p. 292

Liriope muscari
'John Birch'

Plant height: to 18 in.
Partial to full shade
Moist soil
Blue Lily-Turf
p. 364

Yucca filamentosa **'Variegata'**

Plant height: 3–15 ft.
Full sun
Sandy, moist,
well-drained soil
Adam's Needle
p. 418

Iris pallida **var.** ***dalmatica*** **'Variegata'**

Plant height: to 3 ft.
Full sun
Well-drained soil
Orris
p. 355

Yucca glauca

Plant height: to 3 ft.
Full sun
Sandy, moist, well-drained soil
Soapweed
p. 419

***Phormium tenax* 'Variegatum'**

Plant height: 8–15 ft.
Sun to partial shade
Moist soil
New Zealand Flax
p. 383

Iris pseudacorus 'Variegata'

Plant height: to 5 ft.
Outer segments: to 2 in. long
Full sun
Moist to wet soil
Blooms late spring to midsummer
Yellow Flag
p. 355

Sisyrinchium striatum

Plant height: 12–18 in.
Flower width: ¾ in.
Full sun
Well-drained soil
Blooms in summer
Argentine Blue-eyed Grass
p. 404

Iris **'Louisiana'**

Plant height: 3–4 ft.
Outer segments:
3–4 in. long
Sun to partial shade
Moist soil
Blooms in spring
Louisiana Iris
p. 355

Paeonia lactiflora **'Honey Gold'**

Plant height: 2–3 ft.
Flower width: 3–5 in.
Sun to partial shade
Sandy, moist,
well-drained soil
Blooms in late spring
Chinese Peony
p. 377

Helleborus lividus

Plant height: to 2 ft.
Flower width: 2½ in.
Partial to full shade
Moist soil
Blooms in winter or early spring
Corsican Hellebore
p. 347

Euphorbia myrsinites

Plant height: to 6 in.
Flowers: in clusters 1½ in. wide
Full sun
Dry, well-drained soil
Blooms in spring
Myrtle Euphorbia
p. 332

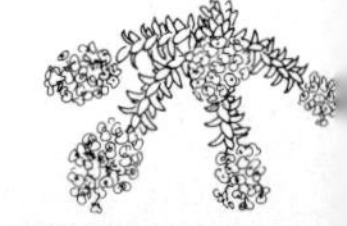

Helleborus foetidus

Plant height: 12–18 in.
Flower width: 1 in.
Partial to full shade
Moist soil
Blooms late winter to early spring
Stinking Hellebore
p. 346

Euphorbia characias 'Wulfenii'

Plant height: 3–4 ft.
Flowers: in clusters 3 in. long
Full sun
Dry, well-drained soil
Blooms in spring
p. 332

Santolina virens

Plant height: 10–18 in.
Flower width: ½ in.
Full sun
Well-drained soil
Blooms midsummer to late summer
Green Lavender Cotton
p. 398

Tanacetum vulgare var. _crispum_

Plant height: 2–3 ft.
Flower width: ⅓ in.
Sun to partial shade
Well-drained soil
Blooms late summer to early fall
Tansy
p. 408

Santolina chamaecyparissus

Plant height: 1–2 ft.
Flower width: ¾ in.
Full sun
Well-drained soil
Blooms midsummer to late summer
Lavender Cotton
p. 398

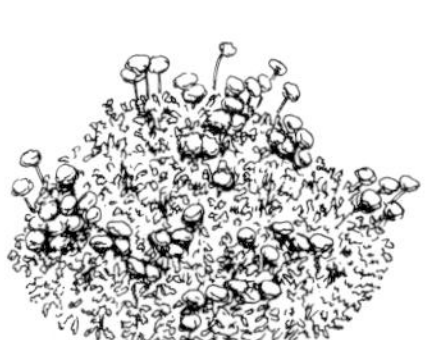

Ruta graveolens

Plant height: 2–3 ft.
Flower width: ½ in.
Full sun
Well-drained soil
Blooms in midsummer
Common Rue
p. 395

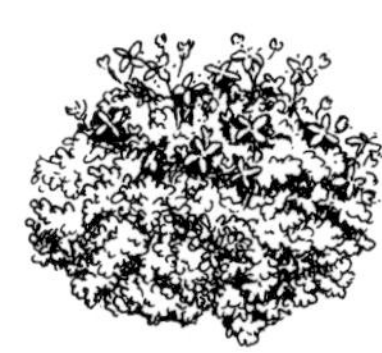

Alchemilla mollis

Plant height: to 15 in.
Flowers: in clusters 2–3 in. wide
Sun to partial shade
Average to moist soil
Blooms late spring to early summer
Lady's-Mantle
p. 281

Primula helodoxa

Plant height: 1½–3 ft.
Flowers: in clusters 2 in. wide
Partial shade
Moist to wet soil
Blooms in early summer
Amber Primrose
p. 389

Rodgersia podophylla

Plant height: to 5 ft.
Flowers: in clusters 12 in. long
Sun to partial shade
Moist soil
Blooms in summer
Bronzeleaf Rodgersflower
p. 392

Phlomis russelliana

Plant height: to 3 ft.
Flowers: in clusters ½–1 in. wide
Full sun
Well-drained soil
Blooms in summer
Sticky Jerusalem-Sage
p. 381

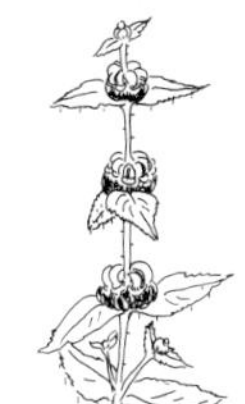

Thalictrum speciosissimum

Plant height: 3–5 ft.
Flower width: ½ in.
Sun to partial shade
Moist, well-drained soil
Blooms midsummer to late summer
Dusty Meadowrue
p. 410

Achillea 'Moonshine'

Plant height: to 2 ft.
Flowers: in clusters 3–4 in. wide
Full sun
Well-drained soil
Blooms in midsummer
Moonshine Yarrow
p. 275

Achillea filipendulina
'Gold Plate'

Plant height: 4–4½ ft.
Flowers: in clusters to 5 in. wide
Full sun
Well-drained soil
Blooms early summer to midsummer
Fernleaf Yarrow
p. 275

Achillea filipendulina
'Coronation Gold'

Plant height: to 3 ft.
Flowers: in clusters 3–4 in. wide
Full sun
Well-drained soil
Blooms early summer to midsummer
Fernleaf Yarrow
p. 275

Helichrysum hybridum
'Sulfur Light'

Plant height: to 18 in.
Flowers: in clusters 2 in. wide
Full sun
Dry, well-drained soil
Blooms in late summer
Everlasting
p. 345

Sedum aizoon

Plant height: 12–18 in.
Flower width: to ½ in.
Full sun
Well-drained soil
Blooms in midsummer
Aizoon Stonecrop
p. 401

Centaurea macrocephala

Plant height: to 3 ft.
Flower width: to 4 in.
Full sun
Dry soil
Blooms in early summer
Globe Centaurea
p. 306

Euphorbia epithymoides

Plant height: to 12 in.
Bract width: 1 in.
Sun to partial shade
Dry, well-drained soil
Blooms in spring
Cushion Spurge
p. 332

Oenothera tetragona

Plant height: to 18 in.
Flower width: 1½ in.
Full sun
Dry to moist soil
Blooms early summer to midsummer
Common Sundrops
p. 373

Trollius ledebourii
'Golden Queen'

Plant height: 2–3 ft.
Flower width: 2 in.
Sun to partial shade
Moist soil
Blooms in spring
Ledebour Globeflower
p. 413

Oenothera missourensis

Plant height: 3–6 in.
Flower width: 4 in.
Full sun
Dry, well-drained soil
Blooms early summer to midsummer
Missouri Primrose
p. 373

Hemerocallis 'Bonanza'

Plant height: to 15 in.
Flower width: 2–6 in.
Full sun
Average to moist soil
Blooms in spring
Daylily
p. 348

Asphodeline lutea

Plant height: 2–3 ft.
Flower width: 1 in.
Full to partial shade
Well-drained soil
Blooms in early summer
Asphodel
p. 295

Ligularia × przewalskii
'The Rocket'

Plant height: 4–6 ft.
Flowers: in clusters 12–18 in. long
Sun to partial shade
Moist soil
Blooms in summer
Rocket Ligularia
p. 361

Lysimachia punctata

Plant height: 2–3 ft.
Flower width: 1 in.
Sun to partial shade
Moist soil
Blooms late spring to early summer
Yellow Loosestrife
p. 366

Thermopsis caroliniana

Plant height: 3–5 ft.
Flower width: ½–¾ in.
Full sun
Well-drained soil
Blooms late spring to early summer
Carolina Thermopsis
p. 410

Kirengeshoma palmata

Plant height: 4 ft.
Flower length: 1½ in.
Partial shade
Moist soil
Blooms late summer to fall
p. 356

Digitalis grandiflora

Plant height: to 3 ft.
Flower length: 2 in.
Partial shade
Moist, well-drained soil
Blooms in early summer
Yellow Foxglove
p. 322

Disporum flavum

Plant height: 2–3 ft.
Flower length: 1 in.
Partial to full shade
Dry soil
Blooms in spring
Fairy-Bells
p. 323

Uvularia grandiflora

Plant height: to 2½ ft.
Flower length: 2 in.
Partial to full shade
Moist soil
Blooms in late spring
Big Merrybells
p. 413

Corydalis lutea

Plant height: to 12 in.
Flower length: ¾ in.
Sun to partial shade
Well-drained soil
Blooms in summer
Yellow Corydalis
p. 316

Primula vulgaris

Plant height: to 6 in.
Flower width: 1½ in.
Partial shade
Moist soil
Blooms in late spring
English Primrose
p. 389

Primula veris

Plant height: 6–8 in.
Flower width: ½ in.
Partial shade
Moist soil
Blooms in late spring
Cowslip Primrose
p. 389

Caltha palustris

Plant height: 1–2 ft.
Flower width: 2 in.
Sun to partial shade
Moist to wet soil
Blooms in spring
Cowslip
p. 303

Sedum kamtschaticum

Plant height: 6–12 in.
Flower width: ¾ in.
Sun to partial shade
Well-drained soil
Blooms in midsummer
Orange Stonecrop
p. 401

Mimulus guttatus

Plant height: to 2 ft.
Flower length: 1½ in.
Full sun
Moist soil
Blooms summer to fall
Common Monkey Flower
p. 370

Opuntia humifusa

Plant height: to 6 in.
Flower width: 2–3 in.
Full sun
Dry soil
Blooms in early summer
Prickly Pear
p. 375

***Calceolaria* 'John Innes'**

Plant height: to 6 in.
Flower length: ½–1 in.
Partial shade
Moist soil
Blooms in early summer
Calceolaria
p. 302

Draba densiflora

Plant height: 2–3 in.
Flower width: 1/8 in.
Sun to partial shade
Well-drained soil
Blooms in spring
Rock Cress Draba
p. 325

Aurinia saxitilis
'Citrina'

Plant height: 6–12 in.
Flower width: 1/8 in.
Full sun
Dry, well-drained soil
Blooms in spring
Basket-of-Gold
p. 298

Euphorbia cyparissias

Plant height: 8–12 in.
Bract width: ¼ in.
Full sun
Dry soil
Blooms in spring
Cypress Spurge
p. 332

Solidago **'Gold Dwarf'**

Plant height: 1–5 ft.
Flower width: ⅛–¼ in.
Sun to partial shade
Moist, well-drained soil
Blooms midsummer to fall
Goldenrod
p. 405

Adonis amurensis

Plant height: to 12 in.
Flower width: 2 in.
Sun to partial shade
Average soil
Blooms in mid-spring
Amur Adonis
p. 278

Chrysogonum virginianum

Plant height: 4–10 in.
Flower width: 1½ in.
Sun to partial shade
Well-drained soil
Blooms late spring to summer
Golden Star
p. 311

Linum flavum

Plant height: 1–2 ft.
Flower width: 1 in.
Full sun
Well-drained soil
Blooms in summer
Golden Flax
p. 363

Potentilla tabernaemontana

Plant height: to 3 in.
Flower width: ½ in.
Full sun
Dry, well-drained soil
Blooms in early summer
Spring Cinquefoil
p. 388

Duchesnea indica

Plant height: 2–3 in.
Flower width: ½ in.
Sun to partial shade
Average soil
Blooms in summer
Barren Strawberry
p. 325

Stylophorum diphyllum

Plant height: to 18 in.
Flower width: 2 in.
Partial shade
Moist, well-drained soil
Blooms in late spring
Celandine Poppy
p. 407

Waldsteinia ternata

Plant height: 6–12 in.
Flower width: ½ in.
Sun to partial shade
Well-drained soil
Blooms in late spring
Barren Strawberry
p. 418

Chelidonium majus

Plant height: to 3 ft.
Flower width: ½ in.
Full sun
Average soil
Blooms in early summer
Celandine
p. 308

Meconopsis cambrica

Plant height: to 2 ft.
Flower width: 2 in.
Partial shade
Moist soil
Blooms late spring to early summer
Welsh Poppy
p. 369

Ranunculus repens
'Pleniflorus'

Plant height: 1–2 ft.
Flower width: ¾ in.
Sun to partial shade
Moist soil
Blooms late spring to early summer
Creeping Buttercup
p. 391

Trollius europaeus

Plant height: to 2 ft.
Flower width: 1–2 in.
Sun to partial shade
Moist soil
Blooms in spring
Common Globeflower
p. 413

Potentilla recta
'Macrantha'

Plant height: to 2 ft.
Flower width: 1 in.
Full sun
Dry, well-drained soil
Blooms in summer
Sulphur Cinquefoil
p. 387

Potentilla × tonguei

Plant height: 8–12 in.
Flower width: 1 in.
Full sun
Dry, well-drained soil
Blooms late spring to early summer
Staghorn Cinquefoil
p. 388

Coreopsis auriculata 'Nana'

Plant height: 12–18 in.
Flower width: 1 in.
Sun to partial shade
Moist, well-drained soil
Blooms in early summer
Eared Coreopsis
p. 314

Coreopsis lanceolata 'Baby Sun'

Plant height: to 3 ft.
Flower width: 2½ in.
Full sun
Dry soil
Blooms early summer to late summer
Lance Coreopsis
p. 315

Coreopsis verticillata 'Golden Shower'

Plant height: 2–3 ft.
Flower width: 2 in.
Sun to partial shade
Dry, well-drained soil
Blooms in midsummer
Threadleaf Coreopsis
p. 315

***Coreopsis verticillata* 'Moonbeam'**

Plant height: 1½–2 ft.
Flower width: 2 in.
Sun to partial shade
Dry, well-drained soil
Blooms in midsummer
Threadleaf Coreopsis
p. 315

Eriophyllum lanatum

Plant height: to 2 ft.
Flower width: 1 in.
Full sun
Dry, well-drained soil
Blooms in summer
Woolly Eriophyllum
p. 330

Chrysanthemum frutescens

Plant height: 2–3 ft.
Flower width: 1½–2½ in.
Full sun
Average soil
Blooms in summer
Marguerite Daisy
p. 310

Anthemis tinctoria 'Moonlight'

Plant height: to 3 ft.
Flower width: 2 in.
Full sun
Well-drained soil
Blooms in summer
Golden Marguerite
p. 286

Arctotheca calendula

Plant height: to 12 in.
Flower width: 2 in.
Full sun
Average soil
Blooms in spring
Cape Weed
p. 289

Buphthalum salicifolium

Plant height: 1–2 ft.
Flower width: 2 in.
Sun to partial shade
Moist soil
Blooms in summer
Yellow Oxeye Daisy
p. 302

Helianthus × multiflorus

Plant height: to 6 ft.
Flower width: 5 in.
Full sun
Moist, well-drained soil
Blooms in summer
Perennial Sunflower
p. 345

Anthemis sancti-johannis

Plant height: 1–3 ft.
Flower width: 2 in.
Full sun
Well-drained soil
Blooms in summer
Saint John's Camomile
p. 286

Heliopsis helianthoides scabra

Plant height: 3–4 ft.
Flower width: 1½–2½ in.
Sun to partial shade
Well-drained soil
Blooms in summer
Orange Sunflower
p. 346

Doronicum cordatum

Plant height: 1–2½ ft.
Flower width: 2 in.
Sun to partial shade
Moist soil
Blooms in spring
Leopard's Bane
p. 324

Inula ensifolia

Plant height: to 12 in.
Flower width: 1½ in.
Full sun
Average to moist soil
Blooms in summer
Swordleaf Inula
p. 354

Chrysopsis mariana

Plant height: 1–3 ft.
Flower width: 1½ in.
Sun to partial shade
Average soil
Blooms midsummer to late summer
p. 312

Helenium autumnale

Plant height: to 5 ft.
Flower width: 2 in.
Full sun
Moist soil
Blooms late summer to early fall
False Sunflower
p. 343

Helianthus angustifolius

Plant height: to 6 ft.
Flower width: 2–3 in.
Full sun
Moist, well-drained soil
Blooms in fall
Swamp Sunflower
p. 345

Rudbeckia fulgida

Plant height: 2–3 ft.
Flower width: 3 in.
Full sun
Well-drained soil
Blooms midsummer to fall
Orange Coneflower
p. 394

Rudbeckia nitida 'Herbstsonne'

Plant height: 4–7 ft.
Flower width: 4 in.
Full sun
Average to moist soil
Blooms midsummer to late summer
p. 394

Chrysanthemum coccineum 'Brenda'

Plant height: 1–3 ft.
Flower width: 2½ in.
Full sun
Well-drained soil
Blooms in early summer
Pyrethrum
p. 310

Gaillardia × grandiflora

Plant height: ⅔–3 ft.
Flower width: 3–4 in.
Full sun
Well-drained soil
Blooms in summer
Blanketflower
p. 335

Monarda didyma

Plant height: 2–3 ft.
Flower width: 2 in.
Sun to partial shade
Average to moist soil
Blooms in summer
Bee Balm
p. 371

Papaver orientale 'China Boy'

Plant height: 3–4 ft.
Flower width: 6 in.
Full sun
Well-drained soil
Blooms in early summer
Oriental Poppy
p. 378

Paeonia lactiflora 'Ms. Wilder Bancroft'

Plant height: 2–3 ft.
Flower width: 4–6 in.
Full sun to partial shade
Moist soil
Blooms in late spring
Chinese Peony
p. 377

Alcea rosea

Plant height: 5–9 ft.
Flower width: 3–5 in.
Full sun
Moist, well-drained soil
Blooms in midsummer
Garden Hollyhock
p. 280

Paeonia tenuifolia

Plant height: to 2 ft.
Flower width: 3–4 in.
Sun to partial shade
Well-drained soil
Blooms in mid-spring
Fernleaf Peony
p. 377

Alstroemeria ligtu

Plant height: to 2 ft.
Flower width: 1½–2 in.
Sun to partial shade
Well-drained soil
Blooms in early summer
p. 282

Hemerocallis
'Admiral Nelson'

Plant height:
2½–3½ ft.
Flower width: 2–6 in.
Full sun
Average to moist soil
Blooms late spring to early summer
Daylily
p. 347

Belamcanda chinensis

Plant height: 2–4 ft.
Flower width: 1½–2 in.
Sun to partial shade
Average soil
Blooms in summer
Blackberry Lily
p. 299

Crocosmia masoniorum

Plant height: to 3 ft.
Flower width: 1½ in.
Full sun
Sandy, well-drained soil
Blooms in late summer
Crocosmia
p. 317

Asclepias tuberosa

Plant height: 1–3 ft.
Flower width: ½ in.
Full sun
Dry to average soil
Blooms in midsummer
Butterfly Weed
p. 294

Euphorbia griffithii 'Fire Glow'

Plant height: to 3 ft.
Bract width: ½–¾ in.
Sun to partial shade
Dry, well-drained soil
Blooms in early summer
Fire Glow Euphorbia
p. 332

Anigozanthos flavidus

Plant height: 3–4 ft.
Flower length: 1½ in.
Full sun
Well-drained soil
Blooms late spring to fall
Kangaroo Paw
p. 285

Physalis alkekengi

Plant height: to 2 ft.
Calyx width: 1½–2 in.
Sun to partial shade
Average soil
Blooms in late spring
Chinese Lantern-Plant
p. 383

Actaea rubra

Plant height: 1½–2 ft.
Berry width: ⅜ in.
Partial to full shade
Moist soil
Blooms mid-spring to late spring
Red Baneberry
p. 277

Eremurus stenophyllus

Plant height: 2–5 ft.
Flowers: in clusters 1–2 ft. long
Full sun
Well-drained soil
Blooms early summer to midsummer
p. 329

***Lupinus* 'Russell Hybrid'**

Plant height: 2–3 ft.
Flowers: in clusters 12–18 in. long
Sun to partial shade
Moist soil
Blooms in early summer
Russell Hybrid Lupine
p. 365

Kniphofia uvaria

Plant height: 2–6 ft.
Flowers: in clusters 6–12 in. long
Full sun
Moist, well-drained soil
Blooms in late summer
Red-hot Poker
p. 357

Lobelia cardinalis

Plant height: 3–6 ft.
Flower length: 1½ in.
Sun to partial shade
Moist soil
Blooms in summer
Cardinal-Flower
p. 364

Astilbe × arendsii 'Fanal'

Plant height: 2–4 ft.
Flowers: in clusters 8–12 in. long
Partial shade
Moist soil
Blooms early summer to midsummer
Astilbe
p. 296

Penstemon barbatus

Plant height: 2–3 ft.
Flower length: 1 in.
Full sun
Well-drained soil
Blooms in midsummer
Beardlip Penstemon
p. 379

Heuchera sanguinea

Plant height: 1–2 ft.
Flower width: ¼–½ in.
Sun to partial shade
Moist soil
Blooms early summer to late summer
Coral Bells
p. 349

Penstemon gloxinioides

Plant height: 2–3 ft.
Flower length: 2 in.
Full sun
Well-drained soil
Blooms in early summer
Gloxinia Penstemon
p. 379

Aquilegia canadensis

Plant height: 1½ ft.
Flower width: 1½ in.
Sun to partial shade
Well-drained soil
Blooms in late spring
Common Columbine
p. 288

Lychnis chalcedonica

Plant height: 1½–
to 2½ ft.
Flowers: in clusters
2–3 in. wide
Sun to partial shade
Moist soil
Blooms early summer
to midsummer
p. 366

Epimedium × warleyense

Plant height: 9–12 in.
Flower width: ¾ in.
Partial to full shade
Moist soil
Blooms in spring
Warley Epimedium
p. 328

Geum reptans

Plant height: 6–8 in.
Flower width: 1½ in.
Sun to partial shade
Dry, well-drained soil
Blooms in spring
Avens
p. 341

Geum quellyon
'Mrs. Bradshaw'

Plant height: to 2 ft.
Flower width: 1½ in.
Sun to partial shade
Moist, well-drained soil
Blooms spring to early summer
Chilean Avens
p. 341

Potentilla nepalensis
'Roxana'

Plant height: to 2 ft.
Flower width: 1 in.
Full sun
Dry, well-drained soil
Blooms midsummer to late summer
Nepal Cinquefoil
p. 387

Lychnis × arkwrightii

Plant height: 12–15 in.
Flower width: 1 in.
Sun to partial shade
Moist soil
Blooms early summer to midsummer
p. 365

***Potentilla atrosanguinea* 'Gibson's Scarlet'**

Plant height: 12–18 in.
Flower width: 1 in.
Full sun
Well-drained soil
Blooms in midsummer
Ruby Cinquefoil
p. 387

Helianthemum nummularium
'Fire Dragon'

Plant height: 9–12 in.
Flower width: 1 in.
Full sun
Dry soil
Blooms in early summer
Rock Rose
p. 344

Sedum spurium

Plant height: to 6 in.
Flowers: in clusters 2 in. wide
Sun to partial shade
Dry, well-drained soil
Blooms in midsummer
Two-row Stonecrop
p. 401

Verbena peruviana

Plant height: 3–4 in.
Flower width: ⅔ in.
Full sun
Well-drained soil
Blooms in summer
p. 415

Sedum 'Ruby Glow'

Plant height: 6–8 in
Flowers: in clusters
2 in. wide
Full sun
Well-drained soil
Blooms in late summer
Ruby Glow Sedum
p. 401

Shortia galacifolia

Plant height: to 8 in.
Flower width: 1 in.
Partial to full shade
Moist soil
Blooms in early summer
Oconee Bells
p. 402

Antennaria dioica var. *rosea*

Plant height: 4–12 in.
Flower width: ¼ in.
Full sun
Dry, well-drained soil
Blooms in summer
Pussytoes
p. 286

Helleborus orientalis

Plant height: to 18 in.
Flower width: 2 in.
Partial to full shade
Moist, well-drained soil
Blooms early spring to mid-spring
Lenten Rose
p. 347

Roscoea humeana

Plant height: 8–12 in.
Flower length: 4 in.
Sun to partial shade
Sandy, well-drained soil
Blooms early summer to midsummer
Hume Roscoea
p. 394

Sedum sieboldii

Plant height: 6–9 in.
Flowers: in clusters
2 in. wide
Sun to partial shade
Well-drained soil
Blooms in fall
October Daphne
p. 401

Phlox subulata
'Sampson'

Plant height: to 6 in.
Flower width: ¾ in.
Full sun to partial shade
Well-drained soil
Blooms in spring
Ground Pink
p. 382

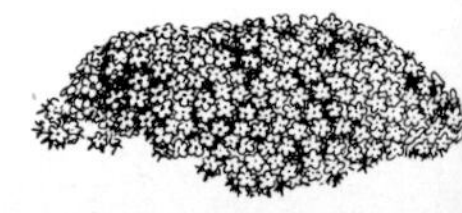

Aubrieta deltoidea

Plant height: to 6 in.
Flower width: ¾ in.
Sun to partial shade
Well-drained soil
Blooms in early spring
False Rockcress
p. 297

aponaria cymoides

Plant height: 4–8 in.
Flower width: ½ in.
Full sun
Sandy, well-drained soil
Blooms late spring to early summer
Rock Soapwort
p. 398

Gypsophila paniculata

Plant height: to 3 ft.
Flower width: ¼ in.
Full sun
Well-drained soil
Blooms in midsummer
Baby's-Breath
p. 343

Petrorhagia saxifraga

Plant height: 6–10 in.
Flower width: ¼–½ in.
Full sun
Well-drained soil
Blooms in summer
Tunic Flower
p. 380

Gypsophila repens 'Rosea'

Plant height: 6–8 in.
Flower width: ¼ in.
Full sun
Moist, well-drained soil
Blooms in summer
Creeping Baby's-Breath
p. 343

Limonium latifolium

Plant height: 1½–2 ft.
Flower width: ⅛ in.
Full sun
Moist, well-drained soil
Blooms in summer
Sea-lavender
p. 362

Goniolimon tataricum

Plant height: to 18 in.
Flower width: ¼ in.
Full sun
Dry, well-drained soil
Blooms in early summer
Tatarian Statice
p. 342

Epimedium grandiflorum
'Rose Queen'

Plant height: to 12 in.
Flower width: 1–2 in.
Partial to full shade
Moist soil
Blooms mid-spring to late spring
Longspur Epimedium
p. 328

Saxifraga* × *urbium

Plant height: to 12 in.
Flower width: ⅓ in.
Partial to full shade
Moist soil
Blooms in spring
London Pride
Saxifrage
p. 399

Epimedium* × *rubrum

Plant height: to 12 in.
Flower width: 1 in.
Partial to full shade
Moist soil
Blooms in spring
Red Epimedium
p. 328

Begonia grandis

Plant height: 1–2 ft.
Flower width: 1–1½ in.
Partial to full shade
Moist soil
Blooms late summer to fall
Hardy Begonia
p. 299

***Anemone vitifolia* 'Robustissima'**

Plant height: 2–3 ft.
Flower width: 2–3 in.
Sun to partial shade
Moist soil
Blooms late summer to fall
Japanese Anemone
p. 285

Thalictrum rochebrunianum

Plant height: 3–5 ft.
Flower width: ½ in.
Sun to partial shade
Moist, well-drained soil
Blooms midsummer to late summer
Lavender Mist Meadowrue
p. 409

Anemone × hybrida

Plant height: 1–5 ft.
Flower width: 2–3 in.
Sun to partial shade
Moist soil
Blooms late summer to early fall
Japanese Anemone
p. 285

Rhexia virginica

Plant height: 9–18 in.
Flower width: 1½ in.
Full sun
Wet soil
Blooms summer to early fall
Deer Grass
p. 392

Hibiscus moscheutos

Plant height: 3–8 ft.
Flower width: 4–12 in.
Full sun
Moist soil
Blooms in summer
Rose Mallow
p. 350

Rhexia mariana

Plant height: 1–2 ft.
Flower width: 1½ in.
Full sun
Wet soil
Blooms summer to early fall
Maryland Meadowbeauty
p. 392

Hibiscus coccineus

Plant height: 6–8 ft.
Flower width: 5–6 in.
Full sun
Moist soil
Blooms in summer
Scarlet Rose Mallow
p. 350

Malva alcea

Plant height: 2–4 ft.
Flower width: 2 in.
Sun to partial shade
Dry soil
Blooms in summer
Hollyhock Mallow
p. 368

Callirhoe involucrata

Plant height: 6–12 in.
Flower width: 1½–2½ in.
Full sun
Dry soil
Blooms in summer
Finger Poppy Mallow
p. 303

Oenothera speciosa

Plant height: 6–18 in.
Flower width: 2 in.
Full sun
Well-drained soil
Blooms in early summer
Showy Primrose
p. 373

Geranium psilostemon

Plant height: to 2 ft.
Flower width: 1½ in.
Sun to partial shade
Moist soil
Blooms in early summer
Armenian Cranesbill
p. 340

Geranium sanguineum* var. *lancastriense

Plant height: 12–18 in.
Flower width: 1 in.
Sun to partial shade
Average soil
Blooms late spring to midsummer
Blood-red Cranesbill
p. 340

Geranium dalmaticum

Plant height: to 6 in.
Flower width: 1 in.
Sun to partial shade
Moist to dry soil
Blooms spring to early summer
p. 339

***Geranium endressii* 'A. T. Johnson'**

Plant height: 12–18 in.
Flower width: ½–1 in.
Sun to partial shade
Moist, well-drained soil
Blooms late spring to early summer
A. T. Johnson Geranium
p. 339

Geranium maculatum

Plant height: 12–20 in.
Flower width: 1 in.
Sun to partial shade
Well-drained soil
Blooms spring to early summer
Wild Geranium
p. 340

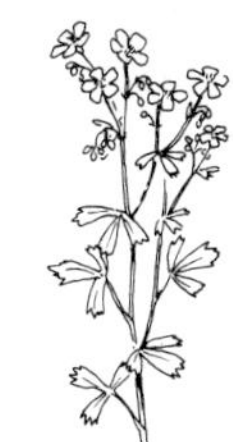

Lychnis coronaria

Plant height: 1½–3 ft.
Flower width: 1 in.
Sun to partial shade
Moist, well-drained soil
Blooms in early summer
Rose Campion
p. 366

Achillea millefolium 'Fire King'

Plant height: to 2 ft.
Flower width: ¼ in.
Full sun
Average soil
Blooms in midsummer
Common Yarrow
p. 275

Armeria maritima

Plant height: 6–10 in.
Flowers: in clusters
¾ in. wide
Full sun
Dry soil
Blooms in mid-spring
Common Thrift
p. 291

Dianthus barbatus

Plant height: 1–2 ft.
Flower width: ½ in.
Sun to partial shade
Well-drained soil
Blooms in early summer
Sweet William
p. 319

Diantbus plumarius 'Agatha'

Plant height: 9–18 in.
Flower width: 1½ in.
Full sun
Well-drained soil
Blooms late spring to early summer
Grass Pink
p. 320

Dianthus × _allwoodii_

Plant height: 12–18 in.
Flower width: 1½–2 in.
Full sun
Well-drained soil
Blooms in summer
Allwood Pink
p. 319

Diantbus deltoides

Plant height: 4–12 in.
Flower width: ¾ in.
Full sun
Well-drained soil
Blooms in late spring
Maiden Pink
p. 319

Dianthus gratianopolitanus 'Tiny Rubies'

Plant height: 6–8 in.
Flower width: ½–¾ in.
Full sun
Well-drained soil
Blooms in late spring
Cheddar Pink
p. 320

Viola cornuta

Plant height: 5–8 in.
Flower width: 1½ in.
Partial shade
Moist, well-drained soil
Blooms in late spring
Horned Violet
p. 417

Primula sieboldii

Plant height: to 12 in.
Flower width: 2 in.
Partial shade
Moist soil
Blooms in late spring
Japanese Star Primrose
p. 389

Silene schafta

Plant height: to 6 in.
Flower width: ¾ in.
Sun to partial shade
Sandy, moist, well-drained soil
Blooms summer to fall
Moss Campion
p. 403

Geranium macrorrhizum

Plant height: 12–18 in.
Flower width: 1 in.
Sun to partial shade
Average soil
Blooms late spring to early summer
Bigroot Cranesbill
p. 340

Incarvillea delavayi

Plant height: to 2 ft.
Flower width: 2 in.
Sun to partial shade
Moist soil
Blooms in early summer
Hardy Gloxinia
p. 353

Digitalis × mertonensis

Plant height: to 3 ft.
Flower length: 2–3 in.
Partial shade
Moist, well-drained soil
Blooms in summer
p. 323

Dicentra spectabilis

Plant height: 1–2 ft.
Flower length: 1½ in.
Partial to full shade
Moist soil
Blooms in spring
Common Bleeding Heart
p. 321

Dicentra 'Luxuriant'

Plant height: 12–18 in.
Flower length: 1 in.
Partial shade
Moist, well-drained soil
Blooms spring to fall
p. 321

Symphytum × rubrum

Plant height: to 18 in.
Flower length: ½–1 in.
Sun to partial shade
Well-drained soil
Blooms in late spring
p. 408

Tradescantia × andersoniana 'Pauline'

Plant height: 2–2½ ft.
Flower width: 1 in.
Sun to partial shade
Well-drained soil
Blooms late spring to early summer
Common Spiderwort
p. 411

helone lyonii

Plant height: to 3 ft.
Flower length: 1 in.
Partial shade
Moist to wet soil
Blooms in late summer
Pink Turtlehead
p. 309

***ergenia* 'Margery ish'**

Plant height: 12–18 in.
Flower width: ¼–½ in.
Sun to partial shade
Moist soil
Blooms in spring
Hybrid Bergenia
p. 300

Dictamnus albus
'Purpureus'

Plant height: 2–3 ft.
Flower width: 1–2 in.
Full sun
Moist soil
Blooms in early summer
Gas Plant
p. 321

Lychnis viscaria
'Splendens Plena'

Plant height: 12–18 in.
Flowers: in clusters 1½–2 in. wide
Full sun
Moist, sandy soil
Blooms late spring to early summer
German Catchfly
p. 366

Aquilegia 'Dragon Fly'

Plant height: 1–3 ft.
Flower width: 2 in.
Sun to partial shade
Average soil
Blooms in late spring
Hybrid Columbine
p. 288

Primula japonica

Plant height: 8–16 in.
Flower width: 1 in.
Partial shade
Moist soil
Blooms in late spring
Japanese Primrose
p. 389

Mimulus lewisii

Plant height: to 2½ ft.
Flower length: 2 in.
Full sun to partial shade
Moist soil
Blooms in midsummer
Lewis' Monkey Flower
p. 371

Saponaria officinalis

Plant height: 1–3 ft.
Flower width: 1 in.
Full sun
Well-drained soil
Blooms in summer
Bouncing Bet
p. 398

Sidalcea malviflora 'Loveliness'

Plant height: 1½–3¼ ft.
Flower width: 1½ in.
Full sun
Well-drained soil
Blooms in midsummer
Checkerbloom
p. 403

Hesperis matronalis

Plant height: 2–3 ft.
Flower width: ½–¾ in.
Sun to partial shade
Moist, well-drained soil
Blooms early summer to midsummer
Dame's-Rocket
p. 348

Bergenia cordifolia

Plant height: 12–18 in.
Flower width: ¼–½ in.
Sun to partial shade
Moist soil
Blooms in spring
Heartleaf Bergenia
p. 300

Coronilla varia

Plant height: to 18 in.
Flower length: ½ in.
Full sun
Dry soil
Blooms in summer
Crown Vetch
p. 315

Indigofera incarnata

Plant height: 12–18 in.
Flower length: ¾ in.
Full sun
Well-drained soil
Blooms midsummer to late summer
Chinese Indigo
p. 353

Galega officinalis

Plant height: 2–3 ft.
Flower length: ½ in.
Sun to partial shade
Average soil
Blooms in summer
Goat's Rue
p. 336

Prunella grandiflora 'Rosea'

Plant height: to 12 in.
Flowers: in clusters 2 in. long
Sun to partial shade
Average to moist soil
Blooms in summer
Self Heal
p. 390

Physostegia virginiana

Plant height: 4–5 ft.
Flower length: 1 in.
Sun to partial shade
Moist soil
Blooms in summer
False Dragonhead
p. 384

Stachys macrantha 'Robusta'

Plant height: 12–18 in.
Flower width: 1½ in.
Sun to partial shade
Well-drained soil
Blooms in midsummer
Big Betony
p. 406

Lythrum salicaria

Plant height: 2–6 ft.
Flower width: ¾ in.
Full sun
Moist soil
Blooms midsummer to late summer
Purple Loosestrife
p. 367

Astilbe tacquetii 'Superba'

Plant height: 3–4 ft.
Flowers: in clusters 6–10 in. long
Partial shade
Moist soil
Blooms in midsummer
p. 297

Centranthus ruber

Plant height: 1–3 ft.
Flowers: in clusters 2 in. wide
Full sun
Well-drained soil
Blooms in summer
Red Valerian
p. 307

Elsholtzia stauntonii

Plant height: to 5 ft.
Flowers: in clusters
6 in. long
Full sun
Well-drained soil
Blooms in early fall
Staunton Elsholtzia
p. 327

Liatris spicata

Plant height: 4–6 ft.
Flowers: in clusters
6–12 in. long
Full sun
Moist soil
Blooms in summer
Gay-Feather
p. 360

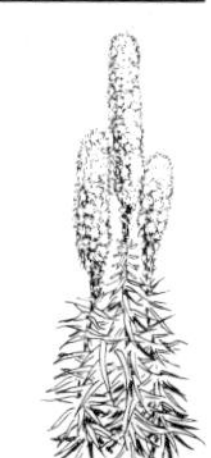

× Heucherella tiarelloides
'Bridget Bloom'

Plant height: to 18 in.
Flower width: ¼–½ in.
Sun to partial shade
Moist soil
Blooms spring to early summer
p. 349

Polygonum affine
'Superbum'

Plant height: to 18 in.
Flowers: in clusters 2–3 in. long
Sun to partial shade
Moist soil
Blooms summer to early fall
p. 386

Teucrium chamaedrys

Plant height: 1–2 ft.
Flower length: ¾ in.
Full sun
Well-drained soil
Blooms in midsummer
Wall Germander
p. 409

***Polygonum bistorta* 'Superbum'**

Plant height: 2–3 ft.
Flowers: in clusters 6 in. long.
Partial to full shade
Moist soil
Blooms in early summer
European Bistort
p. 386

Veronica virginica 'Rosea'

Plant height: 2–6 ft.
Flowers: in clusters 6–8 in. long
Sun to partial shade
Well-drained soil
Blooms in late summer
Culver's Root
p. 416

Veronica spicata

Plant height: 12–18 in.
Flowers: in clusters 6 in. long
Sun to partial shade
Well-drained soil
Blooms in midsummer
Speedwell
p. 416

Linaria purpurea 'Canon Went'

Plant height: 2–3 ft.
Flowers: in clusters 4–6 in. long
Full sun
Sandy, well-drained soil
Blooms in summer
Purple Toadflax
p. 363

Astilbe chinensis 'Pumila'

Plant height: 8–12 in.
Flowers: in clusters 6 in. long
Partial shade
Dry soil
Blooms in late summer
Chinese Astilbe
p. 296

Polygonum cuspidatum var. **compactum**

Plant height: to 2 ft.
Flowers: in clusters 4 in. long
Full sun
Average soil
Blooms late summer to fall
Reynoutria Fleeceflower
p. 387

Filipendula rubra

Plant height: 4–7 ft.
Flowers: in clusters 4 in. wide
Partial shade
Very moist soil
Blooms in summer
Queen-of-the-Prairie
p. 333

Filipendula palmata

Plant height: 2–4 ft.
Flowers: in clusters
4 in. wide
Partial shade
Very moist soil
Blooms in summer
Meadowsweet
p. 333

Valeriana officinalis

Plant height: 2–4 ft.
Flowers: in clusters
4 in. wide
Full sun
Moist, well-drained soil
Blooms in midsummer
Common Valerian
p. 414

Thalictrum aquilegifolium

Plant height: 2–3 ft.
Flowers: in clusters 4 in. wide
Sun to partial shade
Moist, well-drained soil
Blooms late spring to early summer
Columbine Meadowrue
p. 409

Sedum **'Autumn Joy'**

Plant height: to 2 ft.
Flowers: in clusters 3–4 in. wide
Sun to partial shade
Well-drained soil
Blooms midsummer to late summer
Autumn Joy Sedum
p. 401

Sedum spectabile

Plant height: to 2 ft.
Flowers: in clusters
3–4 in. wide
Sun to partial shade
Dry, well-drained soil
Blooms in late summer
Showy Stonecrop
p. 401

'edum maximum
'Atropurpureum'

Plant height: 1–2 ft.
Flowers: in clusters
4 in. wide
Sun to partial shade
Well-drained soil
Blooms late summer to
early fall
Great Stonecrop
p. 401

Paeonia suffruticosa

Plant height: 4–7 ft.
Flower width: 12 in.
Sun to partial shade
Well-drained soil
Blooms in mid-spring
Japanese Tree Peony
p. 377

Aster novae-angliae
'Alma Potschke'

Plant height: 3–5 ft.
Flower width: 1½ in.
Full sun
Average to moist soil
Blooms late summer to fall
New England Aster
p. 296

***Paeonia officinalis* 'Rubra Plena'**

Plant height: to 3 ft.
Flower width: 4 in.
Sun to partial shade
Moist soil
Blooms in late spring
Common Peony
p. 377

hrysanthemum* × *iorifolium

Plant height: to 4 ft.
Flower width: 1–6 in.
Full sun
Moist soil
Blooms in fall
Florists' Chrysanthemum
p. 310

***Centaurea hypoleuca* 'John Coutts'**

Plant height: 1½–2 ft.
Flower width: 2 in.
Full sun
Dry, well-drained soil
Blooms early summer to midsummer
John Coutts Centaurea
p. 306

Echinacea purpurea

Plant height: 2–4 ft.
Flower width: 3 in.
Sun to partial shade
Sandy, well-drained soil
Blooms in midsummer
Purple Coneflower
p. 326

Centaurea montana 'Violetta'

Plant height: 1½–2 ft.
Flower width: 2–3 in.
Full sun
Average soil
Blooms mid-spring to early summer
Mountain Bluet
p. 306

Monarda fistulosa

Plant height: 3–4 ft.
Flower width: 1½–2 in.
Sun to partial shade
Dry to moist soil
Blooms in summer
Wild Bergamot
p. 371

Chrysanthemum zawadskii
'Clara Curtis'

Plant height: to 18 in.
Flower width: 2½ in.
Full sun
Well-drained soil
Blooms midsummer to late summer
p. 311

Scabiosa caucasica
'David Wilkie'

Plant height: to 2½ ft.
Flower width: 2–3 in.
Full sun
Moist soil
Blooms in summer
Pincushion Flower
p. 400

Stokesia laevis

Plant height: to 2 ft.
Flower width: 2–4 in.
Sun to partial shade
Sandy, moist, well-drained soil
Blooms in late summer
Stokes' Aster
p. 406

***Erigeron* 'Walther'**

Plant height: 1–2 ft.
Flower width: 2 in.
Full sun
Sandy, well-drained soil
Blooms in summer
Fleabane
p. 329

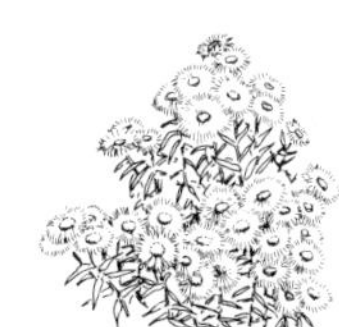

Nepeta mussinii

Plant height: to 12 in.
Flowers: in clusters 3–4 in. high
Full sun
Sandy, well-drained soil
Blooms early summer to midsummer
p. 373

Campanula garganica

Plant height: to 6 in.
Flower width: ½ in.
Full sun
Average to moist soil
Blooms spring to fall
p. 304

Campanula poscharskyana 'E. K. Toogood'

Plant height: 4–6 in.
Flower width: 1 in.
Sun to partial shade
Well-drained soil
Blooms in summer
Serbian Bellflower
p. 305

Campanula portenschlagiana

Plant height: 6–8 in.
Flower width: ¾–1 in.
Partial shade
Well-drained soil
Blooms late spring to summer
Dalmatian Bellflower
p. 305

Viola odorata 'Royal Robe'

Plant height: 6–8 in.
Flower width: ¾–1 in.
Partial shade
Moist, well-drained soil
Blooms in late spring
Sweet Violet
p. 417

Omphalodes cappadocica

Plant height: 6–10 in.
Flower width: ⅓ in.
Partial to full shade
Well-drained soil
Blooms in spring
Navelwort
p. 374

Omphalodes verna

Plant height: to 8 in.
Flower width: ½ in.
Partial to full shade
Moist soil
Blooms in spring
Creeping Forget-Me-Not
p. 374

Cynoglossum nervosum

Plant height: to 2 ft.
Flower width: ½ in.
Full sun
Well-drained soil
Blooms in early summer
Great Houndstongue
p. 317

Brunnera macrophylla

Plant height: 12–18 in.
Flower width: ¼ in.
Partial shade
Moist soil
Blooms in spring
Siberian Bugloss
p. 301

Myosotis scorpioides var. *semperflorens*

Plant height: 12–18 in.
Flower width: ⅓ in.
Sun to partial shade
Moist soil
Blooms spring to fall
True Forget-Me-Not
p. 372

Ceratostigma plumbaginoides

Plant height: to 12 in.
Flower width: ½ in.
Full sun
Well-drained soil
Blooms in late summer
Leadwort
p. 308

Polemonium reptans

Plant height: 8–12 in.
Flower width: ½ in.
Sun to partial shade
Moist, well-drained soil
Blooms in spring
Creeping Polemonium
p. 385

Phlox divaricata

Plant height: to 18 in.
Flower width: 1 in.
Partial to full shade
Moist soil
Blooms in spring
Wild Sweet William
p. 381

Linum perenne

Plant height: 1–2 ft.
Flower width: 1 in.
Full sun
Well-drained soil
Blooms in summer
Perennial Flax
p. 363

Phlox stolonifera
'Blue Ridge'

Plant height: to 12 in.
Flower width: ¾ in.
Partial shade
Moist soil
Blooms in late spring
Creeping Phlox
p. 382

Geranium
'Johnson's Blue'

Plant height: 12 in.
Flower width: 1½–2 in.
Sun to partial shade
Average to moist soil
Blooms late spring to early summer
Johnson's Blue Cranesbill
p. 340

Geranium himalayense

Plant height: 8–15 in.
Flower width: 2 in.
Sun to partial shade
Well-drained soil
Blooms mid-spring to late spring
Lilac Cranesbill
p. 340

Pulmonaria saccharata

Plant height: 8–14 in.
Flower length: ¾–1 in.
Partial to full shade
Moist soil
Blooms mid-spring to late spring
Bethlehem Sage
p. 391

/erbena rigida

Plant height: 1–2 ft.
Flowers: in clusters 1 in. wide
Full sun
Well-drained soil
Blooms in summer
Vervain
p. 415

'ulmonaria •ngifolia

Plant height: to 12 in.
Flower length: ¾–1 in.
Partial to full shade
Moist soil
Blooms late spring to early summer
p. 390

Gentiana asclepiadea

Plant height: to 2 ft.
Flower length: 1½ in.
Partial shade
Moist soil
Blooms midsummer to late summer
Willow Gentian
p. 339

Pulmonaria angustifolia

Plant height: 6–12 in.
Flower length: ¾–1 in.
Partial to full shade
Moist soil
Blooms in spring
Blue Lungwort
p. 390

Campanula glomerata

Plant height: 1–3 ft.
Flowers: in clusters 3 in. wide
Sun to partial shade
Dry to moist soil
Blooms early summer to midsummer
Danesblood Bellflower
p. 304

Polemonium foliosissimum

Plant height: 2–2½ ft.
Flower width: ⅝ in.
Sun to partial shade
Moist, well-drained soil
Blooms late spring to early summer
Leafy Polemonium
p. 385

Campanula carpatica 'Isobel'

Plant height: 6–12 in.
Flower width: 2 in.
Sun to partial shade
Well-drained soil
Blooms late spring to midsummer
Carpathian Harebell
p. 304

Polemonium caeruleum

Plant height: to 3 ft.
Flower width: 1 in.
Sun to partial shade
Moist, well-drained soil
Blooms in spring
Jacob's Ladder
p. 385

Platycodon grandiflorus

Plant height: 1½–2½ in.
Flower width: 2–3 in.
Sun to partial shade
Moist, well-drained soil
Blooms in midsummer
Balloon Flower
p. 384

Anemone pulsatilla

Plant height: to 12 in.
Flower width: 2 in.
Sun to partial shade
Well-drained soil
Blooms in spring
Pasqueflower
p. 285

Tradescantia hirsuticaulis

Plant height: to 12 in.
Flower width: 1 in.
Sun to partial shade
Well-drained soil
Blooms late spring to early summer
p. 411

Iris cristata

Plant height: 4–6 in.
Outer segments: 1½ in. long
Sun to partial shade
Moist soil
Blooms in mid-spring
Crested Iris
p. 354

ris ensata **'Azure'**

Plant height: 2–3 ft.
Outer segments:
3 in. long
Sun to partial shade
Moist soil
Blooms midsummer to late summer
Japanese Iris
p. 355

ris tectorum

Plant height: 8–12 in.
Outer segments:
2 in. long
Sun to partial shade
Sandy soil
Blooms in late spring
Roof Iris
p. 356

Iris sibirica

Plant height: 2–4 ft.
Outer segments:
¾ in. long
Sun to partial shade
Moist soil
Blooms in early summer
p. 356

Iris pumila

Plant height: 4–8 in.
Outer segments:
2–3 in. long
Full sun
Well-drained soil
Blooms in spring
Dwarf Bearded Iris
p. 356

Iris laevigata 'Variegata'

Plant height: 1½–2 ft.
Outer segments: 2½–3 in. long
Full sun
Moist to wet soil
Blooms in summer
Variegated Rabbitear Iris
p. 355

Bearded Iris

Plant height: to 2 ft.
Outer segments: 2–3 in. long
Full sun
Well-drained soil
Blooms in late spring
p. 354

Aquilegia caerulea

Plant height: 2–3 ft.
Flower width: 2 in.
Sun to partial shade
Average soil
Blooms in late spring
Rocky Mountain Columbine
p. 288

Eryngium × zabelii 'Amethyst'

Plant height: 2–2½ ft.
Flower width: 1 in.
Full sun
Dry, well-drained soil
Blooms in summer
Zabel Eryngo
p. 331

Tricyrtis hirta

Plant height: to 3 ft.
Flower length: 1 in.
Partial shade
Moist soil
Blooms in early fall
Toad Lily
p. 411

Echinops ritro 'Taplow Blue'

Plant height: 3–4 ft.
Flower width: 1½–2 in.
Full sun
Well-drained soil
Blooms in midsummer
Globe Thistle
p. 327

Eupatorium coelestinum

Plant height: to 2 ft.
Flower width: ½ in.
Sun to partial shade
Sandy soil
Blooms late summer to early fall
Mist Flower
p. 331

Aster × frikartii

Plant height: 2–3 ft.
Flower width: 2–3 in.
Full sun
Well-drained soil
Blooms midsummer to fall
p. 296

Catananche caerulea

Plant height: to 2 ft.
Flower width: 2 in.
Full sun
Dry soil
Blooms in summer
Cupid's Dart
p. 305

Aster tataricus

Plant height: 6–8 ft.
Flower width: 1 in.
Full sun
Dry to moist soil
Blooms in fall
Tartarian Aster
p. 296

Clematis heracleifolia* var. *davidiana

Plant height: 3–4 ft.
Flower width: 1 in.
Sun to partial shade
Moist soil
Blooms midsummer to late summer
Tube Clematis
p. 313

Anchusa azurea

Plant height: 3½–5 ft.
Flower width: ½ in.
Sun to partial shade
Average soil
Blooms in early summer
Italian Bugloss
p. 284

avandula ngustifolia

Plant height: 1–3 ft.
Flower length: ⅓ in.
Full sun
Dry, well-drained soil
Blooms in summer
Lavender
p. 359

ampanula tundifolia

Plant height: 1–2 ft.
Flower length: 1 in.
Full sun
Well-drained soil
Blooms early summer to late summer
Bluebell
p. 305

Campanula lactiflora **'Superba'**

Plant height: to 4 ft.
Flower width: 1 in.
Sun to partial shade
Moist soil
Blooms in midsummer
Milky Bellflower
p. 304

Mertensia virginica

Plant height: to 2 ft.
Flower length: 1 in.
Partial to full shade
Moist soil
Blooms in early spring
Virginia Bluebells
p. 370

;ampanula latifolia

Plant height: 2–4 ft.
Flower width: 1½ in.
Sun to partial shade
Moist soil
Blooms early summer to midsummer
Great Bellflower
p. 304

ymphytum × plandicum

Plant height: 2–3 ft.
Flower length: ¾–1 in.
Sun to partial shade
Well-drained soil
Blooms late spring to early summer
Russian Comfrey
p. 408

Hosta lancifolia

Plant height: to 2 ft.
Flower length: 2 in.
Partial to full shade
Moist soil
Blooms in late summer
Narrowleaf Plantainlily
p. 351

Adenophora confusa

Plant height: to 3 ft.
Flower length: ¾ in.
Sun to partial shade
Well-drained soil
Blooms midsummer to late summer
Ladybells
p. 278

Penstemon hirsutus

Plant height: 2–3 ft.
Flower length: 1 in.
Full sun
Well-drained soil
Blooms in summer
p. 379

Veronica latifolium 'Crater Lake Blue'

Plant height: 12–18 in.
Flower width: ½ in.
Sun to partial shade
Well-drained soil
Blooms late spring to midsummer
Hungarian Speedwell
p. 416

Delphinium elatum

Plant height: to 6 ft.
Flower width: 1 in.
Full sun
Moist soil
Blooms in early summer
Candle Larkspur
p. 318

Aconitum × bicolor 'Bicolor'

Plant height: 3–4 ft.
Flower length: 1–2 in.
Partial shade
Moist soil
Blooms in late summer
Hybrid Monkshood
p. 276

Aconitum napellus

Plant height: to 4 ft.
Flower length: 1–2 in.
Partial shade
Moist soil
Blooms in late summer
Common Monkshood
p. 277

Aconitum
armichaelii

Plant height: 3–4 ft.
Flower length: 1½ in.
Partial shade
Moist soil
Blooms in late summer
Azure Monkshood
p. 277

Salvia azurea var. **grandiflora**

Plant height: 4–5 ft.
Flower width: 1 in.
Sun to partial shade
Well-drained soil
Blooms late summer to fall
Pitcher's Salvia
p. 396

Baptisia australis

Plant height: 3–5 ft.
Flower width: 1 in.
Full sun
Dry, well-drained soil
Blooms in late spring
Blue False Indigo
p. 298

Lobelia siphilitica

Plant height: 2–4 ft.
Flower length: 1 in.
Sun to partial shade
Moist soil
Blooms in late summer
Blue Lobelia
p. 364

Salvia farinacea
'Catima'

Plant height: to 3 ft.
Flowers: in clusters
3 in. long
Sun to partial shade
Well-drained soil
Blooms in midsummer
Mealy-Cup Sage
p. 396

Salvia × superba 'Mainacht'

Plant height: 1½–3 ft.
Flowers: in clusters 4–8 in. long
Sun to partial shade
Well-drained soil
Blooms in summer
Violet Sage
p. 396

Salvia pratensis

Plant height: to 3 ft.
Flowers: in clusters 4–6 in. long
Sun to partial shade
Well-drained soil
Blooms midsummer to late summer
Meadow Clary
p. 396

Veronica grandis
var. **holophylla**
'Lavender Charm'

Plant height: 2–3 ft.
Flowers: in clusters 6 in. long
Sun to partial shade
Well-drained soil
Blooms in summer
p. 416

Perovskia atriplicifolia

Plant height: 3–5 ft.
Flowers: in clusters 8–12 in. long
Full sun
Well-drained soil
Blooms midsummer to late summer
Azure Sage
p. 379

Crambe cordifolia

Plant height: to 6 ft.
Flower width: 5/16 in.
Full sun
Well-drained soil
Blooms in early summer
Heartleaf Crambe
p. 316

Potentilla tridentata

Plant height: to 12 in.
Flower width: 1/4 in.
Full sun
Sandy, moist soil
Blooms late spring to midsummer
Three-toothed Cinquefoil
p. 388

'ilipendula vulgaris 'Flore Pleno'

Plant height: 2–3 ft.
Flower width: ½–¾ in.
Partial to full shade
Average to dry soil
Blooms in early summer
Dropwort
p. 333

'renaria verna var. 'aespitosa

Plant height: to 2 in.
Flower width: ⅜ in.
Sun to partial shade
Moist soil
Blooms late spring to midsummer
Irish Moss
p. 290

***Arabis caucasica* 'Snow Cap'**

Plant height: to 12 in.
Flower width: ½ in.
Full sun
Dry soil
Blooms in early spring
Wall Cress
p. 288

Iberis sempervirens

Plant height: to 12 in.
Flower width: 1½ in.
Full sun
Well-drained soil
Blooms mid-spring to late spring
Candytuft
p. 352

uphorbia corollata

Plant height: 1½–3 ft.
Flower width: ¼ in.
Full sun
Dry, well-drained soil
Blooms in summer
Flowering Spurge
p. 332

rabis procurrens

Plant height: to 1 ft.
Flower width: 5/16 in.
Sun to partial shade
Dry soil
Blooms in early spring
Rock Cress
p. 289

Saxifraga stolonifera

Plant height: to 2 ft.
Flower width: ¾ in.
Partial to full shade
Moist soil
Blooms in spring
Strawberry Geranium
p. 399

Cerastium tomentosum

Plant height: to 6 in.
Flower width: ½ in.
Full sun
Well-drained soil
Blooms in late spring
Snow-in-Summer
p. 307

Amsonia tabernaemontana

Plant height: to 2 ft.
Flower length: 1/3 in.
Sun to partial shade
Average to moist soil
Blooms in late spring
Blue Star
p. 282

Cerastium biebersteinii

Plant height: to 6 in.
Flower width: 1 in.
Full sun
Well-drained soil
Blooms in early summer
Taurus Cerastium
p. 307

Achillea × lewisii 'King Edward'

Plant height: 8–12 in.
Flower width: ⅛ in.
Full sun
Dry soil
Blooms in midsummer
King Edward Yarrow
p. 275

Chrysanthemum leucanthemum

Plant height: to 2 ft.
Flower width: 1½ in.
Full sun
Average soil
Blooms in early summer
Oxeye Daisy
p. 310

Leontopodium alpinum

Plant height: 6–12 in.
Flower width: ¼ in.
Full sun
Dry soil
Blooms in early summer
Edelweiss
p. 360

Chrysanthemum × superbum 'Little Miss Muffet'

Plant height: 1–2 ft.
Flower width: 2–4 in.
Sun to partial shade
Moist, well-drained soil
Blooms early summer to midsummer
Shasta Daisy
p. 311

Boltonia asteroides 'Snowbank'

Plant height: 3–5 ft.
Flower width: ¾ in.
Full sun
Average soil
Blooms in late summer
White Boltonia
p. 301

Chrysanthemum parthenium

Plant height: 2–3 ft.
Flower width: ¼ in.
Sun to partial shade
Well-drained soil
Blooms late summer to fall
Feverfew
p. 310

Chrysanthemum nipponicum

Plant height: 1½–2 ft.
Flower width: 2–3 in.
Full sun
Well-drained soil
Blooms in fall
Nippon Chrysanthemum
p. 310

Romneya coulteri

Plant height: to 8 ft.
Flower width: 6 in.
Full sun
Well-drained soil
Blooms in late summer
California Tree Poppy
p. 393

Anemone sylvestris 'Snowdrop'

Plant height: to 18 in.
Flower width: 2 in.
Sun to partial shade
Moist soil
Blooms in late spring
Snowdrop Windflower
p. 285

Fragaria chiloensis

Plant height: 6–8 in.
Flower width: ½ in.
Full sun
Well-drained soil
Blooms in summer
Chiloe Strawberry
p. 335

Paeonia mlokosewitschii

Plant height: 1½–2 ft.
Flower width: 5 in.
Sun to partial shade
Well-drained soil
Blooms in spring
Caucasian Peony
p. 377

Helleborus niger

Plant height: to 12 in.
Flower width: 3 in.
Partial to full shade
Moist soil
Blooms winter to early spring
Christmas Rose
p. 347

Zantedeschia aethiopica

Plant height: 1–3 ft.
Spathe length: 5–9 in.
Full sun
Moist soil
Blooms late spring to early summer
Calla Lily
p. 419

Viola striata

Plant height: 4–16 in.
Flower width: ½ in.
Partial shade
Moist, well-drained soil
Blooms in summer
Striped Violet
p. 417

Arisaema riphyllum

Plant height: 1½–2½ ft.
Flower length: 3 in.
Partial to full shade
Moist soil
Blooms late spring to early summer
Jack-in-the-Pulpit
p. 290

rillium randiflorum

Plant height: 12–18 in.
Flower width: 2–3 in.
Partial to full shade
Moist soil
Blooms mid-spring to late spring
Snow Trillium
p. 412

Lamium maculatum
'White Nancy'

Plant height: to 18 in.
Flower length: 1 in.
Full sun to shade
Moist, well-drained soil
Blooms in summer
Spotted Dead Nettle
p. 358

Epimedium × versicolor
'Sulphureum'

Plant height: to 12 in.
Flower width: 1 in.
Partial to full shade
Moist soil
Blooms in spring
Persian Epimedium
p. 328

ymphytum rrandiflorum

Plant height: 8–12 in.
Flower length: ¾ in.
Sun to partial shade
Well-drained soil
Blooms mid-spring to late spring
Ground-cover Comfrey
p. 407

pimedium × voungianum **Niveum'**

Plant height: 8–10 in.
Flower width: ½ in.
Partial to full shade
Moist soil
Blooms in spring
Snowy Epimedium
p. 328

Disporum sessile 'Variegatum'

Plant height: 1½–2 ft.
Flower length: 1 in.
Partial to full shade.
Dry, well-drained soil
Blooms in spring
Variegated Japanese Fairy-Bells
p. 323

Convallaria majalis

Plant height: 6–12 in.
Flower width: ⅜ in.
Partial to full shade
Moist soil
Blooms mid-spring to late spring
Lily-of-the-Valley
p. 314

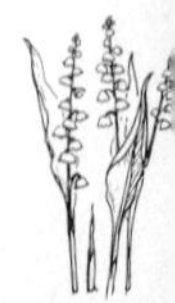

'olygonatum doratum var. ***hunbergii***

Plant height: to 3½ ft.
Flower length: 1 in.
Partial to full shade
Moist soil
Blooms in spring
Variegated Solomon's-Seal
p. 386

)icentra cucullaria

Plant height: 5–8 in.
Flower length: ¾ in.
Partial to full shade
Moist soil
Blooms in spring
Dutchman's-Breeches
p. 320

Dodecatheon meadia

Plant height: 1–2 ft.
Flower length: 1 in.
Partial shade
Well-drained soil
Blooms in late spring
Common Shooting-star
p. 324

Galtonia candicans

Plant height: 3–4 ft.
Flower length: 1 in.
Full sun
Moist, well-drained soil
Blooms in midsummer
Giant Summer Hyacinth
p. 337

[G]aura lindheimeri

Plant height: 4–5 ft.
Flower length: ½–1 in.
Full sun
Dry, well-drained soil
Blooms early summer to fall
White Gaura
p. 338

[G]illenia trifoliata

Plant height: 2–3 ft.
Flower width: 1 in.
Sun to partial shade
Moist soil
Blooms in summer
Bowman's Root
p. 342

Anthericum liliago

Plant height: to 3 ft.
Flower width: ½–¾ in.
Full sun
Moist soil
Blooms early summer to midsummer
St. Bernard's-Lily
p. 287

Campanula persicifolia var. alba

Plant height: 2–3 ft.
Flower length: 1½ in.
Sun to partial shade
Moist soil
Blooms in early summer
Peach-leaved Bellflower
p. 304

'hysostegia 'irginiana 'ummer Snow'

Plant height: to 3 ft.
Flower length: 1 in.
Sun to partial shade
Moist soil
Blooms in summer
False Dragonhead
p. 384

'alva moschata 'Alba'

Plant height: 1–3 ft.
Flower width: 2 in.
Sun to partial shade
Dry soil
Blooms midsummer to late summer
Musk Mallow
p. 368

Phlox carolina
'Miss Lingard'

Plant height: to 3 ft.
Flower width: ¾ in.
Sun to partial shade
Moist, well-drained soil
Blooms in summer
Carolina Phlox
p. 381

Acanthus spinosus

Plant height: 3–4 ft.
Flowers: in clusters
18 in. long
Full sun
Dry soil
Blooms in summer
Spiny Bear's-Breech
p. 274

Dictamnus albus

Plant height: 2–3 ft.
Flowers: in clusters 12–18 in. long
Full sun
Moist soil
Blooms late spring to early summer
Gas Plant
p. 321

Lysimachia clethroides

Plant height: 2–3 ft.
Flowers: in clusters 6–8 in. long
Sun to partial shade
Well-drained soil
Blooms in summer
Gooseneck Loosestrife
p. 366

Cimicifuga simplex

Plant height: 3–4 ft.
Flowers: in clusters 1–3 ft. long
Partial shade
Moist soil
Blooms late summer to fall
Kamchatka Bugbane
p. 313

Galax urceolata

Plant height: to 2½ ft.
Flowers: in clusters 12–18 in. long
Partial to full shade
Moist soil
Blooms in summer
Galaxy
p. 336

Liatris aspera 'Alba'

Plant height: to 3 ft.
Flowers: in clusters 1 in. wide
Full sun
Well-drained soil
Blooms in summer
p. 360

Cimicifuga racemosa

Plant height: to 6 ft.
Flowers: in clusters 1–3 ft. long
Partial shade
Moist soil
Blooms in midsummer
Black Snakeroot
p. 312

Macleaya cordata

Plant height: 6–10 ft.
Flower width: ½ in.
Sun to partial shade
Average soil
Blooms in midsummer
Plume-poppy
p. 368

Artemisia lactiflora

Plant height: to 5 ft.
Flower width: 1/16 in.
Sun to partial shade
Moist, well-drained soil
Blooms midsummer to late summer
Ghostplant
p. 292

Sanguisorba canadensis

Plant height: 3–6 ft.
Flowers: in clusters 3–6 in. long
Sun to partial shade
Moist soil
Blooms late summer to fall
Great Burnet
p. 397

Aruncus dioicus

Plant height: 4–6 ft.
Flower width: ⅛ in.
Partial shade
Moist soil
Blooms in early summer
Goatsbeard
p. 293

Actaea rubra

Plant height: 1½–2 ft.
Flowers: in clusters 1–1½ in. long
Partial to full shade
Moist soil
Blooms mid-spring to late spring
Red Baneberry
p. 277

Filipendula ulmaria 'Plena'

Plant height: 3–5 ft.
Flower length: ⅛ in.
Partial shade
Moist to wet soil
Blooms in midsummer
Queen-of-the-Meadow
p. 333

Rodgersia aesculifolia

Plant height: to 4 ft.
Flowers: in clusters 12–18 in. long
Sun to partial shade
Moist soil
Blooms in summer
Fingerleaf Rodgersflower
p. 392

Clematis recta

Plant height: 2–5 ft.
Flower width: 1 in.
Full sun
Moist soil
Blooms early summer to midsummer
Ground Clematis
p. 313

Smilacina racemosa

Plant height: to 3 ft.
Flowers: in clusters 4–6 in. long
Partial to full shade
Average soil
Blooms in mid-spring to late spring
False Solomon's-Seal
p. 404

Armeria pseudarmeria

Plant height: 1½–2 ft.
Flowers: in clusters 1½ in. wide
Full sun
Well-drained soil
Blooms in midsummer
Plantain Thrift
p. 291

hlox paniculata
Mt. Fujiyama'

Plant height: 3–4 ft.
Flower width: 1 in.
Sun to partial shade
Moist soil
Blooms in summer
Garden Phlox
p. 382

chillea ptarmica
'he Pearl'

Plant height: 1½–2 ft.
Flower width: ½–¾ in.
Full sun
Average soil
Blooms midsummer to late summer
Sneezewort
p. 275

Anaphalis margaritacea

Plant height: to 20 in.
Flower width: ¼ in.
Sun to partial shade
Dry to moist soil
Blooms in summer
Pearly Everlasting
p. 283

Galium odoratum

Plant height: to 1 ft.
Flower width: ¼ in.
Partial to full shade
Moist soil
Blooms in spring
Sweet Woodruff
p. 337

naphalis iplinervis

Plant height: 12–18 in.
Flower width: ½ in.
Sun to partial shade
Average to moist soil
Blooms in midsummer
Pearly Everlasting
p. 283

yngium bourgatii

Plant height: to 2 ft.
Flower width: ¾ in.
Full sun
Dry, well-drained soil
Blooms in late summer
Mediterranean Eryngo
p. 330

Dietes vegeta

Plant height: to 2 ft.
Flower width: 2–2½ in.
Full sun
Well-drained soil
Blooms spring to early summer
African Iris
p. 322

Verbascum chaixii 'Album'

Plant height: to 3 ft.
Flower width: ½–1 in.
Full sun
Well-drained soil
Blooms in summer
Chaix Mullein
p. 415

'acific Coast Iris

Plant height: 9–18 in.
Outer segments:
2–3½ in. long.
Sun to partial shade
Dry soil
Blooms in late spring
p. 355

athyrus latifolius

Plant height: to 9 ft.
Flower width: 1–1½ in.
Sun to partial shade
Well-drained soil
Blooms in summer
Perennial Pea
p. 359

Acanthus

Acanthus family
Acanthaceae

A-kan′thus. Bear's-breech. A genus of about 30 perennial herbs or shrubs, only a few of much horticultural importance in America.

Description
Leaves large, much cut, the segments or large teeth frequently prickly, somewhat thistle-like. Flowers irregular, 1-lipped, in long, erect spikes.

How to Grow
These plants can be grown in sun or shade, but they flower more profusely in the sun. They need well-drained soil; too much water can be fatal. Good in dry areas.

***mollis* 'Latifolius'** *p. 76*
Bear's-breech. 3–4 ft. (1–1.2 m) high. Leaves toothed, not spiny. Flower-spike erect, 18 in. (45 cm) high, the white, lilac, or rose-colored flowers with tiny, spiny bracts beneath. Mediterranean. After division, root pieces that remain will develop into new plants. Also sold as *A. lusitanicus.* Zone 8.

spinosus *p. 258*
Spiny Bear's-breech. 3–4 ft. (1–1.2 m) high. Basal foliage deeply and irregularly cut, each lobe terminating in a rigid white spine. Flowers are pale purple, borne in spikes 18 in. (45 cm) long, atop flower stalks 2–4 ft. (60–120 cm) high. The bracts are tipped with spines. Southern Europe. Also known as *A. spinosissimus.* Zones 5–6.

Achillea

Daisy family
Compositae

A-kil-lee′a. Yarrow. A large genus of perennial herbs, mostly from the north temperate zone, a few grown for their flowers.

Description
Leaves toothed, parted, or divided, and in some species finely dissected. Flowerheads small, but usually numerous, in often flat-topped clusters.

How to Grow
Yarrow is easy to grow in ordinary garden soil; the taller species are attractive in borders. Propagation is by root division in spring or autumn. Many species are rank growers, crowding out other plants.

filipendulina *p. 103*
Fernleaf Yarrow. 3–4 ft. (1–1.2 m) high. Leaves alternate, to 10 in. (25 cm) long, with a strong, spicy odor. Flowerheads are small, yellow, in dense corymbs to 5 in. (12.5 cm) wide. Asia Minor and Caucasus. 'Coronation Gold' grows to 3 ft. (1 m). Flowerheads are mustard-yellow, in corymbs to 4 in. (10 cm) wide. This cultivar requires staking. It is vigorous and tolerates heat well. 'Gold Plate' is a taller form, growing to 4½ ft. (1.35 m). Its stems are hairy and slightly furrowed. Flowerheads are small, yellow, in corymbs to 5 in. (12.5 cm) wide; its flowers are good cut or cut and dried. A number of other cultivars exist. Zone 4.

× *lewisii* 'King Edward' *p. 242*
King Edward Yarrow. 8–12 in. (20–30 cm) high, with alternate gray-green leaves. Leaves 1–2 in. (2.5–5 cm) long, with a pungent, spicy odor when crushed. Daisylike flowers are white and yellow, ⅛ in. (3 mm) wide, and are borne in dense clusters 1½ in. (4 cm) wide. Clusters are borne on top of 6–8 in. (15–20 cm) stalks. Dry, well-drained soil is important for this plant. Zone 4.

***millefolium* 'Fire King'** *p. 168*
Common Yarrow; Milfoil. Plant leafy, to 2 ft. (60 cm) high. Leaves finely dissected, more or less hairy. Flowerheads rose-red to pink, ¼ in. (6 mm) across, in flat-topped corymbs 2–3 in. (5–7.5 cm) across. Rarely cultivated and, in fact, frequently a weed. Eurasia. Flowers best in moist soils. Zone 3.

'Moonshine' *p. 102*
Moonshine Yarrow. 2 ft. (60 cm) high, with silvery-gray leaves. Individual flowers sulfur-yellow, borne in flat clusters 3–4 in. (7.5–10 cm) wide. 'Moonshine' grows well in dry, sunny areas. It is an excellent choice for cutting and drying. Zone 4.

***ptarmica* 'The Pearl'** *p. 267*
Sneezewort. A stout herb 1½–2 ft. (45–60 cm) high. Leaves 1–4 in. (2.5–10 cm) long. Flowers white, ½–¾ in. (13–19 mm) wide; double, resembling miniature

pompoms. Flowers borne in loose clusters 3–6 in. (7.5–15 cm) wide. W. Asia and Europe; naturalized in North America. This invasive plant is not recommended for low-maintenance gardens. It often must be divided annually. Zone 4.

Aconitum

Buttercup family
Ranunculaceae

A-ko-ny′tum. Monkshood or Wolfsbane. A genus of over 100 species of perennial herbs of the north temperate zone, only a handful of which are of garden interest. All are dangerously poisonous (not to the touch).

Description

They usually have thickened or even tuberous roots and leaves that are cleft or divided finger-fashion but not compound. Flowers very irregular, mostly in terminal panicles or racemes, prevailingly blue or purple, but white or yellow in some. Sepals 5, petal-like, one of them large, hood-shaped (hence monkshood) or helmetlike. Petals 2-5, two of them spurlike and contained in the hood, the others small or wanting. Stamens numerous.

How to Grow

Monkshoods are showy garden plants but children should be warned against the poisonous juice. None are happy in warm regions. Partial shade and a rich, moist, well-drained soil, preferably with a pH of 5–6, are best. Full sun is acceptable if the sc moist. The taller sorts need staking, as they are somewhat weak-stemmed plants. They a fine plants for late summer and early autum gardens. All the cultivated kinds are best treated as perennials; they bloom the second or third year from seed, and increase slowly. They can be increased by division, but generally dislike being moved.

× *bicolor* *p. 230*
Hybrid Monkshood. 3–4 ft. (90–120 cm) tall. Flowers violet or blue, sometimes tinge with white, shaped like small helmets with beak in front; flowers are 1–2 in. (2.5–5 cm tall and are borne in a terminal raceme. Als known as *A. cammarum* or *A. napellus* var. *bicolor,* this hybrid group includes many garden selections: 'Bressingham Spire', 3 ft.

(90 cm) tall with violet-blue flowers; 'Blue Sceptre', 3 ft. (90 cm) high with violet-blue and white flowers; and 'Bicolor', 3½–4 ft. (105–120 cm) high, with blue and white flowers. 'Bicolor' may need staking. Zone 5.

carmichaelii *p. 231*

Azure Monkshood. One of the most popular of the garden monkshoods. Normally 3–4 ft. (90 cm–1.2 m) high; occasionally grows to 6 ft. (1.8 m). Leaves 3-lobed, the lobes often notched. Flowers generally blue (rarely white), the helmet extended into a spurlike visor; 1½ in. (4 cm) long borne in a loose raceme 2–8 in. (5–20 cm) tall. A very handsome plant from e. Asia. Also called *A. fischeri*. Zones 3–4.

napellus *p. 231*

Common Monkshood. Source of the drug aconite and cultivated for ornament. Not over 4 ft. (1.2 m) high, the leaves twice- or thrice-divided into narrow segments. Flowers blue, the broad helmet with a beaklike visor; 1–2 in. (2.5–5 cm) long and borne in a loose raceme 2–8 in. (5–20 cm) tall. Europe. An extremely poisonous plant. Zone 5.

Actaea

Buttercup family
Ranunculaceae

Ac-tee'a. Perennial herbs somewhat sparsely scattered over the north temperate zone.

Description

Leaves twice- or thrice-compound, the ultimate leaflets sharply cleft and toothed. Flowers numerous, white, in thick terminal clusters. Fruit a red or white berry.

How to Grow

Useful and attractive herbs for the wild garden, these plants need a moist soil, but not a strongly acid one, and grow best in partial shade. Easily increased by root division in early spring.

rubra *pp. 141, 264*

Red Baneberry; Red Cohosh. 1½–2 ft. (45–75 cm) high. Flowers white, in racemes 1–1½ in. (2.5–4 cm) long. Fruit a cherry-red, poisonous berry on a very slender stalklet. North America. Plant in fertile, organic soil. Zone 4.

Adenophora
Bellflower family
Campanulaceae

A-den-off′o-ra. Ladybell. About 40 species of perennial herbs, mostly from e. Asia.

Description
Closely related to *Campanula*s and grown for their handsome blue flowers.

How to Grow
These plants differ from *Campanula* only in technical characteristics, and their cultivation is the same as for that genus.

confusa *p. 228*
Ladybells. 3 ft. (90 cm) high. Flowers bell-shaped, ¾ in. (19 mm) long, purple, in sparse clusters. Blooms mid- to late summer. Easy to grow in full sun or partial shade in average soil. Keep soil moist but be sure it is well-drained. Zone 4.

Adonis
Buttercup family
Ranunculaceae

A-don′is. Annual or perennial Eurasian herbs, some of them longtime favorites in the flower garden. There are 20 known species.

Description
They have alternate, dissected leaves and a solitary flower with 5–16 petals.

How to Grow
Plants in this family grow best in sandy, loamy soil rich in organic matter. They are well-suited to rock gardens.

amurensis *p. 118*
Amur Adonis. A perennial rock garden plant, 1 ft. (30 cm) high. Flowers golden yellow, 2 in. (5 cm) across. E. Asia. Mid-spring. Needs rich loam. Divide the fibrous roots in spring. The plant is dormant by midsummer. A double-flowered form is known. Zone 4.

Aegopodium
Carrot family
Umbelliferae

Ee-go-po′di-um. A small group of Eurasian perennial herbs, one of which, the Goutweed, is planted (mostly in its variegated form) as a nonevergreen edging or ground cover.

Description
Leaves twice-compound, the ultimate leaflets toothed. Flowers small, white, in a compound umbel.

How to Grow
Easily grown in ordinary soil; prefers partial shade, but tolerates sun. Increased by dividing its slender rootstocks in spring or fall.

podagraria *p. 84*
Goutweed; also called Bishop's Weed. Stout, coarse herb, 12 in. (30 cm) high. Leafstalks, especially the lower ones, winged and clasping. Flowers are white and scarcely 1.8 in. (3.2 mm) wide, usually 12–15 in each umbel. Umbels 1½–3 in. (4–7.5 cm) wide. Most popular is 'Variegatum', which has white-margined leaflets and is a useful foliage plant. Flowers bloom in June but they are not attractive and should be removed to prevent self-seeding. Goutweed thrives in any soil condition, wet or dry, and can become weedy if not controlled. In hot, humid weather, it may contract leaf blight. Zone 4.

Ajuga
Mint family
Labiatae

Aj′oo-ga. Bugleweed. Annual or perennial herbs, sometimes weedy, but a few cultivated in borders and rock gardens for their profusion of white, blue, or sometimes reddish blooms.

Description
Flowers irregular and 2-lipped, in close clusters or spikes.

How to Grow
The bugleweeds, all European, are easy to grow in ordinary, well-drained garden soil. Propagation by spring-sown seeds, division, and, in *A. reptans,* by its free-rooting stems.

reptans *p. 85*
The common blue Bugleweed. It is 3–6 in. (7.5–15 cm) high, but the stems are usually half-prostrate and often rooting. In the typical form the flowers are ¼ in. (6 mm) wide and blue or purplish, but the following are the preferred garden sorts: var. *alba,* with white flowers; var. *atropurpurea,* with bronze foliage and blue flowers; var. *mettalica crispa,* with metallic, crisped leaves and blue flowers in uninterrupted spikes; 'Burgundy Glow' has green, white, and dark pink to purple foliage. Zone 3.

Alcea

Mallow family
Malvaceae

Al-see'a. Hollyhock. Old and popular flower garden plants including the common Garden Hollyhock and the Antwerp Hollyhock. The genus comprises about 60 species of tall, leafy-stemmed biennial or perennial herbs, all from the temperate regions of the Old World.

Description
They have usually hairy, often felty, alternate leaves and a terminal, spirelike cluster (mostly racemes) of very showy flowers, the 5 petals usually notched, originally red or white, but variously colored in the horticultural forms. Below the calyx is a series of 6–9 bracts.

How to Grow
These plants require full sun; moist, well-drained soil; and good air circulation. Sow them in place or in cold-frames in summer and they will flower the following year. After they are established, the plants will grow spontaneously by reseeding. Though they are perennials, they are short-lived and thus often treated as biennials. To promote a longer life span, faded flowering stalks should be cut off as soon as flowering ceases.

rosea *p. 136*
Garden Hollyhock. Originally a tall Chinese perennial herb, but grown mostly as a biennial and even as an annual. It is erect, 5–9 ft. (1.5–2.7 m) high, the stem leafy, spirelike, and hairy. Leaves generally roundish, long-stalked, rough. Flowers essentially stalkless, 3–5 in. (7.5– 12.5 cm)

wide, in long, stiff, but wandlike, terminal clusters. They are single or double, and white, pink, purple, red, or yellow. China. *A. Rosea* is afflicted by red spider mites and rust. Also called *Althaea rosea*. Zone 4.

Alchemilla
Rose family
Rosaceae

Al-ke-mill′a. Of the 200 species of this genus, only a few are of any garden importance.

Description
They are somewhat weedy plants with lobed or compound leaves and small greenish-yellow flowers without petals.

How to Grow
They are very easy to grow in any ordinary garden soil and may be increased by division. Grown only for the silvery or grayish leaves. In hot or dry climates, plant them in moist, humus-enriched soil.

conjuncta *p. 77*
Plants are 4–6 in. (10–15 cm) high with 5-lobed leaves. Leaves have a silvery edge and lower surface. Flowers ⅛ in. (3 mm) wide, borne in compound clusters. They are light greenish-yellow. Europe. Zone 4.

mollis *p. 100*
Lady's-Mantle. Rootstock stout and horizontal; plant grows to 15 in. (40 cm) high, producing a clump of erect, long-stalked, grayish leaves with shallow rounded lobes that are toothed. Flower clusters 2–3 in. (5–7.5 cm) wide. Bears many ⅛ in. (3 mm) chartreuse or yellowish flowers. Europe. Also sold as *A. vulgaris*. Zone 4.

Alstroemeria
Amaryllis family
Amaryllidaceae

Al-stro-meer′i-a. The Peruvian lilies comprise perhaps 50 species of South American herbs, a few of which are grown in the greenhouse or outdoors for their showy, lily-like flowers.

Description
Roots fibrous or tuberous, the stem slender.

Leaves often twisted at the base, narrow. Flowers slightly irregular in a terminal umbe that is sometimes compound. Petals not united into a tube.

How to Grow
Peruvian lilies require special conditions to do well. The species are not hardy but can be grown in a cool greenhouse. In the autumn pot them up very carefully, for the roots are tender. Give occasional feeding with liquid manure. After they bloom, store them in a cool, dry, frost-free place over the winter. Alstroemerias greatly increase their roots during a single season and need plenty of pot space. Divide them when lifting for the resting period and replant in pots or outdoors as needed.

ligtu *p. 137*
About 2 ft. (60 cm) high. Flowers are borne in terminal, bracted clusters of 2–3 flowers. Flowers are 1½–2 in. (4–5 cm) wide; red, with inner segments streaked in purple. Chile. Zone 8.

Amsonia
Dogbane family
Apocynaceae

Am-sown′i-a. A few herbs; the species described below is American; others are Asiatic.

Description
Leaves alternate, without marginal teeth. Flowers small, funnel-shaped, the lobes long and slender, usually pale blue and in terminal branched clusters.

How to Grow
Amsonias are easy to grow in any moist, ordinary garden soil. They are easily divided in spring or fall.

tabernaemontana *p. 241*
Blue Star; Willow Amsonia. A bushy perennial, up to 2 ft. (60 cm) high. Flowers very pale blue, hairy on the outside, in a dense cluster, but each one scarcely ⅓ in. (8 mm) long. Mass. to Tex. Late spring. Grow in a cool, moist place. If growth becomes loose and open, cut back stems by half to induce a denser habit. Often sold as *A. salicifolia.* Zone 4.

Anaphalis
Daisy family
Compositae

A-naff'a-lis. A large genus of wild everlastings, one of which is common as a weedy herb in America.

Description
Leaves stalkless, alternate, white-woolly throughout at first, ultimately dull green above. Flowers crowded in small heads, the bracts of which are pearly white, very numerous and fairly long-keeping.

How to Grow
Most species do best in well-drained, normally fertile soil. The plants divide easily in spring and fall. They make excellent dried flowers.

margaritacea *p.268*
Pearly Everlasting. Perennial erect herb, to 20 in. (50 cm) high. Flowerheads in terminal cluster, the flowers all tubular, the heads ¼ in. (6 mm) in diameter. For everlastings, they are picked before maturity, dried, and then dyed various colors. Throughout north temperate zone. Easily grown in any sandy soil, and as easily transferred from the wild. Zone 4.

triplinervis *p. 269*
Pearly Everlasting. A Himalayan perennial, 12–18 in. (30–45 cm) high. Flowers white, the heads ½ in. (13 mm) in diameter, in loose clusters. This is an excellent choice for moist sites, where other gray foliage plants will not grow. It is not drought tolerant. Zone 4.

Anchusa
Borage family
Boraginaceae

An-koo'sa. Alkanet; also called Bugloss. A genus of perhaps 40 species of Old World herbs, a few of which are grown for their showy flowers.

Description
Plants are all more or less hairy, and have alternate leaves. Flowers small, trumpet-shaped, but somewhat closed at the throat, leafy, usually one-sided, clusters.

How to Grow
Anchusas are easy to grow in any ordinary garden soil in full sun or partial shade. Easily propagated by spring-sown seeds or by division in spring or fall.

azurea *p. 224*
Italian Bugloss. A stout herb, usually 3½–5 ft. (105–150 cm) high. Leaves oblongish or lance-shaped, the base clasping or winged. Flowers bright blue, ½ in. (13 mm) wide, the cluster graceful and one-sided. Mediterranean; now naturalized in North America. A widely cultivated plant grown for its splendid flowers. Though *A. azurea* has no particular soil requirements, it must be watered well during dry periods. Most cultivars require staking. To promote additional flowering, cut back flowering stalks. It is often sold as *A. italica.* The cultivar 'Little John' has deep blue flowers and grows 12–18 in. (30–45 cm) high; 'Lodden Royalist' is 3 ft. (90 cm) high and has royal-blue flowers. Zone 4.

Anemone
Buttercup family
Ranunculaceae

Correctly, a-nee-moe'nee; usually, a-nem-o'nee. Windflower or Anemone; also the Pasque-Flowers, *Anemone patens* and *A. Pulsatilla.* These most popular garden plants comprise a large genus of perennial herbs.

Description
Leaves compound, or if simple, divided or dissected, mostly basal. Flowers usually showy, without petals, but with petal-like sepals.

How to Grow
With very few exceptions, these plants grow best in rich, well-drained soil. Partial shade is necessary for optimum performance; however, most species tolerate full sun if soil is moist. Start new plants in spring so they can establish themselves by winter. Anemones grow slowly and need not be divided for years. In northern regions, protect plants with a loose mulch.

× ***hybrida*** *p. 161*
Japanese Anemone. From 1–5 ft. (30–150 cm) high, depending on the cultivar. Flowers 2–3 in. (5–7.5 cm) wide, solitary, pink or white. Plant in areas protected from the wind. *A. japonica* and *A. hupehensis* are also included in this hybrid group. Zone 6.

pulsatilla *p. 215*
Pasque flower. Nearly 12 in. (30 cm) high. Flowers blue or reddish purple, bell-shaped, and 2 in. (5 cm) wide. Eurasia. Spring. There are also some horticultural forms with lilac or red flowers, and one with variegated foliage. *A. pulsatilla* should be planted in neutral to alkaline soil. Wet soil in winter is detrimental. Zones 5–6.

sylvestris **'Snowdrops'** *p. 246*
Snowdrop Windflower. 18 in. (45 cm) high. Flowers 1 or 2, pure white, 2 in. (5 cm) wide, sometimes nodding, fragrant. Late spring. Suitable for shaded borders or wild gardens. Prefers moist soil. Zone 4.

vitifolia **'Robustissima'** *p. 160*
Japanese Anemone. 2–3 ft. (60–90 cm) high. Flowers pink, 2–3 in. (5–7.5 cm) across and borne, solitary, in cymes. Nepal. Zone 5.

Anigozanthos

Bloodwort family
Haemodoraceae

A-nig-o-zan′thus. A small genus of greenhouse herbs from Australia.

Description
Rootstock fleshy. Leaves narrow, mostly basal. Flowers in 1-sided, woolly racemes, hairy inside, the tube long and flaring, slightly irregular.

How to Grow
Grow in a cool greenhouse, or in a sunny spot with well-drained soil. Propagated by division of the rootstocks, in spring. They need an ample supply of water during spring.

flavidus *p. 140*
Kangaroo Paw. 3–4 ft. (90–120 cm) tall, with a red-woolly stem. Flowers 1½ in. (4 cm) long; tube red and woolly. Flowers in May or June and may continue until fall. Zone 9.

Antennaria
Daisy family
Compositae

An-ten-ar′i-a. A large genus of white-woolly herbs, very common as wild plants.

Description
They have mostly basal leaves and small heads in loose clusters. Flowers all tubular, very minute, dirty white, sometimes dried.

How to Grow
The species are all perennial, mostly somewhat weedy, and very easy to grow in open, dry, sandy places. They spread so rapidly that they may become a nuisance.

dioica* var. *rosea *p. 152*
Pussytoes. 4–12 in. (10–30 cm) high. Leaves hairy, 1½ in. (4 cm) long. Flowerheads pink, ¼ in. (6 mm) wide. Eurasia. A good choice for rock gardens in full sun and other well-drained sites. Var. *rosea* has pink flowerheads. Zones 4–5.

Anthemis
Daisy family
Compositae

An′them-is. A very large genus of Eurasian herbs, some cultivated for ornament, others for fragrant herbage.

Description
Leaves alternate, often mostly basal, dissected or cut (in those described below). Flowerheads with yellow or white rays and yellow disk flowers.

How to Grow
Easily grown in sunny open borders from seeds or by division of roots in spring or fall.

sancti-johannis *p. 129*
Saint John's Camomile. Much-branched, gray-haired, tufted, 1–3 ft. (30–90 cm) high. Flowerheads solitary, orange, 2 in. (5 cm) wide. Bulgaria. Summer. Freely hybridizes with *tinctoria.* Most plants sold as *sancti-johannis* are hybrids. Zone 4.

tinctoria *p. 127*
Golden Marguerite; Yellow Camomile. To 3 ft. (90 cm) high. Flowerheads nearly

2 in. (5 cm) wide, golden yellow. Summer. Tolerates hot, dry climates, and is very easy to grow, but requires yearly plant division. Zone 4.

Anthericum
Lily family
Liliaceae

An-ther′i-kum. A large genus of mostly African herbs, some grown for their clusters of flowers.

Description
Leaves narrow, strap-shaped, basal. Flowers small, white, in a long, loose, leafless raceme, each flower nearly stalkless. Stamens 6.

How to Grow
A. liliago grows best in full sun and fertile, moist soils with organic matter added. Easily propagated by division of its rootstock.

liliago *p. 256*
St. Bernard's-Lily. To 3 ft. (90 cm) high. Flowers ½–¾ in. (13–19 mm) wide, white, flattish, each with small bracts beneath. Europe. Good bloom begins a year after planting. It does poorly in hot, dry areas. Zone 5.

Aquilegia
Buttercup family
Ranunculaceae

A-kwee-lee′je-a. About 75 species of herbaceous perennials, all from the north temperate zone.

Description
Leaves twice- or thrice-compound. Flowers showy, usually at the ends of the branches. Sepals and petals colored alike, the 5 petals with long, hollow spurs. Sepals shorter than spurs.

How to Grow
Some columbines are best suited for rock gardens, others for open borders. They do best in open, sandy loam in perennial borders. All species below require very good drainage and are best increased by division in spring.

caerulea *p. 220*
Rocky Mountain Columbine. A native American columbine, 2–3 ft. (60–90 cm) high. Flowers up to 2 in. (5 cm) wide with bluish purple sepals and white petals. Will not tolerate dry soils; partial shade will prolong flowering. *A. caerulea* is a prey of leaf miners. Zone 4.

canadensis *p. 146*
Common Columbine. A beautiful herb, 1–2 ft. (30–60 cm) high. Flowers 1½ in. (4 cm) wide, with yellow petals, and red sepals and spurs. Where spread is not desired, seed capsules should be removed. Zone 4.

hybrids *p. 179*
Hybrid Columbine. Plants 1–3 ft. (30–90 cm) high. Flowers 2 in. (5 cm) wide, red, yellow, blue, white, or purple. Late spring. Grow where other plants can camouflage the foliage when it fades. Prey to leaf miners. Cultivars include 'Dragon Fly', with large flowers in mixed colors; the white 'Snow Queen'; and 'Nora Barlow', a double flowered strain with petals pink and red tinged with green. Zone 5.

Arabis
Mustard family
Cruciferae

Ar′a-bis. The rock cresses comprise a large genus of herbs much grown for ornament, especially in wall and rock gardens.

Description
They have basal or stem leaves, usually hairy and small, white or purple flowers, often in ample spikes or racemes.

How to Grow
The rock cresses are easy to grow. All prefer open sunlight and warm, sandy soil. Easily propagated by spring or fall division.

caucasica *p. 238*
Wall Cress. A tufted, white-foliaged species from the Caucasus, usually less than 12 in. (30 cm) high. Flowers white, fragrant, ½ in. (13 mm) wide, in loose clusters. There are double-flowered and variegated-leaved forms. Prefers good drainage. In climates with hot, humid summers, it may rot. Zone 4.

procurrens *p. 239*
Rock Cress. Showy, white-flowered, not over 1 ft. (30 cm) high, creeping by short runners. Flowers 5/16 in. (12 mm) wide, in racemes. Se. Europe. It thrives in relatively poor soils. There is a variegated-leaved form. Zone 5.

Arctotheca
Daisy family
Compositae

Arc-to-thee′ca. Only one species is of particular garden interest. Grown almost exclusively in California, it is native to South Africa.

Description
Leaves grayish-green, deeply divided. Flowers yellow, showy, resembling daisies. Usually acts like a ground cover, but growth habit depends on wind and humidity.

How to Grow
A. calendula does not tolerate hot and humid climates or heavy frost. Ideal temperature is 50° F. Self-seeds readily and is easy to grow in sunny, moderately fertile, well-drained soil.

calendula *p. 128*
Cape Weed; Cape-Dandelion. Under 1 ft. (30 cm) high, flowers yellow, 1–2 in. (2.5–5.0 cm) across. Needs a lot of space; good choice for wild gardens, hillsides. Zone 9.

Arenaria
Pink family
Caryophyllaceae

A-re-nay′ri-a. The sandworts comprise a large genus of mostly low herbs.

Description
They have small leaves and mostly small white flowers, with 5 petals, in variously branched clusters, or solitary.

How to Grow
The cultivated sandworts are usually tufted plants of open sunshine. Propagated by root division. Some are offered as *Alsine* and *Minuartia.*

verna* var. *caespitosa *p. 237*
Irish Moss. 2 in. (5 cm) high, in dense, mosslike clumps. Flowers star-shaped, white, ⅜ in. (9 mm) wide, borne in terminal heads. European Mts. and Rocky Mts. In full sun, water almost daily. Variety 'Aurea' has yellow-green foliage. Zone 5.

Arisaema
Arum family
Araceae

A-ri-see′ma. A genus of over 100 species of perennial herbs.

Description
They have tuberous, acrid roots, divided or compound leaves, and tiny flowers crowded on a spadix, which is surrounded by, or has beneath it, a spathe.

How to Grow
The only commonly cultivated species are plants of rich, moist woods; with good humus soil, shade, and a moist site they are easy to grow. Propagated by root division.

triphyllum *p. 249*
Jack-in-the-Pulpit. Root very acrid, but used as a food, when heated, by the Indians. The purplish spathe ("pulpit"), 3 in. (7.5 cm) long, arches over the erect greenish-yellow to white spadix ("Jack"). E. U.S. Zone 4.

Armeria
Plumbago family
Plumbaginaceae

Ar-meer′i-a. Thrift; Sea Pink. Summer-blooming, low, perennial herbs comprising only a few species.

Description
Armerias have small evergreen leaves in basal rosettes, a rigid, stiff, flowering stalk, at the end of which is a dense, globe-shaped flowerhead.

How to Grow
Good plants for borders and rock gardens, sometimes grown in pots (cool greenhouse) for their long-keeping flowers. They are easy to grow in most garden soils, but the species

below do best in well-drained sandy loams in full sun. Easily propagated by division.

maritima *p. 169*
Common Thrift. 6–10 in. (15–25 cm) high. Flowering stalk smooth, the head ¾ in. (19 mm) wide, pink, purple, or white. Europe. If soil is too moist and too fertile, *A. maritima*'s dense mat of leaves will rot in the center. Zone 4.

pseudarmeria *p. 266*
Plantain Thrift. 1½–2 ft. (45–60 cm) high. Flowerheads 1½ in. (4 cm) wide, pink or white. Sw. Europe. Also offered as 'Formosa hybrids', and as *A. latifolia* or *A. formosa.* Zones 6–7.

Artemisia
Daisy family
Compositae

Ar-te-miz′i-a. The wormwoods comprise a very large genus of bitter or aromatic herbs and low shrubs, found in most countries and cultivated since ancient times for their aromatic qualities, for ornament, or as seasoning.

Description
They have alternate, mostly divided or dissected leaves. Flowers in small heads.

How to Grow
Many of the species have a silvery coating on the leaves and do not tolerate much winter moisture. They need full sun and well-drained soils and rot in wet soils or in areas with high humidity. Otherwise they are generally easy to grow and do better in poor and sandy soils than in rich ones. Easily increased by root division.

absinthium *p. 90*
Wormwood. A white-hairy, woody herb, 2½–4 ft. (75–120 cm) high. Flowerheads ⅛ in. (3.2 mm) wide, greenish-yellow, very numerous. 'Lambrook Silver' is a finer-textured form, with silky-gray leaves. Zone 4.

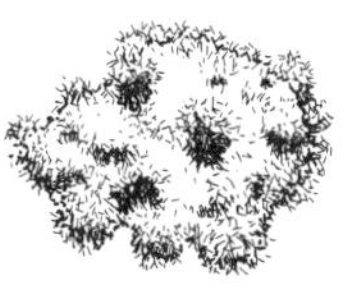

canescens *p. 88*
Plants 12–18 in. (30–45 cm) high. Grown for their foliage. Leaves silver-gray, lacy, branching. Zone 4.

lactiflora *p. 262*
Ghostplant; White Mugwort. To 5 ft. (1.5 m) high. Leaves to 9 in. (22.5 cm) long. Clusters of flowers to 2 ft. (60 cm) long; cream-colored tiny heads 1/16 in. (1.6 mm) across. China. Will tolerate partia shade, but needs a moister, more fertile soil than most artemisias. Prey to rust. Zone 4.

ludoviciana *p. 89*
Silver King Artemisia. Rhizomatous herb, tc 3 ft. (90 cm) high. Leaves white-hairy beneath. Flowerheads to ⅛ in. (3.2 cm) across, grayish-white, borne in dense, branching clusters. Mich. to Wash., Ark., and Mexico. Yearly division will control thi plant's spread. Zone 5.

schmidtiana **'Silver Mound'** *p. 89*
Silver Mound Artemisia. Soft, silky leaves, 4–6 in. (10–15 cm) high, often used in rock gardens. Flowerheads small, white or yellow, not showy. Japan. Delay clumps opening in the middle by pruning foliage before flowering. Japan. Zone 4.

stellerana *p. 91*
Beach Wormwood. A densely white-woolly herb, seldom over 2 ft. (60 cm) high. Flowerheads ¼ in. (6 mm) wide, yellow, crowded in dense racemes. Coasts of ne. U.S and Asia. A splendid beach plant. One of th best gray foliage plants and also one of the least inclined to rot in humid conditions. Zones 3–4.

Arum

Arum family
Araceae

Air'um. Eurasian relatives of the Jack-in-the-Pulpit; most species require the same culture.

Description
A dozen species of tuberous-rooted herbs with mostly arrow-shaped leaves. The flower are borne on a naked spadix that is partly surrounded by the much more showy spathe

How to Grow
Arum grows best in partial shade in humus-rich soil that is moist throughout th growing season. Dormant in the summer.

italicum *p. 81*
Italian Arum. 12–16 in. (30–40 cm) high. Spathe stalked, tubular, 2 in. (5 cm) long, greenish-white with a purplish base and a cream-colored spadix. Orange-red berries borne on stout stalks. Se. Europe. *A. italicum* 'Pictum' has narrow, spear-shaped leaves marbled in gray and cream. Zones 5–6.

Aruncus
Rose family
Rosaceae

A-run′kus. A genus of spirea-like herbs, differing from the closely related *Spiraea* in having compound leaves.

Description
Leaves twice- or thrice-compound. Flowers small, white, crowded into showy panicles, the male and female on different plants. Petals 5. Stamens many. Pistils 3.

How to Grow
A fine plant for borders, it does best in partial shade. Propagated by division.

dioicus *p. 263*
Goatsbeard. A strong-growing plant, 4–6 ft. (1.2–1.8 m) high. Flowers creamy white, ⅛ in. (3.2 mm) wide, nearly stalkless on the branches of a wide-spreading, open cluster 6–10 in. (15–25 cm) high. North America and Asia. Prefers moist soil. Zone 4.

Asarum
Birthwort family
Aristolochiaceae

Ass′a-rum. Woodland plants with aromatic rootstocks, useful only in shady places in the wild garden. Usually called wild ginger because of their strong scent and flavor.

Description
Leaves stalked, heart- or kidney-shaped. Flowers borne at or near the ground and hidden by the relatively dense foliage.

How to Grow
The wild gingers need shade, humus soil, and plenty of moisture. Given these, they spread readily and will cover large areas in a

few years. Easily increased by division of their creeping rootstocks.

canadense *p. 82*
Wild Ginger. 6–8 in. (15–20 cm) high. Leaves 3–6 in. (7.5–15.0 cm) wide. Flowers 1 in. (2.5 cm) wide, bell-shaped, purplish-green on the outside and deep maroon inside. E. North America. Zone 4.

europaeum *p. 81*
European Wild Ginger. 5 in. (12.5 cm) high. Leaves evergreen, glossy. Flowers 1 in. (2.5 cm) wide, bell-shaped, purplish-green outside, deep maroon inside, darker colors predominating. Europe. This evergreen plant may need winter snow cover. Zone 5.

Asclepias
Milkweed family
Asclepiadaceae

As-klee′pi-as. Milkweed. Milky-juiced, rather showy, but sometimes weedy herbs, including about 200 species.

Description
Leaves opposite or in whorls, rarely alternate. Flowers regular, usually in close, roundish umbels. Fruit a pair of follicles, the many seeds with a tuft of silky hairs.

How to Grow
The native species are very easy to grow in full sun in average garden soil or even in drier soils. Propagation by seeds or root cuttings.

tuberosa *p. 139*
Butterfly Weed. Showiest of all native milkweeds. 1–3 ft. (30–90 cm) high, erect or sprawling. Flowers ½ in. (13 mm) wide, bright orange, in terminal cymes 2 in. (5 cm) across. Thrives in dry, sandy soil in North America. Will compete successfully with grasses. Zone 4.

Asphodeline
Lily family
Liliaceae

As-fo-de-line′e. A genus of perhaps 20 species of herbs found in the Mediterranean region and of interest chiefly because it contains Asphodel, a plant that in legend was thought to have covered the Elysian Fields.

Description
Very narrow leaves cluster at the base and resemble blue-gray grass leaves. Flowers yellow, star-shaped, fragrant, borne in a raceme that terminates in a 2–4 ft. (60–120 cm) spike. Racemes are 12–18 in. (30–45 cm) long; flowers 1 in. (2.5 cm) long.

How to Grow
Asphodel is easy to grow in any well-drained garden soil, either in partial shade or in full sun. Propagated by spring or fall root division.

lutea *p. 108*
Asphodel; King's Spear. A thick-rooted herb, 2–3 ft. (60–90 cm) high. Flowers numerous, 1 in. (2.5 cm) across, in racemes. S. Europe and Arabian Peninsula. Asphodel may need winter mulching in northern regions.
Zone 6.

Aster
Daisy family
Compositae

As'ter. The *Aster* is confusing. To many gardeners it implies the Garden, or China Aster, a popular annual that actually belongs to the genus *Callistephus. Aster* is an immense group of mostly perennial herbs.

Description
Most are stout plants of the woods or fields, easily grown and often too weedy for borders or beds. Leaves alternate. Flowerheads usually clustered, made up of ray flowers and often yellow disk flowers. Most bloom in late summer and fall.

How to Grow
Asters do best in full sun in soil that is fertile, moist, and well-drained. During growing season soil must not become dry; during dormant season, soil must not become soggy. Asters self-sow freely; faded flowers should be removed promptly because seeds will not produce true to type plants. Plants need division every other year; divisions from outside of clumps will grow quickly into larger plants.

× ***frikartii*** *p. 222*
A perennial herb, 2–3 ft. (60–90 cm) high. Flowers lavender-blue, 2–3 in. (5.0–7.5 cm) wide, and fragrant. May mildew in humid areas. In northern zones, mulch with evergreen branches in winter. Zone 6.

novae-angliae *p. 196*
New England Aster. 3–5 ft. (90–150 cm) high. Leaves numerous. Ray flowers deep purple, heads crowded and nearly 1½ in. (4 cm) wide. E. North America. The variety "Alma Potschke" has pink flowers. Zone 5.

tataricus *p. 223*
Tartarian Aster. Often 6–8 ft. (1.8–2.4 m) high, wide-spreading. Lower leaves nearly 2 ft. (60 cm) long. Ray flowers blue or violet-purple, heads 1 in. (2.5 cm) wide in profuse clusters. Siberia (U.S.S.R.). A handsome plant that needs plenty of space and is easy to grow. Zone 4.

Astilbe

Saxifrage family
Saxifragaceae

As-til′be. A genus of spirea-like herbs, widely grown as handsome border perennials.

Description
Leaves simple, or twice- or thrice-compound. Flowers borne in profuse, spirelike panicles 6–12 in. (20–30 cm), mostly unisexual. Petals 4–5 (sometimes lacking), white, pink, or reddish. Stamens 8–10. Pistils 2 or 3.

How to Grow
Astilbes are easy to grow in partial shade in any ordinary moist soil. They are heavy feeders, and benefit from extra fertilizer during the summer. They reproduce quickly; divide them every 3 years.

× ***arendsii*** *p. 144*
Astilbe; False Spirea. 2–4 ft. (60–120 cm) high. Leaves dark green or bronze. Flowers minute, red, white, or pink, 1/16 in. (1.6 mm) wide, in clusters. Grows best in moist soil. Zone 5.

chinensis **'Pumila'** *p. 191*
Chinese Astilbe. 8–12 in. (20–30 cm) high. Flowers mauve-pink, minute 1/16 in. (1.6 mm) wide. Panicles create dense, erect

plumes. Can tolerate drier soils than other *Astilbes.* Excellent for rock gardens and border-fronts. Zone 5.

***tacquetii* 'Superba'** *p. 186*
3–4 ft. (90–120 cm) high. Foliage bronze-green. Very small magenta or reddish-purple flowers borne on panicles, which resemble long, feathery spikes. China. More drought-tolerant than × *arendsii.* Zone 5.

Aubrieta
Mustard family
Cruciferae

Au-bree'sha. A small genus of Old World perennial herbs. The only horticultural species is very popular as a mat-forming plant for edgings, rock gardens, or open borders.

Description
They have more or less crowded leaves and relatively large 4-petaled flowers in short terminal clusters.

How to Grow
Grow in partial shade, in light, well-drained soil.

deltoidea *p. 155*
False Rockcress. 6 in. (15 cm) high. Leaves hairy. Flowers ¾ in. (2 cm) wide, typically lilac or purple; borne in terminal racemes. Many varieties are available, some with pink flowers. Zone 5.

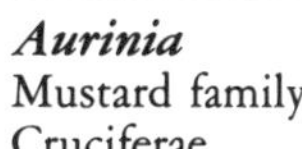

Aurinia
Mustard family
Cruciferae

Aw-ri'nee-a. A group of about 7 species of herbs native to cen. and e. Europe and n. Asia Minor.

Description
Flowers have 4 sepals and 4 petals, and are arranged in racemes or panicles.

How to Grow
Aurinia are easy to grow in most well-drained soils with a sunny exposure.

They need excellent drainage; hot, humid weather can be fatal.

saxitilis *p. 116*
Basket-of-Gold. The most popular of the madworts, 6–12 in. (15–30 cm) high, in dense mats or clumps. Flowers golden yellow, ⅛ in. (3.2 mm) across, in clusters that cover the grayish foliage. Europe. Spring. Over-fertilization will produce a sprawling plant. Cut stems back one-third to one-half after flowering to lengthen life span The many cultivars include 'Compacta', known for its dwarf habit, and 'Citrina' with pale yellow flowers. Zone 4.

Baptisia
Bean family
Leguminosae

Bap-tiz′i-a. False indigo or wild indigo is a general term for about 30 species of perennial North American herbs.

Description
Baptisia are stout plants with compound leaves. Flowers pealike, in showy racemes, followed by short pods.

How to Grow
The 2 species described below are useful plants in drier parts of borders or wild gardens. They need full sun, an open, porous, sandy soil; increase by division.

australis *p. 232*
Blue False Indigo. From 3–5 ft. (90–150 cm) high. Flowers blue, 1 in. (2.5 cm) across, borne in terminal racemes 9–12 in. (22.5–30 cm) long. Zone 4.

perfoliata *p. 87*
To 2 ft. (60 cm) high. Blue- to gray-green, leathery leaves. Flowers tiny, ¼ in. (6 mm) across, yellow, round, borne singularly. Zone 8.

Begonia
Begonia family
Begoniaceae

Bee-go′ni-a. An immense genus of tropical foliage and flowering herbs, with soft or succulent stems, and the only horticultural genus of this family.

Description
Leaves alternate, often brightly colored or with colored veins. Flowers red, pink, yellow, or white, slightly irregular, the male and female separate.

How to Grow
Grow in partially shaded areas, in moist humus-enriched soil. In northern areas, a light mulch will prevent winter damage. Propagated from bulbils developing in the leaf axils that drop to the ground and grow into plants.

grandis *p. 160*
Hardy Begonia. A smooth-leaved, branching plant, 1–2 ft. (30–60 cm) high. Leaves red on the underside with toothed lobes. Flowers large, flesh-pink, 1–1½ in. (2.5–4 cm) across. China and Japan. It can stand temperatures of −18° C (0° F) if the tuberous base is not allowed to freeze. Zone 7.

Belamcanda
Iris family
Iridaceae

Bel-am-kan′da. A single East Asian perennial herb grown for ornament in open borders throughout the U.S.

Description
Long, sword-shaped leaves and red-spotted orange flowers with 6 segments, scarcely distinguishable as petals and sepals. Fruit a 3-valved capsule.

How to Grow
Plants smaller in areas of full sun and low fertility. Ideal condition is moist, fertile soil. Propagate by spring division of its stout rootstock.

chinensis *p. 138*
Blackberry Lily; Leopard Flower. From 2–4 ft. (60–120 cm) high. Leaves iris-like. Flowers 1½–2 in. (4–5 cm) wide, soon withering. *B. flabellata* is a shorter species and includes 'Hello Yellow', which has yellow flowers. Zone 5.

Bergenia
Saxifrage family
Saxifragaceae

Ber-gen′i-a. About 12 Asiatic perennial herbs, several of which are grown in borders for their ornamental foliage and very early-blooming pink or white flowers. The genus is sometimes known as *Megasea.*

Description
In dense clumps or colonies from thickened rootstocks. Leaves mostly basal, thick and fleshy, pitted, half-evergreen. Flowers large, in nodding panicles or racemes.

How to Grow
Grown like *Saxifraga,* a close relative (all the species below are often offered as *Saxifraga*). Bergenia can be grown in any soil. Plant in light shade, or in full sun if enough moisture is provided.

cordifolia *p. 182*
Heartleaf Bergenia. 12–18 in. (30–45 cm) high. Flowers pink, ¼–½ in. (6–13 mm) across, clusters among the leaves. Prey to slugs. Siberia (U.S.S.R.). Zone 3.

hybrids *p. 177*
Hybrid Bergenia. From 9–18 in. (22.5–45 cm) in height. Each variety differs in appearance: 'Abendglut' or 'Evening Glow' to 9 in. (22.5 cm) high; flowers crimson-purple, usually semidouble. 'Margery Fish' 12–18 in. (30–45 cm) high, flowers ¼–½ in. (6–13 mm) wide, pink; 'Morganrote' or 'Morning Blush' 18 in. (45 cm) high, pink flowers. 'Silberlicht' or 'Silver Light' 12 in. (30 cm) high, white flowers with a pale pink calyx. 'Sunningdale' 12 in. (30 cm) high, with carmine flowers on red stalks. All zone 3.

Boltonia
Daisy family
Compositae

Bole-tone′i-a. A small genus of asterlike perennial herbs, the species below native in the U.S. and planted in borders.

Description
Boltonias are erect, leafy plants with alternate leaves. Flowers in short-stalked

heads, the many rays rather showy. Often called False Camomile, False Starwort, or Thousand-flowered Aster.

How to Grow
Boltonias are very easy to grow in average soil. Plant in open sunlight, toward the rear of a bed or border. They bloom profusely in late summer, and are easily propagated by spring or fall division.

***asteroides* 'Snowbank'** *p. 244*
White Boltonia. From 3–5 ft. (1.0–1.5 m) high, and bushy. Leaves pale green. Flowerheads ¾ in. (19 mm) wide, very numerous, generally white, but sometimes violet or purple. Somewhat susceptible to mildew; grow fastest in moist, fertile soil. Sometimes sold as *B. laevigata.* Zone 4.

Brunnera
Borage family
Boraginaceae

Brun′er-ra. An anchusa-like herb of the Caucasus and Siberia, rather commonly cultivated as *Anchusa myosotidiflora.*

Description
It has large, heart-shaped, basal leaves, erect, hairy stems, and flowers in clusters.

How to Grow
Brunnera tolerates many soils. It can survive drier shady sites, but performs best in partial shade and moist soil.

macrophylla *p. 206*
Siberian Bugloss. 12–18 in. (30–45 cm) high. Flowers blue, spring-blooming, not over ¼ in. (6 mm) wide. Starlike flowers borne in loosely branched racemes, and resemble Forget-me-nots. Zone 4.

Buphthalmum
Daisy family
Compositae

Bewf-thal′mum. A small genus of Eurasian herbs, usually called oxeye because of their yellow, dark-centered flowerheads. Grown in perennial borders for their rather large flowers.

Description
Leaves alternate. Ray flowers, long and strap-shaped.

How to Grow
The species below is easy to grow in any ordinary garden soil in full sun to partial shade. Propagate by division in spring.

salicifolium *p. 128*
Yellow Oxeye Daisy. 1–2 ft. (30–60 cm) high. Leaves willowlike. Flowerheads solitary, 2 in. (5 cm) wide, disk darker than the bright yellow rays. Se. Europe. Summer. Also called *B. grandiflorum.* Zone 4.

Calceolaria
Figwort family
Scrophulariaceae

Kal-see-o-lay′ri-a. A very large genus of tropical American herbs or shrubby plants, collectively called slipperworts from the slipper-shaped, showy flowers.

Description
The garden calceolaria is a dwarf, tufted plant. Leaves opposite or in whorls. Flowers in irregular clusters. Stamens 2.

How to Grow
Garden calceolarias are restricted to areas with mild winters and cool summers. Soil must be well-drained. Propagation is by division in the spring or by seeding. Seeds should be sown in May and pots placed in a cold frame in June for flowering plants the following year. Very popular with florists.

'John Innes' *p. 115*
Calceolaria. To 6 in. (15 cm) high. Bright yellow flowers ½–1 in. (1.3–2.5 cm) long, 2-lipped. Upper lip small and slightly pouched; lower lip inflated and slipper-shaped. South America. Prefers moist soil and partial shade. Zone 7.

Callirhoe
Mallow family
Malvaceae

Kal-lir′o. A small genus of North American herbs, well liked for their showy flowers.

Description
Alternate, usually cleft or dissected, leaves. Flowers mostly in leaf axils, petals irregularly cut but not notched at the ends.

How to Grow
The cultivated species are easy to grow in ordinary garden soil, and are propagated by spring or fall division of their clumps. They prefer sunny dry sites.

involucrata *p. 164*
Finger Poppy Mallow. From a deep rootstock, normally 6–12 in. (15–30 cm) high. Flowers 1½–2½ in. (4–6 cm) wide, pale red-purple with purple predominant. Because of its deep taproot it needs water only during droughts. Zone 4.

Caltha
Buttercup family
Ranunculaceae

Kal′tha. About 20 species of marsh or swamp perennial herbs, growing in the north temperate and arctic zones.

Description
Stem hollow, the leaves roundish, heart- or kidney-shaped, without teeth. Flowers 1–2 in. (2.5–5.0 cm) across, without petals, but with pink, white, or yellow petal-like sepals.

How to Grow
The species below is easily transplanted to the wild garden, or will grow in rich, moist soil in borders if given partial shade. Propagated by division or by seeds.

palustris *p. 113*
Cowslip; Marsh Marigold. 1–2 ft. (30–60 cm) high. Flowers 2 in. (5 cm) wide, bright yellow, several together. The most popular cultivar is 'Flore Pleno', with double flowers 2 in. (5 cm) across. Zone 4.

Campanula
Bellflower family
Campanulaceae

Kam-pan′you-la. Bellflowers comprise an important group of garden plants, over 2 dozen of 300 known species in common cultivation for their handsome bloom. No garden plants offer greater variety of blue hues.

Description
Basal leaves often unlike the stem leaves. Flowers typically bell-shaped, often very showy, mostly blue or white.

How to Grow
The species below are easy to grow in ordinary garden soils. Most prefer sunny sites. The foliage of most species is susceptible to slugs.

***carpatica** p. 214*
Carpathian Harebell. 6–12 in. (15–30 cm) high. Flowers solitary, erect, blue, nearly 2 in. (5 cm) wide. S. Europe. Prefers fertile, moist soil. There are many white and sky-blue varieties. Zone 4.

***garganica** p. 202*
Somewhat sprawling, 6 in. (15 cm) long. Flowers wheel-shaped, solitary, blue, ½ in. (13 mm) wide. Flowers early in season, with sporadic flowering until fall. Zone 6.

***glomerata** p. 213*
Danesblood Bellflower. 1–3 ft. (30–90 cm) high. Large, long-stalked leaves. Flowers blue or white, ¾–1 in. (2.0–2.5 cm) long, in dense clusters. Does well even in wet soil. Double-flowered form and variety with deep violet flowers in large clusters are available. Zones 3–4.

***lactiflora** p. 226*
Milky Bellflower. To 4 ft. (120 cm) high. Flowers white or pale blue, 1 in. (2.5 cm) wide, in long, terminal, showy panicles. Needs staking. Prefers moist, fertile soil. 'Superba' has large, violet-blue flowers. Zone 4.

***latifolia** p. 227*
Great Bellflower. 2–4 ft. (60–120 cm) high. Flowers purplish blue, solitary, 1½ in. (4 cm) long. A good choice for shaded area in moist soil. Species self-seeds and does not usually need support. Var. *macrantha* has flowers nearly twice as large. Zone 4.

***persicifolia** p. 256*
Peach-leaved Bellflower. 2–3 ft. (60–90 cm) high. Flowers blue or white, 1½ in. (4 cm) long, in showy terminal racemes. Grow in

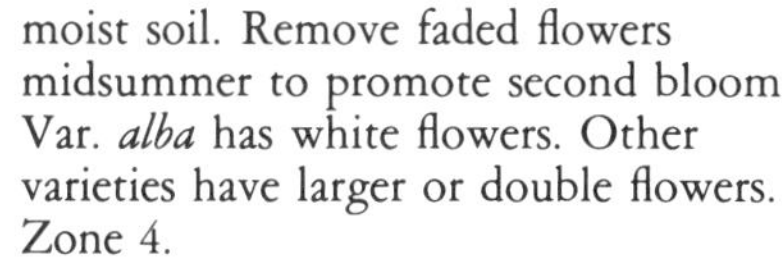

moist soil. Remove faded flowers midsummer to promote second bloom. Var. *alba* has white flowers. Other varieties have larger or double flowers. Zone 4.

portenschlagiana *p. 203*
Dalmatian Bellflower. 6–8 in. (15–20 cm) high. Flowers few, bluish purple, ¾–1 in. (2–2.5 cm) wide. Prefers well-drained, gritty soil. Zone 5.

poscharskyana *p. 203*
Serbian Bellflower. Weak-stemmed or sprawling plant 4–6 in. (10–15 cm) high. Flowers numerous, lilac, 1 in. (2.5 cm) wide. Drought resistant, a good choice for well-drained rock gardens. Cultivars include 'E. K. Toogood.' Zone 4.

rotundifolia *p. 225*
Bluebell; Harebell 1–2 ft. (30–60 cm) high. Flowers bright blue, 1 in. (2.5 cm) long, in a lax, few-flowered cluster. Self-seeds and may become a weed. White variety and another with double flowers and shredded petals available. Zone 3.

Catananche
Daisy family
Compositae

Kat-a-nann'ke. Of the 5 known species, only the Blue Succory is of garden interest.

Description
Leaves mostly basal, narrow. Flowers in handsome long-stalked heads, rays flat and slightly toothed.

How to Grow
Easy to grow in full sun in any ordinary garden soil. Propagated by division or by seeds sown in early spring to flower the same year.

caerulea *p. 223*
Cupid's Dart; Blue Succory. To 2 ft. (60 cm) high. Leaves very hairy. Flowerheads nearly 2 in. (5 cm) wide, rays blue (white or white-margined in a horticultural variety). S. Europe. A drought-tolerant plant. Wet soil in winter may be fatal. Makes a durable dried flower. Zone 5.

Centaurea
Daisy family
Compositae

Sen-tor′ree-a. A genus of chiefly Eurasian herbs comprising over 400 species.

Description
Annuals or perennials of diverse leaf form with flowers in heads. Heads contain only tubular flowers; below a series of overlappin bracts.

How to Grow
In general, they require full sun and dry soil and may need staking.

***hypoleuca* 'John Coutts'** *p. 198*
18–24 in. (45–60 cm) high. Leaves lobed, green on top and gray below. Flowerheads solitary, 2 in. (5 cm) wide; disk flowers white, fringed ray flowers deep rose. Turkey. This species has been incorrectly identified a *C. dealbata.* Zone 4.

macrocephala *p. 105*
Globe Centaurea. 3 ft. (90 cm) high, ovalish leaves toothed. Flowerheads nearly 4 in. (10 cm) wide, yellow, bracts below fringed. Armenia (U.S.S.R.). Usually plante individually because of its stiff, coarse growth. Good choice for drying. Zones 3–4.

montana *p. 199*
Mountain Bluet. 18–24 in. (45–60 cm) high foliage white-hairy when young. Leaves oblongish. Flowerheads blue, often 3 in. (7.5 cm) wide, marginal flowers much enlarged and raylike. Bracts beneath head black-fringed. Invasive and a "floppy" growe with a weak floral display, bearing only a fe blossoms at any one time. Some varieties have pink flowers. Zones 3–4.

Centranthus
Valerian family
Valerianaceae

Sen-tran′thus. A small group of mostly perennial herbs from the Mediterranean.

Description
Leaves opposite, sometimes faintly toothed. Flowers small, red in a dense terminal cluster, the corolla with a slender tube, but

spurred at the base, 5-parted at the top. Stamen only 1.

How to Grow
Easy to cultivate; self-sown seedlings may grow abundantly. Sunny areas with well-drained soil best, and ideal sites include walls and limestone walks or outcroppings.

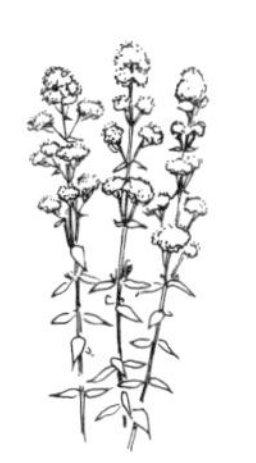

ruber *p. 186*
Red Valerian; Jupiter's Beard. Bushy, 1–3 ft. (30–90 cm) high. Flowers many, fragrant, ½ in. (13 mm) long, the spur slender, usually red but crimson or white in some varieties. A favorite garden plant. Also sold as *Valeriana rubra, V. coccinea,* or *Kentranthus.* Zone 5.

Cerastium
Pink family
Caryophyllaceae

See-ras'tee-um. The 60 or so species of chickweed or mouse-ear chickweed are mostly weedy herbs (sometimes pests), but 3 of them are attractive garden plants.

Description
Leaves opposite, often hairy. Flowers small and white, relatively showy due to the profuse, forked clusters (in cultivated species).

How to Grow
The species below are very easy to grow in full sun in well-drained soil; increased by division. Snow-in-Summer is extremely popular in rock gardens or borders because of its ground-covering habit, mats of white foliage, and white flowers.

biebersteinii *p. 241*
Taurus Cerastium. Creeping plant, not over 6 in. (15 cm) high, leaves grayish-woolly. Flowers white, 1 in. (2.5 cm) across. Asia Minor. A good choice for rock gardens and borders. Zone 4.

tomentosum *p. 240*
Snow-in-Summer. Popular prostrate garden plant, not over 6 in. (15 cm) high, forming large patches. Leaves numerous, conspicuously white-woolly. Flowers white, nearly ½ in. (13 mm) wide. Europe. Invasive. Will grow in pure sand. Zone 4.

Ceratostigma
Plumbago family
Plumbaginaceae

Ser-rat-o-stig′ma. Small genus of herbs or low shrubs from China and Africa, two grown as border plants for their blue flowers

Description
Leaves alternate, hairy on the margins, flowers in loose, headlike clusters surrounded by a series of stiff bracts. Corolla tubular, stamens inserted in tube.

How to Grow
Cultivated species are attractive fall-blooming border plants with no special soil preferences. They do best in full sun and soil with good drainage. Propagated by division.

plumbaginoides *p. 207*
Leadwort. Low or semi-prostrate, to 12 in. (30 cm) high. Flowers deep blue, to ½ in. (13 mm) wide. China. Will not tolerate deep shade. Hardy to zone 6, where winter mulch is required.

Chelidonium
Poppy family
Papaveraceae

Kelly-do′ni-um. Two species of Eurasian biennials; one, *C. majus,* is a frequent escape from old gardens.

Description
Flowers yellow, in small stalked umbels. Sepals 2. Petals 4, the flower to ⅔ in. (17 mm) long.

How to Grow
Thrives in full sun everywhere except very wet locations. Colonizes easily in wooded sites.

majus *p. 121*
Celandine. Forms a basal rosette of deeply divided or cleft leaves. In the second spring 1 or more erect, branching and leafy stems rise from the rosette to 3 ft. (90 cm) high. Stems are filled with a somewhat caustic yellow juice. Yellow flowers ½ in. (13 mm) across. 'Flore Pleno' is a double flowered cultivar that self-sows very easily. Zone 5.

Chelone

Snapdragon family
Scrophulariaceae

Kel-lo′nee. A small group of North American herbs, 2 garden subjects and one, the Pink Turtlehead, a showy plant.

Description
Leaves opposite, toothed. Flowers irregular and 2-lipped, the upper lip arching and notched. Flowers stalkless in a compact terminal spike, only 1 or 2 flowering at a time. Stamens 5, one sterile and shorter than the other 4.

How to Grow
The plants need partial shade and reasonably moist soil. Easily propagated by division.

lyonii *p. 177*
Pink Turtlehead. The most desirable for the garden. To 3 ft. (90 cm) high. Flowers rose-purple, 1 in. (2.5 cm) long. Summer. Species requires humus-enriched, constantly moist soil. Zone 4.

Chrysanthemum

Daisy family
Compositae

Kris-san′thee-mum. An important genus of garden plants, comprising about 100 species, nearly all from the temperate or subtropical regions of the Old World.

Description
Leaves alternate, often more or less divided. Flowers in heads, of all colors except blue and purple. Heads usually showy and of immense size in Florists' Chrysanthemum, but small and button-like in others. Strong-smelling foliage.

How to Grow
Plant in a sunny, well-drained spot. Since chrysanthemums are shallow-rooted, they require moist soil and regular additions of fertilizer. Most species need pinching. When soft growing tip is 4–6 in. (10–15 cm) long, remove it. Stop pinching plants in midsummer, or when they begin flowering. Chrysanthemums benefit from light winter mulch in northern areas. It is safer to dig up plants and store in a cold frame for winter.

In spring, divide plants by digging, then discard the "woody" parts, and replant the fleshy shoots.

coccineum *p. 134*
Pyrethrum; Painted Daisy. Very popular summer-blooming plant, 1–3 ft. (30–90 cm) high. Leaves fernlike. Flowerheads large, often 2½ in. (6 cm) wide; red, pink, lilac, or white, sometimes double. Prey to aphids and red spider mites. Promote second bloom by cutting stems to the ground after flowering. Many named forms. Zone 4.

frutescens *p. 127*
Marguerite Daisy. Tender, very beautiful, much-branched herb, 2–3 ft. (60–90 cm) high. Flowerheads daisylike, 1½–2½ in. (4–6 cm) wide, white, pale yellow, or pink. Canary Islands. Will bloom through summer if stems cut back periodically; do not cut into old woody base. Except in zone 9, species tends to be an annual.

leucanthemum *p. 242*
Oxeye Daisy. Not over 2 ft. (60 cm) high, stems unbranched. Flowerheads long-stalked, usually solitary, 1½ in. (4 cm) wide, white. Often weedy in fields; reseeds easily. Zone 3.

× ***morifolium*** *p. 197*
Florists' Chrysanthemum. Originally 9–15 in. (22.5–38.0 cm) high, but often grown today to 4 ft. (120 cm), and in various shapes (dome-shaped, etc.), due to pinching and disbudding. Leaves grayish-hairy. Flowerheads of many forms, including single, double, pompom; special petal types such as quills and spiders. From 1–6 in. (2.5–15.0 cm) across; all colors but blue. Hybrid. Susceptible to aphids and red spider mites. Zone 5.

nipponicum *p. 245*
Nippon Chrysanthemum or Daisy. Hardy border plant, 1½–2 ft. (45–60 cm) high. Flowerheads solitary at the ends of the branches, white, 2–3 in. (5.0–7.5 cm) wide. Japan. Pinch in southern zones for compact plants. In northern zones, early frost will curtail blooming. Zones 5–6.

parthenium *p. 244*
Feverfew. Bushy, hardy plant for the border, stems leafy, 2–3 ft. (60–90 cm) high. Leaves in varieties, yellowish or crisped. Flowerheads

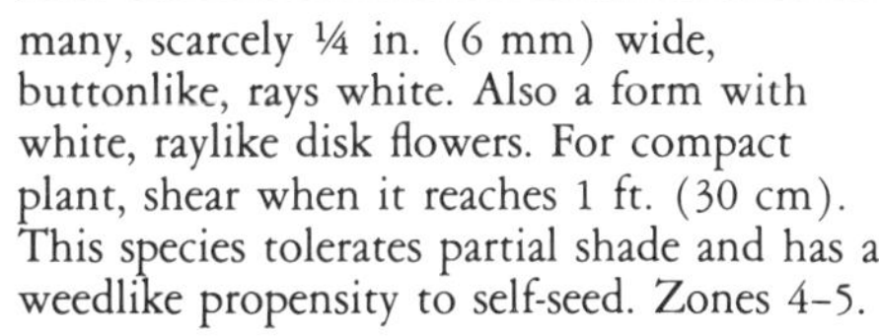

many, scarcely ¼ in. (6 mm) wide, buttonlike, rays white. Also a form with white, raylike disk flowers. For compact plant, shear when it reaches 1 ft. (30 cm). This species tolerates partial shade and has a weedlike propensity to self-seed. Zones 4–5.

× ***superbum*** *p. 243*
Shasta Daisy. 1–2 ft. (30–60 cm) high. Flowerheads 2–4 in. (5–10 cm) wide, white and daisylike. Fine perennial border plant, but soon dies out and is best trained as a biennial. Tolerates partial shade. Aphids may be troublesome. Requires regular division. Many named forms available. Zones 4–5.

zawadskii *p. 200*
To 1½ ft. (45 cm) high, stem bases purplish. Flowerheads solitary, to 2½ in. (6 cm) across, disk yellow, rays white or pink. Spreads rapidly in warm regions and sandy soil. Hybridized with *C.* × *morifolium* to produce Korean Chrysanthemums, very hardy, originally with daisylike heads, but now available with "double" forms. Also sold as *C.* × *rubellum.* Zone 5.

Chrysogonum
Daisy family
Compositae

Kris-sog′o-num. A genus of perennial herbs of the e. U.S., comprising a single species.

Description
A long-stalked herb with opposite, long-stalked, bluntly toothed leaves and yellow flowerheads.

How to Grow
A plant of the rich woods, it prefers such sites, but will grow in partial shade. Not dependably hardy in all northern areas, and will probably be damaged in zone 4 if there is snow cover. Easily propagated by seed or division.

virginianum *p. 118*
Golden Star; Green-and-Gold. 4–10 in. (10–25 cm) high. Flowerheads solitary, or a few, 1½ in. (4 cm) wide, yellow. Pa. to Fla. and La. Needs well-drained soil. Zones 5–6.

Chrysopsis
Daisy family
Compositae

Kris-op'sis. The golden asters (not true asters) comprise a group of North American herbs, almost weedy, grown for their yellow flowerheads and ability to grow in dry, sandy soils.

Description
Low herbs with woolly or hairy leaves and rather large heads of yellow ray and disk flowers, usually in small clusters at the ends of the branches.

How to Grow
Golden asters are very easy to grow in sun or partial shade in any garden soil and can be increased by division in spring. All bloom in midsummer.

mariana *p. 131*
Maryland Golden Aster. 1–3 ft. (30–90 cm) high, silky-hairy. Flowerheads yellow, 1½ in. (4 cm) wide, numerous. Long Island (N.Y.) to Fla. and Tex. A low maintenance species. Also sold as *Heterothaca mariana.* Zone 5.

Cimicifuga
Buttercup family
Ranunculaceae

Sim-mi-siff'you-ga. The bugbanes are tall, rather showy, summer-blooming herbs, well-suited to the wild garden or the shadiest part of the border.

Description
Large, thrice-compound leaves. Flowers small, white, with few or no petals, but crowded in a dense, terminal, finger-shaped cluster at the end of a tall stalk. Stamens many and giving the chief color to the flower.

How to Grow
The 2 species below are best suited to the wild garden. They grow in the woods and should have moist soil (not especially acid) and partial shade. A good mixture is black leaf mold and rotted sods.

racemosa *p. 261*
Black Snakeroot; Black Cohosh. Taller than the other species; sometimes 6 ft. (1.8 m)

high. Flower cluster branched, its main spike 1–3 ft. (30–90 cm) long and showy. Flower spikes may need staking. Zones 3–4.

simplex *p. 260*
Kamchatka Bugbane. Erect, 3–4 ft. (90–120 cm) high. Leaflets unequally toothed, the terminal one 3-lobed. Flowers white or greenish white, in a 1–3 ft. (30–90 cm) long raceme. Midsummer. Plants grown in shade produce thick foliage but few flowers. Also sold as *C. foetida* var. *intermedia.* Zone 4.

Clematis
Buttercup family
Ranunculaceae

Klem′a-tis. A genus of about 270 species of herbs, or shrubby or woody vines.

Description
Leaves opposite, mostly compound, usually with 3–5 or more leaflets, the leafstalk often curling and acting as a tendril. Flowers frequently very showy, with 4 or more petal-like sepals. Stamens numerous. Fruit a collection of 1-seeded achenes, in some species each with a plumed, feathery, and often a showy, tail-like appendage.

How to Grow
Plant in full sun to partial shade, where soil is fertile, cool and moist, never wet or dry. A spring mulch will keep root zone cooler. Light-textured soils need liberal additions of peat moss, leaf mold, or garden compost.

heracleifolia *p. 224*
Tube Clematis. 3–4 ft. (90–120 cm) high. Leaves hairy. Flowers blue, fragrant, hairy on the outside, 1 in. (2.5 cm) wide, in loose clusters not unlike a hyacinth. Most commonly cultivated in var. *davidiana,* which is taller and has deeper blue flowers. Leaf-eating insects may disfigure larger leaves. Zone 4.

recta *p. 265*
Ground Clematis. Erect, 2–5 ft. (60–150 cm) high. Flowers white, fragrant, 1 in. (2.5 cm) wide, in many-flowered clusters. Stake to produce upright plants. Hardy everywhere. Double flowered varieties available. Zone 4.

Convallaria
Lily family
Liliaceae

Kon-va-lair′ee-a. One to 3 species of rhizomatous herbs native in Eurasia and in the mts. of the Southeast from Va. to S.C.

Description
Flowers bell-shaped, borne in a one-sided raceme.

How to Grow
Does best in full to partial shade in moist, fertile soil to which compacted, organic matter is added annually.

majalis *p. 252*
Lily-of-the-Valley. 6–12 in. (15–30 cm) high. Leaves 4–8 in. (10–20 cm) long, 2–3 in. (5.0–7.5 cm) wide, elliptically shaped. Flowers white, ⅜ in. (9 mm) wide, bell-shaped, borne in a terminal raceme; waxy and very fragrant. Zone 4.

Coreopsis
Daisy family
Compositae

Ko-ree-op′sis. Handsome garden flowers commonly called tickseed, comprising a genus of about 100 species of annual or perennial herbs.

Description
Leaves generally opposite, often lobed or dissected but entire in some. Flowerheads solitary or in branched clusters, composed of disk flowers and showy ray flowers, both prevailingly yellow. Double varieties available.

How to Grow
Coreopsis is almost weedlike and very easy to grow in any ordinary well-drained garden soil. It is readily divided in spring or fall. Most are among the most lasting of cut flowers. All are summer bloomers, and many are occasionally offered under the name *Calliopsis.*

auriculata *p. 124*
Eared Coreopsis. Hairy, 12–18 in. (30–45 cm) high, with slender rootstocks. Flowerheads mostly solitary, 1 in. (2.5 cm)

wide, golden yellow. Se. U.S. *C. auriculata* benefits from afternoon shade and will flower into midsummer in cooler regions. Cultivars include *C. auriculata* 'Nana', 9 in. (22.5 cm) high with yellow-orange flowers. Zone 4.

lanceolata *p. 125*

Lance Coreopsis. 2–3 ft. (60–90 cm) high. Flowerheads very long-stalked, to 2½ in. (6 cm) across, disk and ray flowers yellow. Plants grown in moist, fertile soil sprawl and increase rapidly. Cultivars include 'Sunray', 1½–2 ft. (45–60 cm) high and double-flowered; and 'Baby Sun', a more compact plant 12–20 in. (30–50 cm) high. Zone 4.

verticillata *pp. 125, 126*

Threadleaf Coreopsis. 18–30 in. (45–75 cm) high. Flowerheads nearly 2 in. (5 cm) wide, dark yellow. Drought tolerant. Cultivars include 'Golden Shower', most popular, 2–3 ft. (60–90 cm) high, with yellow flowers; 'Moonbeam', 18–24 in. (45–60 cm) high, with light yellow flowers; and 'Zagreb', which is 12–18 in. (30–45 cm) high with yellow flowers. Zone 4.

Coronilla

Bean family
Leguminosae

Kor-ro-nil'la. A genus of about 20 species of herbs or shrubs scattered from the Canary Islands to w. Asia.

Description
Leaves compound, the leaflets arranged feather-fashion. Flowers pealike, in long-stalked umbels from the leaf axils.

How to Grow
The species below is very invasive and is best used as groundcover on steep, sunny banks or in borders. Propagated by seeds.

varia *p. 182*

Crown Vetch. Sprawling vinelike herb, not over 18 in. (45 cm) high. Flowers ½ in. (13 mm) long, pink, rose, and white tricolored, in dense clusters. Europe. Grows best in dry soil. Zone 4.

Corydalis
Fumitory family
Fumariaceae

Kor-rid′a-lis. A large genus of usually weak-stemmed, often prostrate herbs, most from the north temperate zone.

Description
They have lobed or finely dissected leaves, often bluish green. Handsome flowers in dense or lax racemes, the 4 petals spurred. Stamens 6.

How to Grow
Most can be grown in the open border, but preferably in a partly shady section. Mostly spring- and early summer-blooming. Some die down by midsummer.

lutea *p. 112*
Yellow Corydalis. Multi-stemmed, to 12 in. (30 cm) high. Foliage almost lace-like. Flowers yellow, ¾ in. (2 cm) long, in racemes. Europe. Grows well in gravelly or rocky areas; soil should be well-drained. Self-seeds prolifically, but can only be transplanted in small quantities. Zone 5.

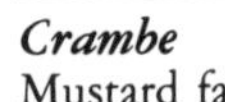

Crambe
Mustard family
Cruciferae

Kram′be. Twenty species of mostly bluish-foliaged herbs ranging from the Canary Islands to w. Asia.

Description
Leaves thick or fleshy, glaucous, very large, up to 2 ft. (60 cm) across, and deeply lobed or cut. Numerous small white flowers are borne on racemes or panicles, each with 4 petals and 4 sepals.

How to Grow
Grows best in full sun and well-drained soil that is slightly alkaline.

cordifolia *p. 236*
Heartleaf Crambe. To 6 ft. (1.8 m) high. Basal leaves bluish-green with stiff hairs. Flowers 5/16 in. (8 mm) across, white, arranged in huge panicles 3–4 ft. (90–120 cm) across, resembling giant baby's breath. Caucasus. Zone 6.

Crocosmia
Iris family
Iridaceae

Kro-kos′mee-a. Five species of gladiolus-like herbs from South Africa.

Description
Leaves broad-linear or sword-shaped, ½–1 in. (1.3–2.5 cm) wide, resembling a gladiolus. Double rows of tubular flowers are borne on an arching stem.

How to Grow
Crocosmia do best in full sun where soil is moist and well-drained. In northern regions, corms should be dug up in fall after the first frost and replanted in spring after all chance of frost has passed; for *C. masoniorum* corms should be dug up in all regions with frost.

masoniorum *p. 139*
Crocosmia. To 3 ft. (90 cm) high. Flowers reddish orange, 1½ in. (4 cm) across, borne on a raceme. South Africa. Prefers sandy loam. Zone 6.

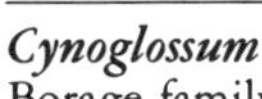

Cynoglossum
Borage family
Boraginaceae

Sin-o-gloss′um. A genus of 90 species of widely scattered herbs, most quite weedy, but the species below often grown for its blue flowers.

Description
Alternate, often roughish leaves, and small flowers in often arching, always one-sided racemes. Corolla funnel-shaped, its limb with 5 rounded lobes. Fruit a collection of small, minutely prickly nutlets.

How to Grow
Plants thrive in full sun and moist soils. Propagate by division in spring or root cuttings in fall.

nervosum *p. 205*
Great Houndstongue. To 2 ft. (60 cm) high. Leaves sparsely hairy. Flowers ½ in. (13 mm) wide, blue, arranged on a one-sided raceme that coils slightly. Prefers average, well-drained soil. In very fertile soil, stems may fall over. Zone 5.

Delphinium
Buttercup family
Ranunculaceae

Del-fin′i-um. The larkspurs comprise a genus of about 300 species, all from the north temperate zone, and include some of the finest hardy garden flowers.

Description
Leaves alternate, always lobed or divided finger-fashion. Flowers very showy, generally in a long terminal raceme or spike, prevailingly blue (other colors in some cultivated forms), and very irregular. Sepals 5, petal-like, one produced into a long spur. Stamens numerous. All have poisonous juice.

How to Grow
Delphinium requires moist soil that is fertilized regularly. Areas of full sun protected from wind are best; plants do poorly in hot areas with long summers. Tall plants with heavy blossoms require staking. Stakes should be in 12 in. (30 cm) of soil, and rise to ⅔ the height of the flower stalk.

elatum *p. 230*
Candle Larkspur. To 6 ft. (1.8 m) high, branches upright. Flowers in long, terminal, spikelike raceme, each flower scarcely over 1 in. (2.5 cm) wide, blue. Petals purple. *D. elatum* is one of the delphiniums used in crosses to develop hybrids, a very popular group of plants that grow to 5 ft. (150 cm) high. Flowers 2–3 in. (5.0–7.5 cm) across, white, pink, lavender, blue, violet, or purple. Plants are susceptible to slugs, red spider mites, leaf spots, stem borers, and powdery mildew, and must be sprayed regularly and require staking. Rebloom will often occur in fall if stalks are cut back. Types include:

1. Giant Pacific Hybrids, flowers usually double with a contrasting set of deeper colored sepals in middle of floret. Heat tolerant. Can be propagated from seed.
2. Blackmore and Langdon Hybrids, flower racemes huge.
3. Belladonna Hybrids, flowers blue or white, compactly arranged. Hardy to Zone 3. Cultivars include 'Belladonna', light blue; 'Bellamosa', dark blue; and 'Casa Blanca', white.
4. 'Connecticut Yankee', shortest type, grows to 2½ ft. (75 cm) high. Bush-type plant with full, branching habit. Flowers white,

blue, lavender, or purple, each resembling a single larkspur. All zone 4.

Dianthus
Pink family
Caryophyllaceae

Dy-an'thus. About 300 species of annual or perennial herbs, mostly Eurasian, some, such as Sweet William, important garden plants.

Description
They have opposite, usually narrow, leaves and swollen joints. Flowers terminal, solitary in the carnation and some others, but usually grouped in small, often dense cymes or panicles. Petals 5 (much doubled in some horticultural forms), fringed or toothed in some species.

How to Grow
Growing the plants below is usually easy in any ordinary garden soil that is extremely well-drained. Most prefer full sun. Plants are inclined to die out if left alone for 2 or 3 years, so avoid this by keeping a fresh stock coming along by division, layering, or cuttings, all easily managed since the plant roots freely. In the mat-forming sorts, it is better to cut off all flowering stalks in fall, nearly to the base of the plant. Also, cut off all faded flowers. Most are spring-blooming.

× ***allwoodii*** *p. 170*
Allwood Pink. Generally tufted bluish-green foliage, 12–18 in. (30–45 cm) high. Flowers red, pink, white or combination, 1½–2 in. (4–5 cm) across, mostly semidouble, petals fringed or not. Soil should be slightly alkaline, with additions of humus. Zone 4.

barbatus *p. 169*
Sweet William. 1–2 ft. (30–60 cm) high, with flat, broad leaves. Flowers not fragrant, ½ in. (13 mm) across, borne in dense cymes 3–5 in. (7.5–12.5 cm) across, red, rose-purple, white, or varicolored; in a few forms double-flowered. Most varieties biennials, although annual self-seeding creates an image of perennial nature. Prefer cool summers and winters mild. Zone 6.

deltoides *p. 171*
Maiden Pink. Forms mats of green foliage, leaves very small and narrow. Flowering

stalks forked, 4–12 in. (10–30 cm) high, flowers nearly ¾ in. (19 mm) wide, red or pink (white with crimson eye in some horticultural forms). Requires alkaline soil, good air circulation. Poorly drained soil in winter can be fatal. Var. *glaucus* has bluish-gray foliage. Zone 4.

gratianopolitanus *p. 171*
Cheddar Pink. 6–8 in. (15–20 cm) high. Flowers solitary, ½–¾ in. (13–19 mm) wide, pink. Drain standing water during winter. Cultivars include 'Tiny Rubies', with a dense, flat mat of leaves topped by stems 2–3 in. (5.0–7.5 cm) high and double-pink flowers. Zone 5.

plumarius *p. 170*
Grass Pink. Mat-forming herb 9–18 in. (22.5–45.0 cm) high, with smooth, bluish-gray foliage. Flowers 1½ in. (4 cm) across, fragrant, rose-pink to purplish, white or variegated colors, petals fringed. Some double-flowered. Eurasia. Add lime to very acid soil and prune after flowering. Light mulch of evergreen branches reduces winter damage. Var. *semperflorens,* with long-continuing bloom, includes many common garden pinks. Zone 4.

Dicentra
Bleeding heart family
Fumariaceae

Dy-sen′tra. A small genus of slender, rather weak, somewhat watery-juiced herbs, some Asiatic, the rest from North America.

Description
They have fleshy rootstocks and feathery, much dissected, often basal leaves that are sometimes compound. Flowers in terminal racemes, very irregular, the petals joined into a heart-shaped or long-spurred corolla.

How to Grow
D. cucullaria should only be grown in the deep shade of wild gardens, preferably in a wind-free place. The others may be grown in open borders or in rock gardens. Increase by division in early spring.

cucullaria *p. 253*
Dutchman's-Breeches. Flowering stalk 5–8 in. (12.5–20.0 cm) high. Flowers white

tipped with yellow, ¾ in. (2 cm) long. Plant in fertile, moist, humus-enriched soil. Dies to the ground by late June in hot climates; may continue to flower in cooler areas. Zone 4.

hybrids *p. 175*
Hybrids of *D. eximia* and *D. formosa.* 12–18 in. (30–45 cm) high. Leaves basal, fine-textured. Flowers pink, heart-shaped, 1 in. (2.5 cm) long, in loose racemes. Varieties include 'Luxuriant', with dark reddish-pink flowers, and 'Bountiful', with red flowers. Zone 4.

spectabilis *p. 175*
Common Bleeding Heart. 1–2 ft. (30–60 cm) high. Flowers 1½ in. (4 cm) long, in a 1-sided raceme 9 in. (22.5 cm) long; rose-colored or red. Needs moist, well-drained soil. In hot or dry climates, foliage will become ragged and should be cut to the ground after flowering. Zones 3–4.

Dictamnus

Citrus family
Rutaceae

Dik-tam′nus. A single hardy Eurasian herb, long cultivated for ornament in open borders, where it may persist for generations.

Description
Somewhat woody, leaves compound, glandular-dotted, leaflets leathery. Flowers in a terminal raceme, white. Petals 5. Stamens 10.

How to Grow
Very easy to grow but does not tolerate change, so plant it where you want it permanently. Dividing should be avoided. Prefers moist soil in full sun. Easiest method of propagation is seeds sown outdoors in fall to sprout the next spring.

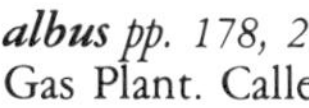

albus *pp. 178, 259*
Gas Plant. Called Gas Plant because the strong vapor of its foliage and flowers will faintly ignite if a lighted match is put to it on a windless summer evening. 2–3 ft. (60–90 cm) high, flowers 1 in. (2.5 cm) long. 'Purpureus' has rose-purple flowers and is otherwise the same as *D. albus.* Var. *rubrus* has red flowers. Zones 3–4.

Dietes
Iris family
Iridaceae

Dy-ee′tees. The 100 species in cultivation ar
South African herbs.

Description
Iris-like. They bear corms or rootstocks and have basal, sword-shaped or narrower leaves. Flowers almost exactly like *Iris.*

How to Grow
Easy to grow in warm regions. In cooler regions, grow as an annual or in a greenhouse.

vegeta *p. 270*
African Iris. 2 ft. (60 cm) high, with leaves spread like a fan. Flowers white with yellow or brown spots and lavender shading, 2–2½ in. (5–6 cm) wide. Needs average well-drained soil and full sun. Blooms last only one day. Zone 8.

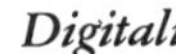

Digitalis
Figwort family
Scrophulariaceae

Di-ji-tay′lis. Handsome, sometimes poisonous or medicinal herbs, some deservedly popular garden flowers.

Description
Erect biennial or perennial herbs, with alternate leaves, or the lower ones sometim crowded. Flowers in long, terminal, often 1-sided racemes, often very showy. Corolla more or less bell-shaped at the base. There are 4 stamens.

How to Grow
If treated as perennials, digitalis can be divided in spring. All are easy to grow in ordinary well-drained garden soil.

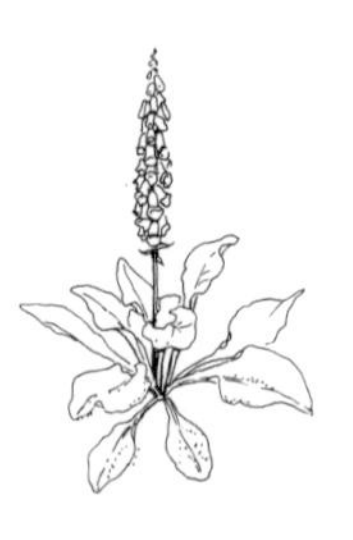

grandiflora *p. 110*
Yellow Foxglove. Hairy, to 3 ft. (1 m) hig Flowers to 2 in. (5 cm) long, yellowish but brown-marked. Europe and w. Asia. Grows best in light shade in moist soils rich in organic matter. Remove faded flowers but leave some seed heads if reseeding is desired Zone 4.

× ***mertonensis*** *p. 174*
To 3 ft. (90 cm) high. Most leaves compose the basal rosette. Flowers rosy-pink, 2–3 in. (5–7.5 cm) long, pendulous, spotted in the throat. Requires frequent division to maintain its perennial character. Zone 5.

Disporum

Lily family
Liliaceae

Dy-spore′um. A genus of perennial herbs. They are sometimes called Fairy-Bells and are woodland plants with creeping rootstocks.

Description
Leaves somewhat downy, nearly stalkless, alternate. Flowers bell-shaped, the 6 segments scarcely identifiable as petals or sepals. Stamens 6, threadlike.

How to Grow
The species below perform best in dry, well-drained, humus-rich soil in partial shade. Easily propagated by seed or by spring division.

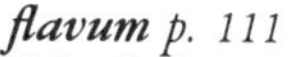

flavum *p. 111*
Fairy-Bells. 2–3 ft. (60–90 cm) high. Leaves shiny, leathery. Flowers 1 in. (2.5 cm) long, yellow. A good choice for dry, shady areas. Zone 4.

sessile **'Variegatum'** *p. 252*
Variegated Japanese Fairy-Bells. 15–24 in. (38–60 cm) high. Leaves edged with white. Flowers white, 1 in. (2.5 cm) across, usually solitary or in groups of 2 or 3. Japan. Zone 4.

Dodecatheon

Primrose family
Primulaceae

Do-deck-kath′ee-on. Beautiful North American wildflowers comprising perhaps 14 species, a few of which are cultivated in the wild garden or in the rock garden.

Description
Leaves wavy-margined, basal. Flowers in a small terminal umbel at the end of a stalk arising from the ground. Corolla with a very

short tube, the 5 lobes turned backwards. Stamens 5.

How to Grow
The species below prefers partial shade and rich, sandy soil high in organic matter and well-drained. Easily propagated by division.

meadia *p. 254*
Common Shooting-star. 1–2 ft. (30–60 cm) high. Leaves to 1 ft. (30 cm) long, forming a basal rosette. Flowers 1 in. (2.5 cm) long, rose-pink or lavender, whitish at the base and pendant, suggesting a falling star. Stamens reddish yellow, anthers purple. Foliage dies down after flowering. Needs moisture during growing season and drier conditions when dormant. Water left standing in crown in winter can be fatal. Zone 5.

Doronicum
Daisy family
Compositae

Do-ron′i-kum. Eurasian herbs comprising 20–30 species, a few of which are widely grown garden plants under the name leopard's bane.

Description
They are stout, often unbranched, herbs with basal leaves and alternate stem leaves. Flowerheads yellow, long-stalked, with a single row of ray flowers.

How to Grow
The leopard's banes are very easy to grow in borders or flower beds. They do better in the North than southward. Easily propagated by division.

cordatum *p. 130*
Leopard's Bane. A single-stemmed herb, 1–2½ ft. (30–75 cm) high. Flowerhead usually single, 2 in. (5 cm) wide, yellow. Partial shade needed in hot climates; may go dormant. Moist soil is best, even during dormancy. Also sold as *D. caucasium.* Varieties include 'Miss Mason' or 'Madame Mason', which retains foliage better during the summer; and 'Spring Beauty', which has a double flower. Zone 4.

Draba
Cabbage family
Cruciferae

Drah′ba. Whitlow grass is a general name for about 250 species of small, usually tufted, herbs, a few of which are cultivated in rock gardens, rarely in borders.

Description
Mostly spring-blooming annuals or perennials from the north temperate zone, with small leaves chiefly in basal rosettes and nearly always hairy. Flowers usually numerous, grouped in racemes; white, yellow, or pinkish-purple. Petals 4.

How to Grow
Does best in sunny or lightly shaded spots. Well-drained soil is very important; soil that is gritty and amended with peat moss is good. During severe winters, *Draba* needs a light mulch.

densiflora *p. 116*
Rock Cress Draba. Dense plant, 2–3 in. (5.0–7.5 cm) high. Flowers yellow, ⅛ in. (3.2 mm) wide, in loose racemes. Blooms in spring. Also sold as *D. globosa, D. nelsonii, D. paysonii, D. sphaerula.* Zone 4.

Duchesnea
Rose family
Rosaceae

Doo-shay′nee-a. Two Asiatic species of herbs, related to *Fragaria.*

Description
Leaves similar to wild strawberry's, trifoliate, ovate, short-stalked and toothed, with silky hair on the lower surface. Flowers yellow with 5 petals.

How to Grow
Very easy to grow. *Duchesnea* may become very invasive in flowerbeds.

indica *p. 120*
Barren Strawberry. 2–3 in. (5–7.5 cm) high, trailing with runners. Flowers yellow, solitary, ½ in. (13 mm) wide. Fruit red, surrounded by the persistent calyx, suggesting a strawberry, but with little flavor. India. Zone 4.

Echinacea
Daisy family
Compositae

Ek-in-a'see-a. Almost weedy North American perennial herbs, commonly called coneflower or purple coneflower and sometimes offered under the name *Brauneria.*

Description
Coarse herbs with black, pungent roots, stout, hairy stems, and alternate leaves, the basal ones long-stalked. Flowerheads solitary on long stalks, the center of the head conical. Ray flowers not numerous, withering but persistent. Below the head a close-set series of small bracts.

How to Grow
The species described below is easy to grow in the open border. It will stand sun and wind, and is most easily propagated by division.

purpurea *p. 198*
Purple Coneflower. 2–4 ft. (60–120 cm) high. Leaves coarsely toothed. Flowers daisy-like, 3 in. (7.5 cm) across, ray flowers pink, sometimes white; disk flowers coppery or orange-brown. Cen. U.S. Susceptible to Japanese beetle. Prefers well-drained, sandy loam soil; drought tolerant. Zone 4.

Echinops
Daisy family
Compositae

Ek'i-nops. Decidedly handsome, thistlelike Old World herbs, commonly called globe thistle and useful in hardy borders. Of the 100 known species several, especially *E. ritro,* are useful both for their handsome, white-woolly foliage and blue flowers.

Description
Leaves alternate, more or less prickly toothec or lobed. Flowerheads with dense spiny bracts, the bracts usually metallic blue.

How to Grow
These bold, showy plants are easy to grow ir any ordinary garden soil, and can be increased by division or raised from seed. They need plenty of space.

ritro *p. 221*
Globe Thistle. 3–4 ft. (90–120 cm) high. Leaves white-felty underneath. Flowerheads blue, 1½–2 in. (4–5 cm) across. Eurasia. This species tolerates hot climates. It prefers sun and may need staking if soil is too fertile and moist. There is little difference between the cultivar 'Taplow Blue' and other seed selections of *E. ritro.* Zone 4.

Elsholtzia
Mint family
Labiatae

El-sholt′zi-a. A genus of over 30 species of chiefly Asiatic aromatic subshrubs.

Description
Foliage has a mint-like appearance and fragrance. Leaves bright green, oblong to lance-shaped, toothed, 3–5 in. (7.5–12.5 cm) long. Numerous small flowers borne in one-sided terminal spikes.

How to Grow
These plants perform best in southern zones. Sunny spots with well-drained soil are ideal.

stauntonii *p. 187*
Staunton Elsholtzia. A low shrub or shrubby herb, to 5 ft. (1.5 m) high. Flowers lavender, ¼ in. (6 mm) long, 1-sided spike to 6 in. (15 cm) long. Corolla only slightly 2-lipped, its stamens long-protruding. N. China. The plant is easily grown in open borders south of zone 6; not reliably hardy to the north. Propagate by greenwood cuttings, or by seed, and cut back to the ground each winter. Zone 7.

Epimedium
Barberry family
Berberidaceae

Ep-i-mee′di-um. Rather woody perennial herbs; all of the 20 known species from the north temperate zone.

Description
Leaves compound, the leaflets finely toothed and arranged feather-fashion. Flowers in clusters, either terminal or opposite the leaves.

How to Grow
Called barrenwort, these plants are mostly used in rock gardens, and are good as ground cover. They tolerate sun but prefer partial shade, and, with a little protection, their foliage may keep green over the winter They do best in moist soil. Cut back old wiry stems in spring. Propagated by division.

grandiflorum *p. 158*
Longspur Epimedium. Stems to 12 in. (30 cm) high. Flowers 1–2 in. (2.5–5.0 cm) across, pink with white tipped spurs. 'Rose Queen' has large flowers and long, white tipped spurs. Also sold as *E. macranthum.* Zone 5.

× ***rubrum*** *p. 159*
Red Epimedium. To 12 in. (30 cm) high. Flowers to 1 in. (2.5 cm) across, bright pink to crimson with white spurs. Also sold as *E. alpinum.* Zone 5,

× ***versicolor*** *p. 250*
Persian Epimedium. To 12 in. (30 cm) high Flowers to 1 in. (2.5 cm) across, petals yellow, spurs tinged with red. 'Sulphureum' is an excellent cultivar with foliage less mottled, yellow petals and sepals. Zone 5.

× ***warleyense*** *p. 147*
Warley Epimedium. 9–12 in. (22.5–30 cm) high. Flowers ¾ in. (19 mm) across, composed of 8 orange sepals, 4 spurlike brownish petals. Zone 5.

× ***youngianum*** **'Niveum'** *p. 251*
Snowy Epimedium. 8–10 in. (20–25 cm) high. Flowers pendulous, white, ½ in. (13 mm) across, composed of 8 sepals and 4 petals. Zone 5.

Eremurus
Lily family
Liliaceae

E-ree-mure′us. Foxtail lilies. Magnificent Asiatic herbs with thick, cordlike or fibrous roots. Few border herbs are so striking or showy. Generally known as foxtail lily or desert candle.

Description
Leaves all basal, rather narrow, without teeth, forming tufts or rosettes. Flowering

stalks from 4–10 ft. (1.2–3.0 m) high, the spire-like raceme usually 1–3 ft. (30–90 cm) long. Flowers are very numerous and bell-shaped.

How to Grow
Soil should be very rich and well-drained in full sun. Roots are peculiarly brittle, so *Eremurus* should be planted very carefully. North of zone 6 plants are not quite hardy and should be mulched.

stenophyllus *p. 142*
To 2–5 ft. (60–150 cm) high. Leaves to 1 ft. (30 cm) long. Flowers golden-orange, 1 in. (2.5 cm) across. Sw. Asia. Not very winter-hardy in northern sites if soil is wet. Buds and new leaves sensitive to frosts. Often sold as *E. stenophyllus bungei* or *E. stenophyllus* var. *bungei*. Zone 7.

Erigeron
Sunflower family
Compositae

E-rij′er-on. The fleabanes comprise about 200 species of annual or perennial herbs of wide distribution.

Description
Plants sometimes nearly stemless with basal leaves. Flowerheads solitary or in branched clusters, the disk flowers yellow, the rays numerous.

How to Grow
The ordinary border fleabanes are very easy to grow in any well-drained garden soil, and can be propagated by division in spring or fall. Best suited to the rock garden.

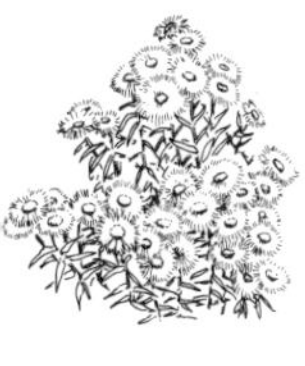

hybrids *p. 201*
Fleabane. 1–2 ft. (30–60 cm) high. Flowers daisylike, 2 in. (5 cm) across, with numerous ray flowers and some disk flowers. Common colors are pink, violet, and lavender, though many others are available. Prefers light, well-drained sandy soil of low fertility. Best growth in maritime climates. ‘Walther’ has light pink flowers. Zone 5.

Eriophyllum
Sunflower family
Compositae

E-ri-o-fill′um. Western North American herbs, often called woolly sunflower, because of their often white-woolly foliage and sunflowerlike heads.

Description
They have alternate leaves. Flowerheads small, resembling a miniature sunflower.

How to Grow
The woolly sunflowers are not happy in slushy or wet eastern winters. In the Far West they do well in open, sandy borders.

lanatum *p. 126*
Woolly Eriophyllum. To 2 ft. (60 cm) high. Flowerheads chiefly solitary, 1 in. (2.5 cm) wide, golden yellow. Idaho and British Columbia to Calif. Needs dry, well-drained soil, especially in winter. Zone 5.

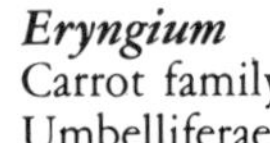

Eryngium
Carrot family
Umbelliferae

Er-rin′ji-um. Very striking and handsome herbs, widely cultivated for borders or rock gardens, and commonly called eryngo or sea holly. Very tall, bold plants.

Description
Unlike most plants of the carrot family, *Eryngiums* have simple leaves, generally cut or lobed, usually spiny-edged. Flowers crowded in dense headlike clusters.

How to Grow
Sea hollies thrive in full sun, in well-drained, sandy soil of moderate to low fertility. They are difficult to transplant; root cuttings are the best means of propagation since not all plants come true from seed. They need plenty of space. Most are summer-blooming.

bourgatii *p. 269*
Mediterranean Eryngo. To 24 in. (60 cm) high. Leaves nearly round, stiff, the veins marked with white. Flowerheads ¾ in. (19 mm) long, blue, the showy bracts beneath silver-white, long and spine-tipped. Zone 5.

× ***zabelii*** *p. 220*
Zabel Eryngo. 2–2½ ft. (60–75 cm) high. Flowers blue, 1 in. (25 mm) wide. This is probably a hybrid of *E. alpinium* and *E. bourgatii.* More tolerant of clay-loam soils and light shade than other *Eryngiums*. Many garden selections are listed under this heading. Zone 5.

Eupatorium
Sunflower family
Compositae

You-pa-toe′ri-um. The bonesets or thoroughworts comprise a genus of over 500 species of chiefly tropical American herbs, a few reaching temperate regions and grown in flower gardens.

Description
Hardy species with opposite or whorled leaves. Flowers showy, in numerous small heads crowded in clusters. Head composed of many small, tubular flowers.

How to Grow
All bonesets are easy to grow in ordinary garden soils. Grown for their profuse, usually late summer or fall, bloom. Propagated by division in spring.

coelestinum *p. 222*
Mist Flower; Hardy Ageratum. To 2 ft. (60 cm) high. Leaves thin, coarsely toothed. Flowerheads numerous, small, light blue or violet-blue. Grows best in wild gardens. Spreads quickly in sandy loam soil, more slowly in clay-loam soil. Zone 5.

Euphorbia
Spurge family
Euphorbiaceae

You-for′bi-a. Probably over 1600 species of wide distribution and great diversity of habit, including the annual Snow-on-the-Mountain and the gorgeous Poinsettia. Some tropical, cactuslike succulents, others weeds.

Description
The cactuslike species from Africa and the East Indies are widely planted for hedges in warm regions, and are usually as leafless as

most cacti. The herb species have flowers with no petals or sepals that are showy only because of their often highly colored bracts. Fruit a capsule.

How to Grow
Euphorbias are easy to grow in dry, well-drained garden soil. Plant in full sun. Plants release a milky sap when a stem, leaf, or root is broken. Sap may cause an allergic reaction, and should be kept away from eyes, mouth, and open cuts.

characias *p. 97*
3–4 ft. (90–120 cm) high. Leaves narrow, blue-gray. Flowers ½ in. (1.3 cm) wide, with reddish-brown glands surrounded by showy yellow-green bracts; arranged in dense, upright clusters. Mediterranean. Var. *wulfenii* has wider spikes, and yellowish-green flowers with yellow centers. Hardy and evergreen to zone 8.

corollata *p. 239*
Flowering Spurge. 1½–3 ft. (45–90 cm) high. Flower cluster with showy white appendages, for which the plant is grown; flowers ¼ in. (6 mm) across, white. Best grown for cutting or as a bedding plant. Zone 4.

cyparissias *p. 117*
Cypress Spurge. 8–12 in. (20–30 cm) high. Flowers and bracts greenish yellow, in a dense umbel. Bracts ¼ in. (6 mm) wide. In moist, fertile soil, plants may become rampant spreaders. Zone 4.

epithymoides *p. 105*
Cushion Spurge. 12 in. (30 cm) high, stems usually form a cushion-shaped or roundish clump. Flowers are greenish, small, in a dense cluster. Yellow bracts, 1 in. (2.5 cm) wide, are showy. Will not thrive in hot, humid climates. Also sold as *E. polychroma.* Zone 5.

griffithii **'Fire Glow'** *p. 140*
Fire Glow Euphorbia. To 3 ft. (90 cm) high. Leaves medium green with pale pink midribs. Flowers borne in clusters 2–4 in. (5–10 cm) across, with showy, red bracts. Himalayas. Zone 5.

myrsinites *p. 96*
Myrtle Euphorbia. 3–6 in. (7.5–15 cm) high. Grown for its foliage. Leaves numerous,

fleshy, bluish green. Small, greenish, unattractive flowers and chartreuse bracts. Needs dry soil, and is hardiest in well-drained sites. Its sprawling habit makes it good for raised beds, rock gardens, or rock walls. Zone 5.

Filipendula

Rose family
Rosaceae

Fill-i-pen′dew-la. A genus of herbs of the rose family, all from the north temperate zone, half of the 10 species grown for ornament in the border and sometimes sold as *Spiraea.*

Description
They have alternate, compound leaves, the leaflets arranged feather-fashion. Flowers small, numerous, in large terminal panicles or corymbs, usually with 5 petals. Stamens numerous.

How to Grow
All the species below except *F. vulgaris* are easy to grow in very moist garden soil and can be propagated by division of the clumps in early spring. *F. vulgaris* needs drier soil. All prefer partial shade.

palmata *p. 193*
Meadowsweet. 2–4 ft. (60–120 cm) high. Rose-pink flowers ⅜ in. (9 mm) across, in 6 in. (15 cm) plumes. Japan. Meadowsweet can be grown in full sun if soil is kept very moist. Also sold as *F. purpurea* or *Spiraea gigantea.* Zone 4.

rubra *p. 192*
Queen-of-the-Prairie. A stout but graceful herb, 4–7 ft. (1.2–2.1 m) high. Flowers magenta-pink, ⅜ in. (9 mm) across, and arranged in a very fine-textured cluster. Zone 3.

ulmaria *p. 264*
Queen-of-the-Meadow. A feathery, beautiful herb, 3–5 ft. (1.0–1.5 m) high. Leaflets toothed, white-felty beneath. Flowers white, tiny, branches terminating in feathery plumes. Also sold as *Spiraea ulmaria.* Zone 4.

vulgaris *p. 237*
Dropwort. 2–3 ft. (60–90 cm) high, the rootstocks tuberous. Leaves finely dissected

and fernlike. Flowers white, ½–¾ in. (13–19 mm) across, in a loose raceme. Not as fine or densely growing as on other species. Dropwort self-sows. 'Flore Pleno' is the double form. Also sold as *F. hexapetala* and *Spiraea filipendula.* Zone 4.

Foeniculum
Carrot family
Umbelliferae

Fee-nick'you-lum. An Old World genus consisting of three species of herbs.

Description
Twice-compound leaves, the leaflets arranged feather-fashion. Small flowers in umbels.

How to Grow
Any well-drained soil with a sunny exposure will do. Can be transplanted in spring or fall propagation is by spring division or by seed.

vulgare *p. 88*
Common Fennel. A perennial, but usually grown as an annual or biennial. Stems 3–5 ft. (1.0–1.5 m) high, bluish green. Ultimate leaflets very numerous, threadlike. Flowers yellow, ⅛ in. (3.2 mm) across, in large umbels. Southern Europe. Summer. Valued for its ornamental foliage. The var. *purpureum* turns deep purple when grown in the sun. Zone 4.

Fragaria
Rose family
Rosaceae

Fra-gay'ri-a. Strawberry. Perennial herbs comprising about 12 species. They are essentially stemless plants except for the long runners.

Description
Leaves compound, with 3 leaflets. Flowers generally white (rarely reddish), arising from the ground. Calyx 5-toothed, the lobes spreading and forming the hull of the strawberry. Petals 5, mostly broad and rounded. Stamens many. Fruit (in the ordinary sense) the much-enlarged, juicy, very fleshy and delicious receptacle, in which or upon the surface of which, are embedded

the true fruits, which are small achenes, commonly, but incorrectly, called the seeds.

How to Grow
Grows well in full sun in most garden soil, particularly if soil is slightly acid. Plants should be treated as biennials, and plowed under after second year for better yield. Plant in rows, which produce more fruit, or hills, which produce better fruit. In zones 3–6, these plants may require mulching in winter.

chiloensis *p. 246*
Chiloe Strawberry. A low bushy plant, 6–8 in. (15–20 cm) high, its runners usually forming after fruit is set. Leaves green and glossy above, pale bluish white beneath. Flowers white, ½ in. (1.3 cm) wide, inclined to droop, standing below the foliage. Fruit firm, large, dark red, the hull large. Zone 5.

Gaillardia
Daisy family
Compositae

Gay-lar′di-a. Fourteen species of showy North American herbs, some very popular flower garden plants from the w. U.S.

Description
They are leafy, erect, branching herbs with alternate or basal leaves that are more or less dotted. Flowerheads extremely handsome, the rays 3-toothed or almost fringed. Disk flowers purple.

How to Grow
Gaillardias prefer light, open soils and full sunlight. They are propagated by division, spring or fall, and are chiefly summer-bloomers.

× ***grandiflora*** *p. 134*
Blanketflower. 8–36 in. (20–90 cm) high. Leaves slightly hairy. Flowers red and yellow, 3–4 in. (7.5–10 cm) wide. Blanketflowers need well-drained soil and will not survive in heavy, wet soils during winter. The crown in the center of the plant often dies; new growth appearing away from the old crown can be dug up and transplanted. If planted from seed, it often flowers in first year. There is a wide variety of color selections. Zone 4.

Galax
Galax family
Diapensiaceae

Gay'lacks. A single perennial evergreen herb from e. North America.

Description
Plant forms a clump of scaly rhizomes, from which arises the cluster of evergreen leaves.

How to Grow
Galax needs full to partial shade and moist soil. Optimum growth requires acid soil with abundant organic matter; add peat moss to enrich the soil.

urceolata *p. 260*
Galaxy. A stemless, tufted herb, 2½ ft. (75 cm) high. Leaves nearly round, green, but bronze with age, and widely used for funeral decorations. Flowers white, 1/16 in. (1.5 mm) across, in a spike-like raceme, on a slender stalk that may be 30 in. (75 cm) high. Petals 5. Stamens 10, five of them sterile and petal-like. Also sold as *G. aphylla.* Zone 5.

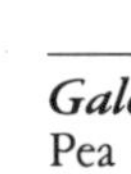

Galega
Pea family
Leguminosae

Ga-lee'ga. A small genus of Eurasian perennial herbs.

Description
Leaves pinnately compound. Flowers pea-shaped and borne in racemes.

How to Grow
Grows well in ordinary soil in full sun or light shade. Plant will form a large, loose clump, 3 ft. (90 cm) high, and may need support.

officinalis *p. 183*
Goat's Rue. An erect herb, 2–3 ft. (60–90 cm) high, the leaflets arranged feather-fashion. Flowers pealike, pink and white or purplish, ½ in. (13 mm) long, arranged in racemes. Summer. Cen. Europe to Iran. There are forms with variegated leaves. Zone 5.

Galium
Madder family
Rubiaceae

Gay′li-um. Weak, almost weedy perennial herbs, commonly known as bedstraw or cleavers. They are suited only to informal plantings in borders or rock gardens.

Description
Stems often prostrate or arching. Leaves stalkless. Flowers very numerous, but small, white, yellow, or maroon, the corolla wheel-shaped or deeply 4-parted. Stamens 4.

How to Grow
Galium requires a moist, well-drained, shady site with slightly acid soil. In such places, the foliage remains shiny-green into the fall. However, if grown in a sunny, dry site, plants will become stunted and may die down.

odoratum *p. 268*
Sweet Woodruff. To 1 ft. (30 cm) high. Leaves in whorls, fragrant when dried. Flowers white, to ¼ in. (6 mm) across, in clusters. Eurasia. Zone 5.

Galtonia
Lily family
Liliaceae

Gall-to′ni-a. A small genus of South African bulbous herbs.

Description
Large, drooping, whitish flowers on a tall raceme. Leaves large, basal, fleshy, and straplike, 2½ ft. (75 cm) long.

How to Grow
Easily grown in humus-enriched, well-drained, moist soil. Does best in full sun. In northern areas, bulbs should be mulched. In severe winter climates, it is best to dry bulbs and replant them in spring.

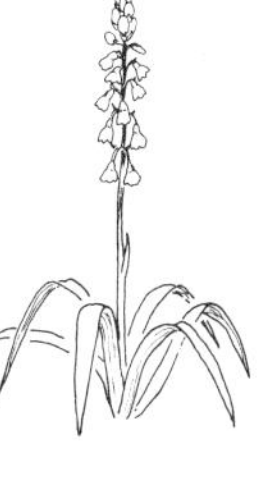

candicans *p. 254*
Giant Summer Hyacinth. 3–4 ft. (90–120 cm) high, with showy white flowers. Leaves narrowly pointed, semi-erect and grayish green. Single, erect flower stem (scope) carries about 12 whitish bell-shaped flowers, each 1 in. (2.5 cm) long. Stamens 6.

South Africa. Increased by offsets and often sold as *Hyacinthus candicans.* Not really hard north of zone 5 unless well mulched.

Gaura

Evening primrose family
Onagraceae

Gau′ra. About 20 species of rather coarse, chiefly perennial North and South American herbs, the one below grown for ornament in more informal borders.

Description
They are stout herbs with alternate leaves and summer-blooming flowers in terminal spikes or racemes. Petals slightly unequal, separate, the base narrowed into a claw.

How to Grow
This species is very easy to grow in full sun in any ordinary garden soil and is readily increased by spring or fall division. Needs a mulch north of zone 7.

lindheimeri *p. 255*
White Gaura. To 5 ft. (1.5 m) high; bushy. Flowers white fading to light pink, ½–1 in. (1.3–2.5 cm) long, in erect, wandlike stalks. Louisiana, Texas. Well-drained soil is of paramount importance. In poorly drained areas, raise the bed. *Gaura* has a long taproot, and needs watering only in the driest part of summer. Zone 6.

Gentiana

Gentian family
Gentianiaceae

Jen-she-a′na. The gentians constitute a genus of about 350 species of herbs, some of them choice plants for rock gardens, borders, or wild gardens, and all of them needing somewhat specialized culture. They are chiefly plants of cool, moist regions, especially mountain meadows, and some grow on alpine summits.

Description
Leaves opposite. Flowers showy, often solitary or in few-flowered clusters. Corolla 4 to 5-lobed, often with teeth between the lobes. Stamens 5.

How to Grow
Culture varies with species. Most do well in loam soil, although some require a scree (loose, stony material with little soil), and others prefer moist, humus-enriched, almost boglike soil. Generally, the soil should be moist and cool and the site should be in partial shade or full sun.

asclepiadea *p. 212*

Willow Gentian. 2 ft. (60 cm) high and suited to the shadier parts of the herbaceous border. Flowers dark blue, 1½ in. (4 cm) long. Summer. Best growth will occur in acid, humus-rich soil that is kept moist and cool. Zones 6–7.

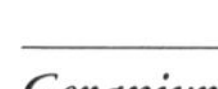

Geranium
Geranium family
Geraniaceae

Ger-ray′ni-um. About 300 species of hardy perennial, biennial, or (rarely) annual herbs, commonly called cranesbill. The genus does not include the common garden geranium, *Pelargonium.*

Description
Generally low, often half-prostrate herbs with forking stems and dissected or lobed roundish leaves divided finger-fashion. Flowers with 5 petals and 10 stamens. Fruit a collection of elastically splitting beaked capsules (carpels) that persist.

How to Grow
Cranesbills are easy to grow and readily increased by division of clumps in spring or fall. Some are woodland plants (as noted below), and should be grown in partially shaded parts of the wild garden. Nearly all bloom in spring and early summer.

dalmaticum *p. 166*

To 6 in.(15 cm) high, with clusters of 2–4 flowers, petals rose-colored. Flowers to 1 in. (2.5 cm) across. Yugoslavia. In areas where summers are hot, plant in partial shade and moist, fertile soil. Where summers are cooler, full sun and drier soils are acceptable. Zone 5.

endressii *p. 167*

Pyrenean Cranesbill. 12–18 in. (30–45 cm) high. Flowers ½–1 in. (1.3–2.5 cm) wide,

rose-pink. Pyrenees. Requires well-drained soil of average fertility. Where summers are cool, it will flower most of the season; in hot areas, flowering is restricted to late spring and early summer. Cultivars include 'A. T. Johnson', 12 in. (30 cm) high, with light, silvery-pink flowers. Zone 4.

himalayense *p. 210*
Lilac Cranesbill. 8–15 in. (20–38 cm) high. Flowers almost 2 in. (5 cm) wide, blue with purple veins. Also sold as *G. grandiflorum* and *G. meeboldii.* Zone 4.

hybrid 'Johnson's Blue' *p. 209*
Johnson's Blue Cranesbill. Grows to 12 in. (30 cm) high. Flowers profuse, 1½–2 in. (4–5 cm) wide, fine blue petals with darker blue veins. Hot, dry summers require moist soil and partial shade. This species is probably a hybrid of *G. pratense* and *G. himalayense.* Zone 4.

macrorrhizum *p. 173*
Bigroot Cranesbill. 12–18 in. (30–45 cm) high, roots thick. Flowers magenta or pink, to 1 in. (2.5 cm) across. Aromatic when crushed. S. Europe. Cultivars include 'Album', which has white flowers with red calyxes. Zone 4.

maculatum *p. 167*
Wild Geranium. 12–20 in. (30–50 cm) high. Flowers 1 in. (2.5 cm) wide, pale lilac. E. U.S., especially in rocky woods. Zone 5.

psilostemon *p. 165*
Armenian Cranesbill. To 2 ft. (60 cm) high. Flowers magenta with a black center, to 1½ in. (4 cm) across. Armenian S.S.R. (U.S.S.R.). Cultivars are lilac-pink. Zone 4.

sanguineum *p. 166*
Blood-red Cranesbill. 12–18 in. (30–45 cm) high. Flowers 1 in. (2.5 cm) wide, reddish purple to pale pink. Best of the cranesbills for open borders. Highly adaptable to climates, and will tolerate full sun even in hot, dry summers. Var. *lancastriense* is lower, with light pink flowers veined in crimson; there is also a white-flowered variety. Zone 4.

Geum
Rose family
Rosaceae

Jee′um. Avens. Most of the 50 known species from the cooler parts of the north temperate zone.

Description
They have chiefly basal leaves that are compound or so deeply cut or lobed as to appear so, the terminal segment or leaflet much larger than the others. Flowers solitary or a few, in corymbs, yellow, white, or red. Petals 5, rather broad. Stamens numerous. Fruit a collection of silky-plumed achenes that are often as showy as the flowers.

How to Grow
The avens are easy to grow in sun or partial shade in most garden soils, and are readily increased by division. Some of the taller ones are striking in borders. Mostly summer-blooming.

quellyon *p. 148*
Chilean Avens. To 2 ft. (60 cm) high. Flowers orange, red, or yellow, 1½ in. (4 cm) across, in erect stalks, alone or in clusters, single or double. Chile. Also sold as *G. chiloense.* Cultivars include *G.* 'Borisii', a hardier hybrid 12–18 in. (30–45 cm) high, and 'Mrs. Bradshaw' with brick-red semi-double flowers. Zones 5–6.

reptans *p. 147*
Avens. 6–8 in. (15–20 cm) high. Flowers yellow and orange, 1½ in. (4 cm) across. Europe. Plants spread by runners. In hot climates, amend the soil with organic matter. Zones 5–6.

Gillenia
Rose family
Rosaceae

Gil-len′i-a. North American perennial herbs, both species grown in the wild garden.

Description
Erect, branching plants with compound leaves or simple leaves deeply 3-parted. Flowers in loose terminal panicles. Petals 5, narrow and spreading, a little unequal. Stamens 10–20, not protruding.

How to Grow
These woodland plants prefer partial shade and should have moist, rich soil that is not too acid. Propagated by division of the clumps in spring.

trifoliata *p. 255*
Bowman's Root. 2–3 ft. (60–90 cm) high. Flowers star-shaped, white, 1 in. (2.5 cm) across. After white petals drop, red calyxes enlarge and become decorative. E. U.S. Can be grown in full sun except in very hot regions. Also sold as *Spiraea trifoliata.* Zone 5.

Goniolimon
Plumbago family
Plumbaginaceae

Go-nee-o-li′mun. A genus of 20 species of mostly Eurasian plants, differing from *Limonium* in technical characteristics.

Description
An excellent dwarf plant with lance-shaped leaves and flower clusters that stand erect.

How to Grow
Easy to grow in sunny sites with well-drained soil.

tataricum *p. 158*
Tatarian Statice. To 18 in. (45 cm) high. Flower panicle with the branches narrowly winged; flowers rosy-pink, ¼ in. (6 mm) across. Calyx remains on plant after petals drop. Calyx white, green-veined, the corolla red. S. Europe. Also offered as *Limonium tatarica.* Zone 4.

Gypsophila
Pink family
Caryophyllaceae

Jip-sof′fill-a. Handsome annual or perennial herbs, some very popular garden plants generally known as baby's-breath from the profusion of flowers.

Description
They are bluish-green herbs with opposite, small leaves and slightly swollen joints. Flowers many, in usually profuse branched

panicles. Petals 5, sometimes toothed, usually with a minute claw. Stamens 10.

How to Grow
Gypsophilas are very popular garden plants because they are easy to grow and bloom profusely. Start as plants or sow seeds directly. These plants do not transplant easily. Propagate by division. All need full sunlight and open, not too rich, soils.

paniculata *p. 156*
Baby's-Breath. To 3 ft. (1 m) high. Flowers very numerous, ¼ in. (6 mm) across, white. Spring and summer. Eurasia. Soil should be moist, well-drained, and pH should be neutral to slightly alkaline. Plants taller than 18 in (45 cm) need staking in open, windy sites. In areas with long growing seasons, plants will rebloom if cut back before flowers go to seed. Zone 4.

repens *p. 157*
Creeping Baby's-Breath. 6–8 in. (15–20 cm) high. Flowers ¼ in. (6 mm) wide, white. Mts. of Europe. Good ground cover for sunny areas; also does well in well-drained rock gardens and walls. The variety 'Rosea' has pink flowers. Zone 4.

Helenium
Daisy family
Compositae

Hell-lee'ni-um. The sneezeweeds are rather tall, coarse New World herbs, useful chiefly toward the rear of the informal herbaceous border or in open places in the wild garden.

Description
All the cultivated species except *H. amarum* are stout perennials with alternate leaves and profuse heads of flowers. Clusters usually flat, blooming in late summer and fall.

How to Grow
Almost any garden soil will suit sneezeweed, but it does best in moist, fertile soil in full sun; *H. autumnale* may need curtailing, since it tends to become weedy. Propagate by spring division of the clumps.

autumnale *p. 132*
False Sunflower. To 5 ft. (1.5 m) high. Flowerheads nearly 2 in. (5 cm) wide, the

rays lemon-yellow, orange, or mahogany, the disk flowers darker. E. U.S. Taller cultivars will stay short if tips are pinched in spring. Zone 4.

Helianthemum

Rock rose family
Cistaceae

He-li-an′thee-mum. Usually prostrate or sprawling woody plants or herbs, a few of which are cultivated for their roselike flowers. They are usually called frostweed or sun-rose.

Description
Evergreen leaves. Flowers very fleeting. Some flower earlier and are larger with showy petals; the later flowers are smaller and may have no petals. Large-flowered petals usually 5. Stamens numerous.

How to Grow
Best growth occurs in full sun in alkaline soil that is well-drained and sandy. Protect the plants in regions with severe winters.

nummularium *p. 150*
Rock Rose. 9–12 in. (22.5–30.0 cm) high. Flowers yellow, round, 1 in. (2.5 cm) across crepe-papery in texture, with 5 petals. Cut back after first bloom to promote autumn bloom. Cultivars can be pink, red, orange, o white. 'Fire Dragon' has bright red flowers. Zone 6.

Helianthus

Daisy family
Compositae

He-li-an′thus. Rather coarse, hardy annual or perennial herbs comprising about 150 species, found mostly in North America. They are very diverse in size and character.

Description
Leaves alternate, sometimes opposite above, the margins usually coarsely toothed. Flowers in terminal heads, from 3–12 in. (7.5–30.0 cm) across, the ray florets yellow, the disk florets yellow, brown, or purple.

How to Grow
The species below are easily grown in moist soils and full sun. Plants spread quickly and require regular division.

angustifolius *p. 132*
Swamp Sunflower. To 6 ft. (1.8 m) high, covered with stiff hairs. Flowerheads 2–3 in. (5.0–7.5 cm) across, solitary, or 2 or 3, yellow, the disk florets purple. Though native to wet soils, plants are fairly drought tolerant. Zones 6–7.

× ***multiflorus*** *p. 129*
Perennial Sunflower. To 6 ft. (1.8 m) high, with stiff hairs. Flowerheads yellow, to 5 in. (12.5 cm) across, single or double. This species is hardier than *H. angustifolius* and performs best in moist, well-drained soils. Zone 5.

Helichrysum
Daisy family
Compositae

Hell-i-kry'zum. One of the better-known groups of everlastings, and comprising a genus of over 300 species.

Description
They are herbs or shrubs with flowerheads composed wholly of disk flowers, the parts chaffy and holding their color long after drying. The bracts are also colored.

How to Grow
Grow species below in an open, sunny site with well-drained soil.

hybridium **'Sulfur Light'** *p. 104*
Everlasting. To 18 in. (45 cm) high. Flowers ¼ in. (6 mm) across, sulfur yellow, in terminal clusters. Foliage may do poorly in hot, humid climates. Zone 5.

Heliopsis
Daisy family
Compositae

He-li-op'sis. Sunflowerlike North American herbs, useful for informal borders or wild gardens.

Description
They have opposite, rather coarsely toothed, 3-veined leaves, often very rough. The flowerheads long-stalked, showy, the long rays generally yellow, the disk flowers darker

How to Grow
Easy to grow in average soil, preferably in full sun. Added humus will make the soil more water retentive, which helps growth. Propagated by seed (may self-sow) and by division.

helianthoides *p. 130*
False Sunflower. 3–4 ft. (1.0–1.5 m) high. Flowerheads 1½–2½ in. (4–6 cm) wide, yellow, rays 1 in. (2.5 cm) long. Tolerates shade; needs well-drained soil. In var. *scabra,* the Orange Sunflower, flowerheads fewer and orange-yellow. There are several horticultural varieties. A durable and showy plant that is a mainstay of the late summer perennial garden. Zones 4–5.

Helleborus
Buttercup family
Ranunculaceae

Hell-e-bore′rus. A small genus of Eurasian herbs, one, the ever-popular Christmas Rose, named for its very late bloom. These are the true hellebores that yield drugs; the root of *H. niger* is also a violent poison.

Description
Nearly stemless plants with thick fibrous roots and chiefly basal, long-stalked leaves. Flowers solitary or few, showy, with 5 petal-like sepals. Numerous stamens.

How to Grow
Grows in most garden soils, but prefers moist ones and partial shade. Propagated by division of the roots in late summer. Division must be done carefully because the roots are brittle. The Christmas Rose may also be forced in the greenhouse.

foetidus *p. 97*
Stinking Hellebore. 12–18 in. (30–45 cm) high; evergreen. Flowers cup-shaped, 1 in. (2.5 cm) long, green but sometimes purplish, unpleasantly scented. W. Europe. Will not tolerate full sun or heat. Zones 6–7.

lividus *p. 96*
Corsican Hellebore. To 24 in. (60 cm) high. Evergreen. Flowers nodding, nearly 2½ in. (6 cm) wide, greenish yellow, borne in a profuse cluster of 15–20 flowers. At temperatures below 5° F., foliage becomes tattered. Also sold as *H. corsicus.* A good choice for zone 8 and south.

niger *p. 247*
Christmas Rose. To 12 in. (30 cm) high. Flowers nearly 3 in. (7.5 cm) wide, white or pinkish green. Europe. Depending on locality, plant blooms in late fall, Christmas, or early spring, sometimes under snow. A translucent cover over plants will prevent damage from snow, ice, and rain. Zone 4.

orientalis *p. 153*
Lenten Rose. To 18 in. (45 cm) high with a cluster of 2–6 flowers, 2 in. (5 cm) wide, cream, purplish pink, or greenish white fading to brown, on a branched, leafless stem. Very popular in Europe. The easiest species of the genus to grow. Zone 5.

Hemerocallis
Lily family
Liliaceae

Hem-mer-o-kal′lis. About 15 wild species of herbs, found from Central Europe to Japan, with many hybrid forms.

Description
Leaves nearly all basal, narrow, sword-shaped, and keeled. Stem or stalk of flower cluster often branched and usually exceeds leaves. Flowers funnel-form or bell-shaped, widely expanding above.

How to Grow
Best planted in spring or fall, in a sunny spot, in moist but well-drained soil. Divide newer hybrids about every 3 years.

hybrids *pp. 107, 138*
Daylily. To 2½–3½ ft. (75–105 cm) high, with dwarf forms less than 12 in. (30 cm) high. Flowers 2–6 in. (60–180 cm) wide, in every color except blue and true white. Cultivars available that flower in spring, summer, or fall; some are repeat bloomers. 'Admiral Nelson' is 3 ft. (90 cm) high, red.

'Bonanza' is 15 in. (38 cm) high, light orange with maroon to brown center. All zone 4.

Hesperis
Mustard family
Cruciferae

Hes′per-is. Attractive Old World biennial or perennial herbs comprising about 25 species, generally called rocket or damewort. The species below is widely grown.

Description
Erect, branching plants with alternate, usually finely toothed, leaves, and showy, fragrant flowers in long terminal racemes. Petals 4.

How to Grow
Grow as ordinary garden perennials or biennials, starting seeds a season before expected bloom. *H. matronalis* is often a biennial and not long-lived; replace plants that die out after blooming with seedlings. Plant in sun or partial shade.

matronalis *p. 181*
Dame's-Rocket. 2–3 ft. (60–90 cm) high. Flowers resemble *Phlox,* normally purple, lilac-purple, or mauve, ½–¾ in. (13–19 mm), delightfully night-fragrant. Needs heavy fertilization and prefers moist, well-drained soil. Double-flowered form and white-flowered forms available. Zone 4.

Heuchera
Saxifrage family
Saxifragaceae

Hew′ker-a. Alumroot. Attractive North American perennial herbs comprising about 40 species, chiefly from the Rocky Mt. region.

Description
Stout rootstocks and mostly basal, long-stalked, often roundish or lobed leaves. Stalk of flower cluster arising from the rootstock, often leafy, crowned with a narrow panicle or raceme of bell- or saucer-shaped flowers. Most color comes from the conspicuous 5-lobed calyx.

How to Grow
Blooming most of the summer, this plant is well suited for the open (partly shaded) border. It requires fertile, well-drained soil with a high humus content. In winter, drainage is very important, and mulching may be needed. In hot climates, it grows best in filtered shade. Can be forced.

sanguinea *p. 145*
Coral Bells. Best known and easiest to grow of all alumroots. 1–2 ft. (30–60 cm) high. Small, red, bell-shaped flowers, ¼–½ in. (6–13 mm) wide. N. Mex., Ariz., and Mexico. Most Coral Bells are cultivars or hybrids of *H. sanguinea.* Zone 4.

Heucherella
Saxifrage family
Saxifragaceae

Hew-ker-ell′a. A hybrid genus created from crossing the genera *Heuchera* and *Tiarella.*

Description
Leaves borne on long petioles, round to heart shaped, lobed. Flowers small, pink, in panicles.

How to Grow
Prefers full sun to partial shade in moist soil. Otherwise, treat in the same way as *Heuchera sanguinea.*

× ***tiarelloides*** *p. 188*
To 18 in. (45 cm) high. Flowers pink, ¼–½ in. (6–13 mm) across, borne in a panicle atop a 16 in. (40.5 cm) stalk. Zone 4.

Hibiscus
Mallow family
Malvaceae

Hy-bis′kus. An important genus of over 250 species, of great horticultural interest because it yields many garden annuals, musky-seeded perfume plants, some food plants, showy perennials, a few shrubs, and some gorgeously colored tropical trees.

Description
Leaves alternate, always with the veins arranged finger-fashion, sometimes lobed or

parted. Flowers usually large, generally bell-shaped, with 5 petals and sepals. There is often a series of bracts beneath the calyx.

How to Grow
The species described below prefer full sun in moist to wet soil but tolerate dry sites.

coccineus *p. 163*
Scarlet Rose Mallow. An extremely showy perennial, 6–8 ft. (1.8–2.4 m) high. Long-stalked bluish-green leaves cut into 5 slender lobes. Flowers 5–6 in. (12.5–15.0 cm) wide, brilliant scarlet. Fine petals and long-protruding stamens. Native to wet, low grounds, Fla. and Ga. Zone 6.

moscheutos *p. 162*
Rose Mallow; Swamp Mallow. 3–8 ft. (1.0–2.4 m) high. Flowers white, pink, or red, but with no eye, generally 4–7 in. (10–18 cm) wide but can grow to 12 in. (30 cm). Useless for picking since they wilt within an hour. Also sold as *H. oculiroseus* and *H. palustris.* Most garden selections are now hybrids of *H. moscheutos.* Zone 5.

Hosta
Lily family
Liliaceae

Hos′ta. Plantainlily. Widely cultivated herbs, often known under the names of *Funkia* and *Niobe*. 40 known species, all from China, Korea, and Japan. They are sometimes known as daylily.

Description
Tufted plants, grown both for their handsome basal leaves and their white, lilac, or blue flowers. Flowers are in spikes or racemes terminating a usually bracted stalk that arises from the leaves. Flowers tubular, the 6 lobes not distinguishable as petals and sepals, all petal-like.

How to Grow
Plantainlilies are very easy to grow and are common in old-fashioned gardens; they also grow perfectly in the open border. They prefer shade or partial shade and soil that is moist in summer; they are readily increased by spring or fall division of the clumps. Wet soil in winter can damage these plants. They are susceptible to slugs and snails.

fortunei *p. 79*
Fortune's Plantainlily. To 2 ft. (60 cm) or more high. Leaf blades to 5 in. (12.5 cm) long, egg-shaped, with a heart-shaped base. Flowers lilac to violet, to 1½ in. (4 cm) long. Midsummer. Japan. Prefers shade or partial shade, and moist soil. Cultivar 'Aureo-marginata' has green leaves with yellow or gold border. Zone 4.

'Krossa Regal' *p. 78*
Krossa Regal Plantainlily. To 3 ft. (90 cm) high. Leaf blades silvery blue, boldly veined, in basal cluster. Flowers lavender, trumpet-shaped, 2–3 in. (5.0–7.5 cm) long, at top of stalk to 5 ft. (1.5 m) high. Late summer. Zone 4.

lancifolia *p. 228*
Narrow Plantainlily. To 2 ft. (60 cm) high. Leaf blades 4–6 in. (10–15 cm) long, oval lance-shaped or narrower, often with a long point. Flowers violet, to 2 in. (5 cm) long. Japan. Also called *H. cathayana.* Zone 4.

sieboldiana *pp. 77, 78*
Siebold Plantainlily. To 30 in. (75 cm) high. Leaf blades 10–15 in. (25–38 cm) long, oval heart-shaped. Flowers lilac, to 1½ in. (4 cm) long, on a stalk generally shorter than the leaves. Midsummer. Japan. Cultivar 'Frances Williams' has large, rounded, heavy-textured blue leaves with a gold border, and white flowers. Zone 4.

undulata *p. 80*
Wavyleaf Plantainlily. Tallest of all the cultivated species, the flowering stalk often 3 ft. (1 m) high. Leaf blades to 6 in. (15 cm) long, elliptic to egg-shaped, striped with cream or white. Flowers lavender, to 2 in. (5 cm) long. Midsummer. Zone 4.

Houttuynia
Lizard's tail family
Saururaceae

Hoo-too-in′ee-a. This genus consists of a single species native to Japan. It is grown for its foliage.

Description
Alternate leaves variegated with yellow and pink margins. Flowers densely clustered on lateral spikes.

How to Grow
Easy to grow in sun or shade, but soil must be moist, or even boggy.

***cordata* 'Variegata'** *p. 84*
1 ft. (30 cm) high. Flowers ½ in. (13 mm) wide. Quite invasive, especially when grown in wetter soils. Bruised foliage emits a strong odor of orange or citrus, which is very penetrating. Zone 5.

Iberis
Mustard family
Cruciferae

Eye-beer′is. These herbs comprise perhaps 30 species, mostly from the Mediterranean region, about equally divided between annuals and perennials.

Description
Leaves divided or undivided and alternate. Flowers either in flat-topped or finger-shaped clusters, the 4 petals separate.

How to Grow
Perennials are easily propagated by division and are very useful for edging or for rock gardens. Will stop flowering if kept too dry. In cold and windy northern climates, mulch lightly to protect foliage from browning.

sempervirens *p. 238*
Candytuft. Usually evergreen, to 12 in. (30 cm) high. Flowers white, 1½ in. (4 cm) across, in lateral, finger-shaped racemes, elongating into fruit. Europe. Prevent formation of a noticeable space in the center of the plant by pruning stems after flowering. Zone 4.

Incarvillea
Trumpet-vine family
Bignoniaceae

In-kar-vil′lee-a. Tender herbaceous perennials native to Tibet and China.

Description
Leaves alternate, pinnate, segments narrow. Flowers trumpet-shaped, five-lobed, spreading, somewhat irregular, in terminal clusters.

How to Grow
These plants need a sheltered position in a sunny, warm spot with well-drained soil, preferably sandy and enriched with humus. They require winter protection.

delavayi *p. 174*
Hardy Gloxinia. Semihardy perennial with graceful leaves to 1 ft. (30 cm) long. Flowerstalk to 2 ft. (60 cm) high, bearing 2–12 large trumpet-shaped flowers, rosy purple with a yellow throat, the individual flower 1–3 in. (2.5–7.5 cm) long and wide. China. Needs moist soil during flowering season. Propagated by seeds and by division. Zone 6.

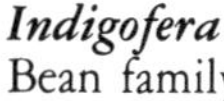

Indigofera
Bean family
Leguminosae

In-di-goff′er-a. Herbaceous perennials and shrubs, with 700–800 species widely distributed through the tropical regions of the world. Some species were formerly used in the manufacture of indigo dye.

Description
Leaves compound. Flowers pealike, in racemes.

How to Grow
All species grow best in well-drained soil and sunny sites. Propagate by tip cuttings in summer or by seed in spring.

incarnata *p. 183*
Chinese Indigo. 12–18 in. (30–45 cm) high. Leaflets elliptical, 2 in. (5 cm) long, and in 3–6 pairs. Flowers rosy, ¾ in. (2 cm) long, carried on 8-in. (20-cm) racemes. Zone 8.

Inula
Daisy family
Compositae

In′you-la. About 100 species of hardy herbs, natives of Asia, Europe, and Africa, some even naturalized in North America.

Description
Leaves mostly hairy, alternate or basal. Flowerheads solitary or few, yellow, seldom white.

How to Grow
Easy to grow, they thrive in ordinary garden soil, but prefer a sunny position. Propagated by division.

ensifolia *p. 131*
Swordleaf Inula. To 12 in. (30 cm) high. Flowerheads yellow, 1½ in. (4 cm) wide. A hardy border plant that will bloom the first year if sown early. Europe and n. Asia. May mildew. Zone 4.

Iris
Iris family
Iridaceae

Eye′ris. Over 150 species of herbs, mostly from the north temperate zone, with thousands of horticultural varieties, which are far more important to the gardener.

Description
Irises have stout rhizomes or bulbous rootstocks and narrow, often sword-shaped leaves. Flowers in 6 segments arising from spathelike bracts. 3 outer segments reflexed, generally called the *falls,* inner 3 usually smaller and erect and known as standards. Both have a narrow claw at the base.

How to Grow
The care of iris varies greatly from species to species. Most need sun, but some tolerate shade. Plant rhizome-producing irises with the rhizome showing and the fan of leaves pointing in the direction you want the plant to grow. Irises rarely need mulching. Propagate species by seed and hybrids by division.

Bearded Iris *p. 219*
Bearded Iris cultivars. 16–30 in. (40.5–75.0 cm) high, in a wide range of colors. Flowers solitary or a few per stem, with 6 petals, usually 3 erect and 3 falling, outer segments 2–3 in. (5.0–7.5 cm) long. Easy to grow in very well-drained soil. Prey to bacterial soft rot and iris borer. 'Frost and Flame' has pure white flowers with bright orange beard. Other cultivars include 'Gentle Rain'. Zone 4.

cristata *p. 216*
Crested Iris. 4–6 in. (10–15 cm) high. Flowers lavender blue with yellow crest,

outer segments 1½ in. (4 cm) long, faintly fragrant. Plant in partial shade, where soil is humus rich and moist; can tolerate full sun if soil is moist. White and light blue horticultural varieties available. Prey to slugs. Zone 4.

ensata *p. 217*
Japanese Iris. Stems 2–3 ft. (60–90 cm) high. Leaves have prominent midrib. Flowers 2–4, white, blue, purple, or red-violet, and often marked with a contrasting color. Outer segments to 3 in. (7.5 cm) long. Source of many varieties called Japanese irises. Plant in lime-free soil and keep constantly moist. Also sold as *I. kaempferi.* Zone 5.

laevigata **'Variegata'** *p. 219*
Variegated Rabbitear Iris. Used to produce Japanese iris hybrids. 18–24 in. (45–60 cm) high. Flower bluish-purple, outer segments 2½–3 in. (6–7.5 cm) long. E. Asia. Will tolerate lime soil; keep soil permanently damp. Zone 5.

× **'Louisiana'** *p. 95*
Louisiana Iris. 3–4 ft. (90–120 cm) high. Flowers many colors, outer segments 3–4 in. (7.5–10.0 cm) long, tend to droop and be flat. Good for areas with hot, humid summers; should be mulched. Zone 5.

Pacific Coast *p. 271*
Pacific Coast hybrid irises. 9–18 in. (22.5–45.0 cm) high, with dark evergreen leaves. Flowers dainty, orchidlike, purple, yellow, orange, or lavender, outer segments 2–3½ in. (5–9 cm) long. Needs dry, acid, well-drained soil. Hardy to Zone 4, but leaves are deciduous north of Zone 7.

pallida **var.** ***dalmatica*** *p. 92*
Orris. Stems to 3 ft. (90 cm) high. Flowers 2–3, fragrant, lilac; falls to 2 in. (5 cm) long. A strong species, foliage will not brown at tips as badly as other species. Cultivars include 'Variegata', with white-striped foliage; and 'Aurea-variegata', with yellow-striped foliage. Zone 6.

pseudacorus *p. 94*
Yellow Flag. To 5 ft. (1.5 m) high, leaves bluish green. Flowers yellow; outer segments to 2 in. (5 cm) long, often violet-veined. Cultivar 'Variegata' has yellow-striped leaves in spring, turning green by summer. Many horticultural varieties. Zones 5–6.

pumila *p. 218*
Dwarf Bearded Iris. Practically stemless, 4–8 in. (10–20 cm) high. Leaves grow longer after flowering. Flowers yellow to lilac, outer segments 2–3 in. (5.0–7.5 cm) long, the beard dense on lower part of the falls. Several horticultural forms. Prey to iris borer. Zone 4.

sibirica *p. 218*
Siberian Iris. Parent species of many forms and hybrids. Hollow-stemmed, stems 2–4 ft. (60–120 cm) high. Flowers 2–3, white to lilac to purple; outer segments to ¾ in. (2 cm) long. Cen. Europe and U.S.S.R. Grows best in slightly acid, moist soil, but will do well in less than ideal conditions. Zone 4.

tectorum *p. 217*
Roof Iris. Stems 8–12 in. (20–30 cm) high. Flowers lavender-blue or bluish purple; outer segments nearly round, 2 in. (5 cm) long, dark-mottled, the crest violet-white. China and Japan. Prey to slugs. Grows best in sandy, moist, low-fertility soil; evergreen to 20° F. Needs a winter mulch in frosty regions. There is a white-flowered variety. Zones 5–6.

Kirengeshoma

Saxifrage family
Saxifragaceae

Keer-en-gay-show′ma. One or two perennial rhizomatous herbs native in Japan and Korea and related to *Hydrangea.*

Description
Leaves opposite, resembling a maple leaf. Bell-shaped flowers borne in clusters from the axils of stems. Flowers 1½ in. (4 cm) long with 5 petals.

How to Grow
Does best in partially shady sites, where soil is moisture-retentive and high in organic matter.

palmata *p. 110*
To 4 ft. (1.2 m) high. Leaves lobed and toothed. Flowers to 1½ in. (4 cm) long, nodding, in branched clusters at stem tips. Abundant additions of peat moss to soil will improve growth. Zone 5.

Kniphofia
Lily family
Liliaceae

Nip-ho′fi-a. African herbaceous perennials, called torch lily, flame flower, or poker-plant, comprising about 65 species.

Description
Long, linear basal leaves; flowers rising in long red or yellow clusters above leaves, blooming from early summer to frost. Corolla drooping, tubular. Stamens 6.

How to Grow
Torch lilies should be heavily mulched with hay or similar material, to keep moisture out of the crown and to prevent freezing. North of zone 5, it is safest to overwinter plants in boxes of soil in a cold but frost-free cellar. Propagated by division, offsets, and seed.

uvaria *p. 143*
Red-hot Poker; Torch Lily. 2–4 ft. (60–120 cm) high. Unusual flowers composed of drooping florets 1½–2 in. (4–5 cm) long, borne in a spikelike raceme 6–12 in. (15–30 cm) long. Colors red and yellow. In winter, avoid wet soil and tie remaining leaves into canopylike bundle to protect crown, or dig up rhizomes and replant following spring. Cultivars are yellow, orange, scarlet, or coral. All Zone 5.

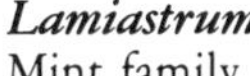

Lamiastrum
Mint family
Labiatae

Lay-mee-as′trum. A single perennial herb, differing from *Lamium* in its yellow flowers.

Description
Leaves opposite, coarsely toothed. Foliage has a pungent odor when bruised. Flowers are hooded and double lipped, in whorls of 5–15 flowers.

How to Grow
Lamiastrum is a durable, rampant-growing ground cover, easy to grow in almost any average soil.

galeobdolon *p. 83*
Yellow Archangel. 1–2 ft. (30–60 cm) high, frequently with stolons. Leaves heart-shaped

to ovate, spotted with silver, 1½ in. (4 cm) long, the margins doubly toothed. Flowers ¾ in. (2 cm) long, in dense clusters in leaf axils. Europe. Prey to slugs. Also sold as *Lamium galeobdolon* and *Galeobdolon luteum.* Zone 4.

Lamium
Mint family
Labiatae

Lay'mi-um. Dead Nettle. Somewhat weedy Old World herbs; 40 known species.

Descriptions
They have opposite, stalked leaves and a square stem. Flowers in close whorls crowde in the leaf axils, or terminal. The corolla is irregular and 2-lipped. Stamens 4.

How to Grow
L. maculatum is easy to grow in any ordinary garden soil. Propagate it by division.

maculatum *p. 250*
Spotted Dead Nettle. To 18 in. (45 cm) high. Flowers purple-red or white, nearly 1 in. (2.5 cm) long. Europe. Grows best in moist soil. Cultivars include 'Beacon Silver', with showy silver leaves and pink flowers; 'White Nancy', with white flowers; and 'Aureum', with yellow-tinted leaves. Zone 4.

Lathyrus
Pea family
Leguminosae

La'thi-russ. An important group of herbs, comprising over 100 species, one the ever-popular Sweet Pea, and several others also widely grown for ornament.

Description
All our cultivated species are vinelike plants, usually with winged or angled stems. Leaves alternate, compound. Flowers typically pealike, often very showy.

How to Grow
Although they adapt to a wide range of soil and climate conditions, these plants flower best in full sun. Durable plants, they become naturalized in low-maintenance sites.

Increased by seeds. To produce the best flowers, young pods should be picked off plants, leaving only a few pods for seed supply.

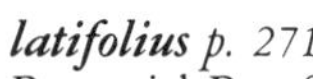

latifolius *p. 271*
Perennial Pea; Sweet Pea. Climbs by tendrils to 9 ft. (2.7 m) or more. Flowers several in a long-stalked cluster, rose-pink, red, or white, 1–1½ in. (2.5–4.0 cm) wide. Europe. So rampant that without control, it can become a nuisance. Zone 4.

Lavandula
Mint family
Labiatae

La-van′dew-la. Lavender. Aromatic Old World herbs or shrubs, chiefly grown for their aromatic oil.

Description
Leaves opposite, without marginal teeth (in ours), and narrow. Flowers lavender or dark purple, crowded into dense clusters in the leaf axils.

How to Grow
Plant in sunny areas with well-drained, sandy soil. Soil that is too fertile will reduce hardiness. Mulch in winter. In spring, prune back the old wood.

angustifolia *p. 225*
Lavender. 1–3 ft. (30–90 cm) high. Leaves lance-shaped or narrower, all white-felty. Flowers lavender, ⅓ in. (8 mm) long, in clusters. Mediterranean region. In mild climates beautiful hedges can be made of lavender. Zones 5–6.

Leontopodium
Daisy family
Compositae

Lee-on-to-po′di-um. A genus of low, tufted alpine herbs related to *Antennaria.*

Description
Leaves basal or alternate, gray, woolly on both upper and lower surfaces. Disk flowers small, clustered tightly into a cyme; cyme surrounded by a tuft of white-woolly bracts.

How to Grow
Plant in well-drained, gritty soil, in full sun. Wet winters or standing water will kill the crowns.

alpinum *p. 243*
Edelweiss. Erect or ascending stems usually 6–12 in. (15–30 cm) high. Flowers ¼ in. (6 mm) across, yellow, borne at the end of the stem in 7–9 heads, each 1½ in. (4 cm) across. Surrounding gray or white woolly bracts are showier. Europe and Asia. Alkaline soil is ideal. Zone 4.

Liatris
Daisy family
Compositae

Ly-a'tris. A genus of about 40 species of rather weedy, but very showy North American herbs.

Description
Rather coarse plants with alternate, usually stiffish, narrow leaves and button-shaped heads of exclusively disk flowers, the head close and surrounded by many greenish bracts. Heads handsome, borne in spikes or racemes. All bloom in summer or early fall and are mostly rose-purple. Commonly called button snakeroot and sometimes offered under the name *Lacinaria.*

How to Grow
All are easy to grow in open sun, light soils, and are increased by division.

aspera *p. 261*
To 3 ft. (90 cm) high. Flowers purple, borne in 1 in. (2.5 cm) heads of 20–40. Incurved, paper-like bracts grow between heads. North America. 'Alba' has white flowers. Zone 4.

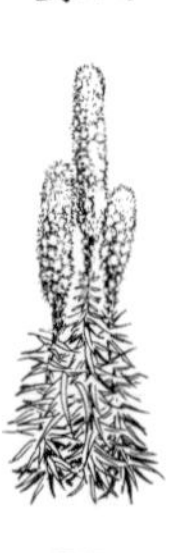

spicata *p. 187*
Gay-Feather. Very leafy-stemmed, 4–6 ft. (1.2–1.8 m) high. Flowerheads purple or white, ½ in. (13 mm) long, dense spikes 6–12 in. (15–30 cm) long. E. North America. Fairly drought-tolerant. Cultivars include 'Kobold', 18–24 in. (45–60 cm) high, with dark purple flowers. Also sold as *L. callilepis.* Zone 4.

Ligularia
Daisy family
Compositae

Lig-you-lay′ri-a. Handsome Eurasian herbs cultivated for their showy flower heads or (in cultivars) for the variegated foliage.

Description
Leaves alternate, or often basal and long-stalked, roundish or kidney-shaped, those on the stem sheathed and smaller. Flowerheads usually nodding, arranged in racemes or corymbs, rays usually yellow and strap-shaped.

How to Grow
These plants are easy to grow and do well in ordinary to moist garden soil. Propagate by cuttings or by division.

dentata *p. 83*
Bigleaf Goldenray. Stout, to 4 ft. (1.2 m) high, rusty-hairy in youth, ultimately nearly smooth. Lower leaves sharply toothed. Flowerheads numerous, composed of 12–14 orange ray flowers and brown disk florets, nearly 2½–5 in. (6.0–12.5 cm) wide. China and Japan. Plant in shade in climates with temperatures above 80° F. Needs deep watering. Cultivars include 'Desdemona', more compact with leaves brownish green above and mahogany red below. Also sold as *L. clivorum* and *Senecio clivorum.* Zone 4.

× ***przewalskii*** **'The Rocket'** *p. 108*
Rocket Ligularia. 4–6 ft. (120–180 cm) high. Leaves triangular to round, sharply toothed; stems a blackish purple. Flowers yellow, ½ in. (13 mm) wide, in spikes 12–18 in. (30–45 cm) long. Zone 4.

tussilaginea *p. 80*
Leopard Plant. To 2 ft. (60 cm) high. Many leaves on slender white-woolly stalks. Flowerheads 1½–2 in. (4–5 cm) wide, light yellow, in branched clusters on white-woolly stalks. Needs partial to full shade. Cultivar 'Aureo-maculata' has yellow, white, or pink-blotched leaves, and is a favorite plant for window boxes. Also sold as *L. kaempferi* and *Senecio kaempferi.* Zones 6–7.

Limonium
Plumbago family
Plumbaginaceae

Ly-mo′ni-um. Sea lavenders or sea pinks comprise a genus of about 150 species of mainly annual or perennial herbs.

Description
Mostly basal, often tufted, leaves. Flowers small, but numerous, in open loose panicles or in branching spikes, mostly lavender, rose-pink, or bluish, sometimes yellow or white. Calyx tubular, often membranous or colored. Corolla 5 nearly separate and often clawed petals.

How to Grow
Mostly found in salt-marshes in the wild, these plants are easy to grow in flower gardens, preferably in full sun in somewhat sandy, moist soil. Since the chaffy flowers hold their color for long periods, they are often used in dried bouquets. Easily increased by division. All bloom in summer or early autumn. Confused with the name *Statice.*

latifolium *p. 157*
Sea-lavender. Hairy, 18–24 in. (45–60 cm) high. Flowers lavender-blue, calyx ⅛ in. (3.2 mm) long, in many branched clusters. Eurasia. Resistant to salt spray. May need staking in fertile soil. Zone 4.

Linaria
Snapdragon family
Scrophulariaceae

Ly-nay′ri-a. Toadflax. A genus of about 100 species of annual or perennial herbs, all from the north temperate zone.

Description
Rather slender herbs with opposite or whorled leaves, upper ones sometimes alternate. Flowers usually showy, in terminal spikes or racemes, the corolla irregular, with a long tube, and long-spurred. Stamens 4.

How to Grow
Toadflax is easily grown in most ordinary garden soils. Readily increased by division, they can also be grown from seed and should bloom the second season.

purpurea *p. 191*
Purple Toadflax. Showy, 2–3 ft. (60–90 cm) high. Flowers purple, to ¼ in. (6 mm) long. Lower lip somewhat white-bearded. S. Europe. Plant in full sun in light, well-drained soil. Cultivars include 'Canon Went', with pink flowers. Zone 5.

Linum
Flax family
Linaceae

Ly′num. Flax. Nearly 200 species of rather slender annual or perennial herbs. Grown only for ornament except for Common Flax, which yields linseed oil and linen.

Description
Leaves generally alternate, stalkless and narrow. Flowers in racemes or cymes, day-blooming and rather fleeting. Sepals and petals each 5, separate. Stamens 5, alternating with the petals.

How to Grow
The ornamental linums are very easy to grow. They need full sun and well-drained soil. Propagate by division or cuttings.

flavum *p. 119*
Golden Flax. 1–2 ft. (30–60 cm) high. Flowers 1 in. (2.5 cm) wide, golden yellow. Europe. Cultivar 'Compactum' is the dwarf form. *Reinwardtia indica* is sometimes sold as *L. flavum.* Zone 5.

perenne *p. 208*
Perennial Flax. 1–2 ft. (30–60 cm) high. Flowers to 1 in. (2.5 cm) across, clear sky-blue. The subspecies *alpinum* is 2–12 in. (5–30 cm) high, with flowers to ¾ in. (2 cm) wide. Europe. Zone 5.

Liriope
Lily family
Liliaceae

Li-ri′o-pe. Lily-turf. Asiatic herbs, sometimes grown as ground covers in warm regions.

Description
Thick but grasslike leaves are evergreen and very numerous, often forming thick mats.

Flowers in spikes or racemes. Corolla small, white, blue, or violet. Stamens 6.

How to Grow
Plant in fertile, moist soil amended with organic matter in partial or full shade. Foliage may become tattered or brown in northern winters. Roots will probably survive; mow foliage to ground to promote a good second growth. Increased by division.

muscari *p. 91*
Blue Lily-Turf. To 18 in. (45 cm) high. Flowers lilac-purple to white, ⅛ in. (3.2 mm) wide, the stalk of the flower cluster as long as the leaves. Forms available with white or yellow variegated leaves. Prey to slugs and snails. North of Zone 6 foliage may be unattractive.

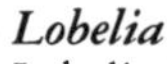

Lobelia
Lobelia family
Lobeliaceae

Lo-bee'li-a. Showy-flowered perennial or annual herbs comprising about 375 species, some popular for borders, wild gardens, and edgings.

Description
Leaves alternate. Flowers in terminal, often very beautiful, clusters, nearly always bracted. Corolla tubular below, split to the base. Stamens united by their anthers into a ring around the style.

How to Grow
Lobelias are easy to grow in open borders. Increased by division of clumps in spring or fall.

cardinalis *p. 143*
Cardinal-Flower. 3–6 ft. (1.0–1.8 m) high. Flowers scarlet, 1½ in. (4 cm) long. E. North America. Best in a moist, shaded wild garden, but can take sun. Mulch year-round. Flower is not long-lived and will self-seed. Zone 3.

siphilitica *p. 233*
Blue, or Great, Lobelia. 2–4 ft. (60–120 cm) high. Flowers 1 in. (2.5 cm) long, blue. E. U.S. Needs moist soil and sun or partial shade. Prey to rust. A good late-flowering plant for late-summer gardens. Zone 5.

Lupinus
Pea family
Leguminosae

Loo-pine′us. A genus of many species, found nearly worldwide. All are hardy.

Description
Leaves finger-shaped, grayish or bright green. Flowers pealike, in dense terminal racemes.

How to Grow
Propagate from seeds or divide in early spring. Good drainage is essential in winter. Perhaps the finest members of the genus are the plants imported from England known as Russell Lupines.

'Russell Hybrid' *p. 142*
Russell Hybrid Lupine. 2–3 ft. (60–90 cm) high. Flowers showy, ½–1 in. (1.3–2.5 cm) wide, some bicolor, others white, yellow, pink, red, blue, and purple. They need moist soil and sun or partial shade. Aphids may be a pest. Not a good choice for areas with hot or dry summers. Seeds difficult to germinate unless nicked with a file and apt to rot if left too long in the soil. Best to sprout seeds in pure sand. Zone 5.

Lychnis
Pink family
Caryophyllaceae

Lick′nis. Catchfly; Campion. About 35 herbs, mostly from the north temperate zone, some old garden favorites cultivated for centuries.

Description
Erect plants, often with sticky hairs. Calyx with 5 teeth. Petals 5, with a claw at the base. Stamens 10.

How to Grow
Species below are very easy to grow in any moist soil in sun or partial shade. Mostly summer-blooming, they are increased by division. Sometimes offered as *Agrostemma.*

× ***arkwrightii*** *p. 149*
12–15 in. (30–38 cm) high. Leaves mahogany-colored. Scarlet flowers 1 in. (2.5 cm) wide. A hybrid of *L. chalcedonica.* Zone 5.

chalcedonica, *p. 146*
Maltese Cross. Hairy, 18–30 in. (45–75 cm) high. Flowers 1 in. (2.5 cm) wide, scarlet, in dense terminal heads. Siberia (U.S.S.R.). Zone 4.

coronaria *p. 168*
Rose Campion. A white-woolly biennial or perennial herb, 18–36 in. (45–90 cm) high. Flowers solitary, terminal, 1 in. (2.5 cm) wide, red-pink to crimson. S. Europe. Grows well in alkaline soil. Short-lived, but seedlings will provide flowering plants within a year. White and double-flowered forms available. Zone 4.

viscaria *p. 178*
German Catchfly. 12–18 in. (30–45 cm) high, stem sticky beneath flowers. Flowers red or purple, ½ in. (13 mm) across, in interrupted clusters, petals somewhat notched. Eurasia. Best in moist, sandy soil, but will tolerate drought. White and double-flowered varieties available. Zone 4.

Lysimachia
Primrose family
Primulaceae

Ly-si-mack'i-a. Loosestrife. A genus of about 165 species of widely distributed herbs, a few grown for ornament.

Description
Leaves without marginal teeth. Flowers solitary or in clusters, either terminal or in the leaf axils. Corolla bell- or wheel-shaped. Stamens 5–7.

How to Grow
Grow these plants in moist, well-drained sites in open borders. They prefer sun or partial shade. Most bloom in summer. All are easily increased by spring or fall division.

clethroides *p. 259*
Gooseneck Loosestrife. Hairy, 2–3 ft. (60–90 cm) high. Flowers ½ in. (13 mm) wide, white, in narrow terminal spikes. E. Asia. *L. clethroides* will spread, especially in moist soil. Zone 4.

punctata, *p. 109*
Yellow Loosestrife. Erect, 2–3 ft. (60–90 cm) high. Flowers 1 in. (2.5 cm) wide, in whorls

in leaf axils, the corolla yellow. Europe. Best in moist to wet soil, but will tolerate drier soil when planted in partial shade. Zone 5.

Lythrum
Loosestrife family
Lythraceae

Lith′rum. Loosestrife. A group of annual or perennial herbs, comprising about 30 widely scattered species.

Description
Leaves mostly opposite. Flowers in terminal spikes or racemes or solitary in leaf axils, bright purple or pink. Petals 4–6 (in cultivated species). Stamens 4–12.

How to Grow
L. salicaria grows best along the edges of pools or streams, although it may be grown in open borders. Increased by division, it blooms in the summer.

salicaria *p. 185*
Purple Loosestrife. 2–6 ft. (60–180 cm) high. Leaves willowlike. Flowers in dense, terminal spikes, the corolla pink or bright purple, ¾ in. (2 cm) wide. Eurasia. A common marsh plant that may choke out native plants. Grow in full sun. Cultivars are not invasive. They include 'Happy', with dark pink flowers, 18 in. (45 cm) high; and 'Robert', with rose-red flowers. Zone 4.

Macleaya
Poppy family
Papaveraceae

Mack-lay′a. Showy border plants native to Asia, both known species grown for ornament, often under the name of *Bocconia.*

Description
Leaves alternate, gray-green on upper surface, with white hairs on lower surface. Many small flowers in a terminal, erect panicle, 1 ft. (30 cm) long. Sepals 2, petals none, stamens many and showy.

How to Grow
Easy to grow in full sun and average soil. Where soil is fertile, plants increase easily

by roots or self-seeding and should be isolated to prevent spreading.

cordata *p. 262*
Plume-poppy. 6–10 ft. (1.8–3.0 m) high. Leaves rounded, silver on the underside. Flowers white, ½ in. (13 mm) across, in clusters 1 ft. (30 cm) long, very showy. Tolerates partial shade. Zone 4.

Malva
Mallow family
Malvaceae

Mal′va. Mallow. About 30 species of widely distributed herbs, some rather weedy, others grown for ornament.

Description
Leaves alternate. Flowers mostly in leaf axils, solitary or clustered, most with 2 or 3 bracts. Petals 5, with a notch at the tip, mostly pink or white. Fruit in a cluster.

How to Grow
These mallows are far less satisfactory than those found in the closely related genus *Hibiscus.* Easy to grow in any ordinary garden soil, but prefers dry soil in sun or partial shade. Divide in spring or fall.

alcea *p. 164*
Hollyhock Mallow. 2–4 ft. (60–120 cm) high. Resembles *M. moschata,* but leaves only once-parted, with star-shaped hairs. Europe. Zone 4.

moschata *p. 257*
Musk Mallow; Musk Rose. Hairy, 1–3 ft. (30–90 cm) high. Stem leaves 5-parted. Flowers pink or white, nearly 2 in. (5 cm) wide, mostly in upper leaf axils. Europe. Does well in any soil and is drought tolerant. Cultivars include 'Alba', with white flowers. Zone 4.

Marrubium
Mint family
Labiatae

Mar-rew′bi-um. Horehound. Thirty species of white-hairy, aromatic herbs, native in the temperate areas of the Old World.

Description
Leaves opposite, sometimes dissected, wrinkled. Flower corolla 2-lipped, with upper lip erect and often notched, lower lip spreading. Numerous flowers in a globular cluster.

How to Grow
Well-drained soil and full sun are best. Plant in autumn or spring, propagate by division, basal cuttings, or seeds.

incanum *p. 82*
Silver Horehound. 2–3 ft. (60–90 cm) high. Leaves to 2 in. (5 cm) long, finely toothed, with white-woolly surface. Flowers ⅛ in. (3.2 mm) wide, white. Italy. Drought tolerant. To avoid rot in hot, humid summers, plant in full sun in sandy, well-drained soil. Zone 4.

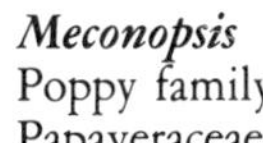

Meconopsis
Poppy family
Papaveraceae

Me-ko-nop′sis. About 45 species of annual or perennial herbs, single-stemmed or branched, with a yellow juice.

Description
Leaves alternate, divided or cut, short-stalked or stalkless. Flowers borne singly, or in flat-topped or branching terminal clusters, yellow, reddish, or blue. Petals 4, sometimes 5 to 9.

How to Grow
They are difficult to grow and require at least partial shade and moist but well-drained soil. Mostly hardy and grow from seed sown in the open in spring.

cambrica *p. 122*
Welsh Poppy. 2 ft. (60 cm) high, pale green, slightly hairy, forming large tufts. Leaves cut feather-fashion. Flowers pale yellow or orange, 2 in. (5 cm) wide, borne singly high above foliage. W. Europe. The Welsh Poppy needs soil very rich in humus. Zone 6.

Mertensia
Borage family
Boraginaceae

Mer-ten′si-a. Bluebells; Lungwort. Many of the 40 known species are showy and native in North America.

Description
Foliage often bluish-green, leaves alternate, often dotted. Flowers usually drooping, in loose, terminal racemes or cymes. Corolla funnel-shaped, blue or purplish, sometimes bearded. Stamens 5.

How to Grow
The species below needs partial shade and a moist site. Division is very difficult; instead, propagate from seed, which should be sown as soon as harvested.

virginica *p. 226*
Virginia Bluebells. To 2 ft. (60 cm) high, foliage pale green. Flowers 1 in. (2.5 cm) long, the tube purplish to blue. Ontario to Ala. and westward. Grow in cool soil rich in organic matter. Dormant in summer when it loses its foliage. Cultivar 'Alba' has white flowers; a pink-flowered cultivar also available. Zone 4.

Mimulus
Figwort family
Scrophulariaceae

Mim′you-lus. About 150 annual or perennial herbs, sometimes subshrubs. Plants often sticky or clammy.

Description
Leaves opposite, with or without marginal teeth. Flowers showy, 2-lipped, often spotted, giving the effect of a face (hence the name monkey flower), growing singly from the axils of the leaves, or in terminal racemes. Sometimes called *Diplacus.*

How to Grow
The species below require full sun and moist soil. They are very tender and treated as annuals in northern areas.

guttatus *p. 114*
Common Monkey Flower. To 2 ft. (60 cm) high. Flowers yellow, generally with red or

brown dots on throat, 1½ in. (4 cm) long. Calyx much swollen in fruit. Ala. to Mexico. Easily transplanted or grown from seed. Zone 9.

lewisii *p. 180*
Lewis' Monkey Flower. Sticky and hairy, nearly 2½ ft. (45 cm) high. Flowers rose-red or rose-purple, to 2 in. (5 cm) long. British Columbia to Calif. and Utah. In warmer areas, plant in partial shade. Zone 9.

Monarda

Mint family
Labiatae

Mo-nar'da. A North American genus of 12 aromatic herbs, some grown for their showy flowers.

Description
Leaves opposite, with marginal teeth. Flowers rather large, white, red, purplish, yellow, or mottled, often with showy, colored bracts. Known as horse mint and bergamot.

How to Grow
Coarse plants but often very brilliant in color. Easily grown in any good soil in full sun or partial shade. Spreading quickly, they should be divided often in spring. Fall-divided clumps will often suffer or die in winter.

didyma *p. 135*
Bee Balm; Oswego Tea. Somewhat hairy, 2–3 ft. (60–90 cm) high. Flowers scarlet, nearly 2 in. (5 cm) long, in terminal clusters, surrounded by red-tinged bracts. Quebec to Ga. and Tenn. Susceptible to rust and powdery mildew. Full sun is acceptable if soil is sufficiently moist. Zone 4.

fistulosa *p. 199*
Wild Bergamot. Softly hairy, 3–4 ft. (90–120 cm) high. Flowers lilac to purple, 1½ in. (4 cm) long, in terminal clusters, the surrounding bracts whitish or purplish. E. North America. Does well in both dry and moist soil; quite drought resistant. Zone 4.

Myosotis
Borage family
Boraginaceae

My-o-so′tis. Forget-me-not. Annual or perennial herbs, most of the 50 species European, but a few through the north temperate zone.

Description
Flowers small, in branched or unbranched clusters. Corolla tubular and spreading, 5-lobed, the throat crested and often of a different color (with an eye).

How to Grow
Most garden forget-me-nots are best treated as hardy annuals or biennials. *M. scorpioides* is a true perennial and prefers partial shade and plenty of moisture; it tolerates full sun if soil is sufficiently moist. Divide in early spring. It is a very attractive bedding plant, especially as a carpet under bulbs, and does better when a bit crowded.

scorpioides *p. 206*
True Forget-Me-Not. The stems more or less prostrate and 12–18 in. (30–45 cm) long. Leaves and stems create a mat. Flowers blue, with a yellow, pink, or white eye, ⅓ in. (8 mm) wide, borne in loose, 1-sided clusters at the end of the stems. Europe, U.S. Prey to red spider mites and mildew. Keep soil moist at all times. Var. *semperflorens* blooms until frost. Zone 5.

Nepeta
Mint family
Labiatae

Nep′e-ta. About 250 species of perennial and annual herbs, found throughout the northern hemisphere.

Description
Leaves mostly heart-shaped. Flowers in close clusters on the stems, often in whorls. Corolla 2-lipped. Stamens 4, two longer than the others.

How to Grow
Easy to grow in sandy, well-drained soil. Usually propagated from seeds sown during spring or summer, or by division of roots, but sometimes from the runners.

mussinii *p. 202*
Mauve Catmint. Stems to 1 ft. (30 cm) high, the whole plant gray-hairy. Flowers blue or white in dense whorls, corolla to ¼ in. (6 mm) long. Has a sprawling habit. Often confused with *N.* × *faassenii,* a sterile hybrid that is 18 in. (45 cm) high, and is a more attractive ground cover. Zone 4.

Oenothera

Evening primrose family
Onagraceae

Ee-no-thee′ra or ee-noth′er-ra. Evening primroses and their day-blooming relatives, the sundrops. This genus comprises 80 species of herbs, all American.

Description
Flowers very showy, day- or night-blooming, mostly yellow, but also white or rose in some species, generally 1 or 2 in the leaf axils. Petals 4, mostly very broad.

How to Grow
Evening primroses are easy to grow in sunny, sandy or loamy sites. Increase by division. All bloom in summer.

missourensis *p. 107*
Missouri Primrose; Ozark Sundrops. Trailing branches 3–6 in. (7.5–15 cm) long. Flowers yellow, to 7 in. (18 cm) long and 4 in. (10 cm) across. They open in the evening, and remain open until the end of the next day. Cen. U.S. Tolerant of poor soil and sunny, dry sites, this plant may rot in wet soil. A garden favorite. Zone 5.

speciosa *p. 165*
Showy Primrose. Day-blooming stems 6–18 in. (15–45 cm), erect or spreading and finely hairy. Flowers nearly 2 in. (7.5 cm) wide, white or pink. Cen. U.S. Should be planted only where spreading will not be troublesome. Also sold as *Hartmannia.* Zone 5.

tetragona *p. 106*
Common Sundrop. 18 in. (45 cm) high. Leaves shiny green, lance-shaped. Flowers 1½ in. (4 cm) wide, bright yellow, saucer-shaped with 4 petals. Eastern North America. Also sold as *O. fruticosa* var. *youngii.* Zone 5.

Omphalodes
Borage family
Boraginaceae

Om-fal-lo′dez. Navelwort. Low annual or perennial herbs, comprising about 25 species, natives of Europe and Asia.

Description
Basal leaves long-stalked, lance- or heart-shaped. Flowers arranged in loose 1-sided racemes. Corolla a short tube, usually white, with veinlike markings radiating from the center, giving it a starlike appearance.

How to Grow
They require moist, well-drained soil that is neutral or slightly alkaline, and partial shade. Seeds should be sown in spring, or plants can be propagated by division of roots in spring or fall.

cappadocica *p. 204*
Navelwort. Rhizomatous, 6–10 in. (15–25 cm) high. Leaves with silky hairs. Flowers small, bright blue, with markings at the throat. Tolerates dry shade. Needs protection in northern winters. Spring. Asia Minor. Zone 6.

verna *p. 205*
Creeping Forget-Me-Not. To 8 in. (20 cm) high, main stems prostrate, but with erect, flowering stems. Leaves pointed. Flowers borne in pairs in loose racemes; individual flowers blue, ½ in. (13 mm) wide. Spring. Europe. Best in full shade, in cool, moist, organic-amended soil. Often used as ground cover. Zone 6.

Opuntia
Cactus family
Cactaceae

O-pun′ti-a; also o-pun′she-a. Prickly Pear, some of them also called tuna and cholla. A very large genus of cacti, spread from New England to Tierra del Fuego and comprising 300 species.

Description
There are 2 general types of cultivated specimens: (1) those with flat or broad joints (some known as tuna) and (2) those with cylindrical or roundish joints (some

known as cholla). Some are prostrate or clambering without a trunk; others, mostly tropical, are treelike. Leaves are small and usually deciduous. Flowers generally solitary. Fruit usually a juicy berry, and edible in some.

How to Grow
Full sun and well-drained, sandy soil are ideal for *O. humifusa.* Moist soil may cause root rot. Very drought tolerant. Exercise care when handling, because the small, red-brown hairs on the surface of the joints lodge easily under the skin.

humifusa *p. 115*
Prickly Pear. Joints flat, oblong, or ovalish, 2–6 in. (5–15 cm) long, the whole plant prostrate. The areoles (depressions) are sparse, spines 1–2 at each cluster, ¾ in. (2 cm) long. Flowers yellow, 2–3 in. (5.0–7.5 cm) wide. Also sold as *O. compressa* and *O. vulgaris.* Zones 5–6.

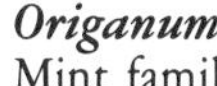

Origanum
Mint family
Labiatae

Or-rig′a-num. A genus of annual to perennial herbs or dwarf shrubs, native from the Mediterranean region to cen. Asia.

Description
Leaves are usually slightly hairy and often toothed. Flowers are tubular, two-lipped, and arranged in small, compact spikes.

How to Grow
All species do well in sunny, well-drained areas. Propagate by division, seeds, or basal cuttings, all in spring.

vulgare **'Aureum'** *p. 86*
Pot Marjoram. Hardy, to 30 in. (75 cm) high, with aromatic foliage and creeping rootstocks. Young leaves are golden yellow. Flowers small, irregular, 2-lipped, purplish pink, borne in spikelike clusters. Europe to cen. Asia. One of the ingredients of imported oregano. Zone 4.

Pachysandra
Box family
Buxaceae

Pack-i-san′dra. Low-growing perennial herbs or subshrubs comprising 5 species, natives of North America and e. Asia.

Description
Stems fleshy. Leaves spoon-shaped, the upper half with teethlike margins. Flowers greenish white in spikes. Fruit a small, whitish, oval berry.

How to Grow
Pachysandra is easy to grow in moist ordinary soil. It is one of the best evergreen ground covers for partly shady places; foliage yellows in full sun. Easily propagated by cuttings taken in summer, planted in a mixture of one-half sand and one-half soil. They should be well watered and shaded until rooted. For a quick ground covering, plant them 8–12 in. (20–30 cm) apart.

procumbens *p. 86*
Allegheny Spurge. Evergreen in the South, deciduous in the North. Stems trailing at first and then becoming erect, 8–10 in. (20–25 cm) high. Flowers white or purplish, ½ in. (13 mm), borne on 5–6 in. (12.5–15.0 cm) long spikes. Ky. to Fla. and La. Needs humus-enriched soil. Zone 5.

terminalis *p. 87*
Japanese Spurge. To 1 ft. (30 cm), the stems beneath the surface sending out runners. Leaves thick, dark, glossy-green, spoon-shaped, alternate. Flowers white, ½ in. (13 mm), in terminal spikes. Japan. Susceptible to canker disease. May need spraying in spring. Zone 5.

Paeonia
Peony family
Paeoniaceae

Pee-o′nee-a. Peony. These outstanding and very beautiful garden flowers are derived from perennial herbs and shrubs, which comprise about 33 species, chiefly Eurasian.

Description
All are erect herbs or shrubs from tuberous or thickened roots. Leaves large, basal or on

stems, all compound. Flowers large, showy, usually solitary and terminal (rarely a few in a cluster). Sepals 5. Petals 5–10, but double-flowered types are available.

How to Grow
The species below are easy to grow in well-drained, moisture-retentive, average soil in full sun to partial shade. All below bloom in spring to early summer.

lactiflora *pp. 95, 136*
The chief source of the Chinese, or Common, Peony. Usually 2–3 ft. (60–90 cm) high. Stems erect, with solitary flower or 2–5. Flowers 3–5 in. (7.5–12.5 cm) wide. Petals 8, or much more in some horticultural varieties. Stamens golden yellow. Japan, China, and Siberia. 'Honey Gold' is 30 in. (75 cm) high, double-blooms have creamy white petals surrounded by split yellow petals; 'Ms. Wilder Bancroft' is 30–36 in. (75–90 cm) high, flowers pom-pom shaped, dark red with gold specks in center, 5–6 in. (12.5–15.0 cm) wide. Susceptible to Botrytis blight. Zone 5.

mlokosewitschii *p. 247*
Caucasian Peony. 18–24 in. (45–60 cm) high. Flowers nearly 5 in. (12.5 cm) wide, yellow. Caucasus. Zone 5.

officinalis *p. 197*
Common Peony. To 3 ft. (90 cm) high. Flowers nearly 4 in. (10 cm) wide, crimson, white, or yellowish. S. Europe and w. Asia. Blooms in late spring. Light shade will prolong blooming in southern areas. Requires a chilling period, so it cannot be grown in extreme southern states. 'Rubra Plena', a double, deep red flower, is popularly called the Memorial Day Peony. Susceptible to Botrytis blight. Zone 5.

suffruticosa *p. 196*
Japanese Tree Peony. 4–7 ft. (1.2–2.1 m) high, often less as cultivated. A much-branched, shrubby plant. Flowers to 12 in. (30 cm) wide, rose-red or white. Fruit densely hairy. China. There are many color forms and varieties. Full sun will fade flowers. Zone 5.

tenuifolia *p. 137*
Fernleaf Peony. To 2 ft. (60 cm) high, with creeping rootstocks. Leaves fernlike. Flowers

3–4 in. (7.5–10.0 cm) wide, crimson or purple. Se. Europe and w. Asia. Zone 5.

Papaver
Poppy family
Papaveraceae

Pap-a′ver. The true poppies comprise a genus of about 50 species of annual or perennial herbs, found mostly in the temperate regions of Europe and Asia, a few in w. North America.

Description
They vary in height from 6–48 in. (15–120 cm). Leaves basal, generally numerous and hairy. Flowers solitary, on long flowering stalk, nodding when in bud but straightening as flower opens. Corolla of 5 petals, vividly colored red, violet, yellow, or white, sometimes blotched at the base. Stamens numerous. Any part of the plant, if cut or broken, exudes a milky substance.

How to Grow
P. orientale is easy to grow in ordinary, well-drained soil in full sun; drainage is vital in winter, when standing water will cause greatest damage.

orientale *p. 135*
Oriental Poppy. 3–4 ft. (0.9–1.2 m) high. Flowers scarlet, purplish black at base, 6 in. (15 cm) wide. Blooms in early summer, then becomes dormant. Also known as *P. bracteatum.* 'China Boy' and 'White King' have white flowers. Zone 4.

Penstemon
Snapdragon family
Scrophulariaceae

Pen-ste′mon. Beardtongue. 250 species of perennial herbs (rarely shrubs), one Asiatic, the rest North American, chiefly from the West.

Description
Leaves opposite or whorled and showy. Flowers 2-lipped, tubular, mostly in terminal racemes or panicles that bloom in summer. Stamens 5, four fertile, one sterile and often bearded.

How to Grow
The beardtongues often flower quickly from seed, some maturing the first year, especially *P. gloxinioides.* The species below are easy to grow in sun or partial shade in well-drained soil. In full sun they tend to die out in about a year. Most do better if given a light mulch in winter.

barbatus *p. 144*
Beardlip Penstemon. 2–3 ft. (60–90 cm) high. Flowers 1 in. (2.5 cm) long, red, lower lip bearded, stamen not bearded. Utah to Mexico. Subspecies *torreyi* has lower lip without a beard. Crown rot may be a problem. Zone 4.

gloxinioides *p. 145*
Gloxinia Penstemon. 2–3 ft. (60–90 cm) high. A group of cultivars very popular on the West Coast and in England. Flowers 2 in. (5 cm) long, white through crimson to blue. 'Firebird' has scarlet flowers. Zone 9.

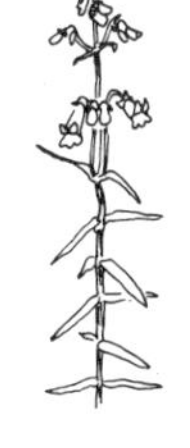

hirsutus *p. 229*
Sticky-hairy, 2–3 ft. (60–90 cm) high. Flowers purple or violet, 1 in. (2.5 cm) long, stamen and throat densely bearded. Quebec to Va. and Tex. Zone 5.

Perovskia
Mint family
Labiatae

Per-ov'skee-a. Russian sage. A small central Asian genus of salvialike herbs or subshrubs.

Description
Leaves incised or dissected, covered with grey-white hairs. Small flowers arranged in whorl-like terminal racemes or panicles; individual flowers tubular.

How to Grow
Easy to grow in full sun and well-drained soil. Plants in shade will sprawl. Propagate by summer cuttings.

atriplicifolia *p. 235*
Azure Sage. Shrubby, 3–5 ft. (1.0–1.5 m) high. Bruised foliage has sagelike odor. Flowers blue, ¼ in. (6 mm) wide, in scattered and widely spaced whorls, ultimately spikelike at tip. Cut to the ground

each spring to promote strength and good flowers. Zones 5–6.

Petrorhagia

Pink family
Caryophyllaceae

Pet-ro-ra′gee-a. A genus of 25 species of annual and perennial herbs, native from the Canary Islands to the w. Himalayas.

Description
Low-growing, tufted and spreading plants. Leaves opposite, small, lance-shaped or oblong. Flowers small, pale pink, lilac, or white, in heads or solitary. Corolla of 5 petals. Stamens 10.

How to Grow
Easy to grow in any well-drained, average soil in full sun. Propagate by seeds or root division in spring.

saxifraga *p. 156*
Tunic Flower; Coat Flower. Hardy, 6–10 in. (15–25 cm) high. Stems thin and wiry. Leaf margins covered with bristles. Flowers white or pink, ¼–½ in. (6–13 mm) wide, resembling those of Baby's Breath, in terminal-branching clusters. Petals deeply notched. S. Europe. Several horticultural color forms are available, one double-flowered. Also known as *Tunica saxifraga.* Zone 5.

Phlomis

Mint family
Labiatae

Flow′mis. Jerusalem Sage. Strong-growing perennial herbs or subshrubs comprising about 100 species, of the Mediterranean region east to China. Grown for their flowers.

Description
Stems coarse and square, 1½–6 ft. (45–180 cm) high. Leaves large, oval, or heart-shaped, opposite. Flowers yellow, purple, or white, in whorls in the axils. 4 stamens, 2 long and 2 short.

How to Grow
Easily propagated by seeds, cuttings, or

division of tubers. Grow in full sun in well-drained, sandy loam with low fertility. Fertile soil weakens plant stems and joints.

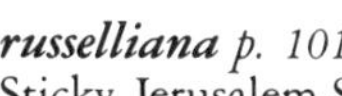

russelliana *p. 101*
Sticky Jerusalem-Sage. 3 ft. (90 cm) high. Leaves wrinkled and woolly. Flowers ½–1 in. (1.3–2.5 cm) wide, yellow, hooded, in whorls along a tall spike. Asia. Zone 6.

Phlox

Phlox family
Polemoniaceae

Flocks. Perennial and annual herbs, usually hardy, comprising about 60 species found mostly in North America, one in Siberia.

Description
Some strong and erect, others trailing. Leaves lance-shaped, opposite and in pairs, or alternate. Flowers showy, in loose terminal or closely packed clusters, usually with a conspicuous eyelike marking at opening of corolla tube. Corolla of 5 united petals forming a short, narrow tube. Stamens 5.

How to Grow
Garden favorites, they are easy to grow and flower for a long time. All but *P. subulata* benefit from humus-enriched, moist soil. Most prefer sun or partial shade. Propagate from seeds, cuttings, or division.

carolina *p. 258*
Carolina Phlox. To 3 ft. (90 cm) high. Flowers purple, sometimes rose or white, ¾ in. (2 cm) across, in loose clusters. Mostly cultivated in horticultural forms. E. U.S. Prey to spider mites, particularly in dry soil. Needs well-drained soil and sun or partial shade. Often offered as *P. suffruticosa.* 'Miss Lingard' does not produce seeds. Zone 5.

divaricata *p. 208*
Wild Sweet William. To 18 in. (45 cm) high, with creeping, flowerless stems that root, thus increasing the size of the plant rapidly. Flowers mauve, to 1 in. (2.5 cm) across, in loose clusters. Spring. E. North America. Shade or partial shade and moist soil are important; susceptible to powdery mildew. Zone 4.

paniculata *p. 267*
Garden Phlox; Perennial Phlox. Strong stems, 3–4 ft. (1.0–1.2 m) high. Flowers pink, white, red, or pale blue, 1 in. (2.5 cm) across, in large spreading clusters. E. U.S. Difficult to grow; prey to powdery mildew and spider mites. Grows in sun or partial shade. Remove faded flowers to prevent self-seeding, which crowds out choicer cultivars. 'Mt. Fujiyama' has large white flowerheads. Zone 4.

stolonifera *p. 209*
Creeping Phlox. To 12 in. (30 cm) high, increasing with creeping, flowerless stems that root. Flowers purple or violet. ¾ in. (2 cm) across, in dense clusters. Pa. to Ga. and westward. Needs partial shade. 'Blue Ridge' has blue flowers. Zone 4.

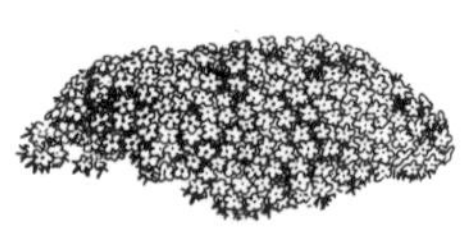

subulata *p. 154*
Ground Pink; Moss Pink. Evergreen creeper to 6 in. (15 cm) high, forming a dense mat. Leaves small, crowded, needle-like. Flowers bright purple, pink, or white, ¾ in. (2 cm) across, in dense clusters. N.Y. to Tenn. and westward. Prefers average, well-drained soil. Shear stems back halfway after flowering to promote denser plants. 'Sampson' has pink flowers. Zone 4.

Phormium
Agave family
Agavaceae

For′mi-um. Two species of large herbs, grown for ornament in Fla. and Calif., and one for its valuable fiber in New Zealand, where they are native.

Description
They have basal, two-part, very tough, long, sword-shaped leaves. Flowering stalk usually exceeding leaves, with alternate and bracted branches that bear the flowers. Flowers red or yellow, tubular, somewhat curved, with 6 stamens protruding.

How to Grow
Grow outdoors only in extreme southern regions. Sow seeds in early spring so they germinate in time to be set out that year, or increase by dividing roots. In borders, they need plenty of space.

tenax *p. 93*
New Zealand Flax; Flax Lily. 8–15 ft. (2.4–4.5 m) high. Striking leaves up to 9 ft. (2.7 m) high, 5 in. (12.5 cm) wide, leathery, usually red-margined, and shreddy at tip. Flowers dull red, 2 in. (5 cm) long, whole cluster well above foliage. Easy to grow in sun or partial shade in moist soil. 'Variegatum' has yellow and green leaves. Zone 9.

Physalis
Potato family
Solanaceae

Fiss′a-lis. Husk Tomato; Ground Cherry. 80 species of annual or perennial herbs found throughout warm and temperate regions.

Description
Leaves alternate, ovalish, or heart-shaped. Flowers inconspicuous, 1–2 produced in axils of leaves. Blue or whitish yellow. After fertilization, calyx becomes inflated and colored, enclosing a round, yellow or green, sometimes sticky berry containing seeds.

How to Grow
Mostly grown for ornamental calyx, which becomes pale yellow to deep orange or red in fall; when cut, calyx keeps for weeks indoors. They will grow in ordinary garden soil in sun or partial shade. Easily propagated by seeds or by division of roots in early spring.

alkekengi, *p. 141*
Chinese Lantern-Plant. To 2 ft. (60 cm) high. Long, creeping underground stems quickly grow out-of-bounds. Flowers small, whitish. Inflated calyx to 2 in. (5 cm) wide, red, resembling a fruit, develops in late summer. Se. Europe to Japan. Prey to flea beetles. Zone 5.

Physostegia
Mint family
Labiatae

Fy-so-stee′gee-a. An herbaceous perennial, native in se. U.S.

Description
Leaves opposite, oblongish, toothed. Flowers

in leafless spikes, corolla much longer than calyx.

How to Grow
Easy to grow in moist soil in full sun; plant in drier soil in shadier sites. Propagate by seed or division of clumps.

virginiana *pp. 184, 257*
False Dragonhead; Obedient Plant. Tall, wandlike, 4–5 ft. (1.2–1.5 m) high. Flowers purple-red, rose-pink, or even lilac, 1 in. (2.5 cm) long, in terminal leafy spike nearly 8 in. (20 cm) long. In dry soil and full sun, height will be reduced. E. North America. Sometimes known as *Dracocephalum.* The cultivar 'Summer Snow' is 3 ft. (90 cm) high and has earlier blooming white flowers. Zone 4.

Platycodon
Bellflower family
Campanulaceae

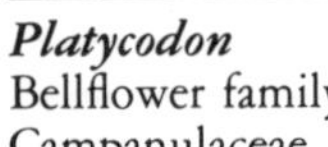

Plat-i-ko′don. A single, showy perennial herb from E. Asia. *Platycodon* is loosely allied to the genus *Campanula.*

Description
Leaves alternate, ovalish or narrower. Flowers usually solitary, long-stalked, broadly bell-shaped or deeply saucer-shaped.

How to Grow
This handsome border plant blooms in the summer and is easy to grow in moist well-drained soils. Increase by spring division. Because it is slow to emerge in the spring, mark its location to prevent accidentally digging it up during spring clean-up. The Balloon Flower takes 2 years to flower when grown from seed.

grandiflorus *p. 215*
Balloon Flower. Erect herb, 18–30 in. (45–75 cm) high. Flowers 2–3 in. (5–7.5 cm) wide, dark blue, white, or pink. Var. *mariesii* is a dwarf form. There are also double and semidoubled flowered forms available. Zone 4.

Polemonium
Phlox family
Polemoniaceae

Po-lee-mo'ni-um. Hardy North American perennial (rarely annual) herbs comprising about 20 species. A few in Europe and Asia.

Description
Leaves long, with many opposite, narrow, lance-shaped leaflets giving leaves a ladderlike appearance. Flowers blue, purple, yellow, or white, in loose, branching clusters. Corolla broadly bell-shaped. Stamens 5.

How to Grow
The species below are easy to grow in sun or partial shade in moist, humus-enriched, well-drained soil. Very moist soil in summer will prevent foliage tips from browning. Sow seeds in sandy soil in early spring; divide rootstocks in early spring, except for *P. caeruleum,* which should be divided in fall. Grow in ordinary garden soil.

caeruleum *p. 214*
Jacob's Ladder. Strong-growing, to 3 ft. (90 cm). Flowers purple or blue, 1 in. (2.5 cm) across, drooping in large clusters. Europe. A good border plant. Var. *album* has white flowers. Zone 4.

foliosissimum *p. 213*
Leafy Polemonium. 2–2½ ft. (60–75 cm) high. Flowers deep violet, ⅝ in. (16 mm) wide, in loose sprays. W. U.S. Zone 4.

reptans *p. 207*
Creeping Polemonium. 8–12 in. (20–30 cm) high, with a spreading habit, not creeping. Flowers light blue, to ½ in. (2 cm) wide, in loose clusters. E. North America. Zone 4.

Polygonatum
Lily family
Liliaceae

Pol-lig-o-nay'tum. Solomon's-Seal. About 30 species of generally hardy herbaceous perennials distributed throughout the northern hemisphere.

Description
Rootstocks thick and branching, 2 in. (5 cm) below the surface of the soil. From

them aerial stems are produced each spring; stems die down in fall. Leaves on upper part of stem only, in 2 rows, alternate, simple, broadly lance-shaped or ovalish, parallel-veined. Flowers tubular, in hanging, 1-to-many-flowered clusters growing from the axils of the leaves.

How to Grow
Easy to grow in partial or full shade in moist soil. The species below will tolerate dry soil in full shade. Propagate by division of rootstocks in fall or spring.

odoratum* var. *thunbergii *p. 253*
Solomon's-Seal. To 3½ ft. (105 cm) high. Flowers white, 2 in a cluster, 1 in. (2.5 cm) long. Japan. Will tolerate drier soils in full shade. 'Variegatum' is smaller, with white-tipped, white-edged leaves. Zone 5.

Polygonum
Knotweed family
Polygonaceae

Pol-lig′o-num. Smartweed, Knotweed. Erect, trailing, or climbing, annual or perennial herbs, comprising about 150 species found throughout the world.

Description
Stems angled, swollen at leaf joints sometimes spotted or streaked brown. Leaves alternate and simple. Flowers small, in terminal spikes or loose racemes. Calyx of 5 sepals generally colored pink or white. Stamens 3–9.

How to Grow
All of these plants are good for attracting bees and all prefer moist soil. Propagate by cuttings in Dec. or by seeds and division of rootstocks in early spring.

affine *p. 188*
Himalayan Fleeceflower. Creeping rootstock, to 18 in. (45 cm) high, leaves brownish. Flowers in dense spikes, 2–3 in. (5.0–7.5 cm) long, bright rose. High Himalayas. Fall. 'Superbum' has dense spikes of deep, dark pink flowers. Zone 4.

***bistorta* 'Superbum'** *p. 189*
European Bistort. 2–3 ft. (60–90 cm) high. Basal leaves resemble large paddles. Pink

flowers closely set on a 6 in. (15 cm) long spike. Europe, Great Britain. Early summer; may bloom again in late summer. Needs shade; in cool summers, will grow in full sun. Zone 4.

cuspidatum *p. 192*
Reynoutria Fleeceflower. Strong-growing, hardy, to 8 ft. (2.4 m) high. Flowers ¼ in. (6 mm) wide, greenish white, numerous, in loose clusters. Japan. Very invasive; not suitable for small borders. Var. *compactum* is a dwarf form 2 ft. (60 cm) high, with pink to pinkish-red flowers. Zone 4.

Potentilla
Rose family
Rosaceae

Po-ten-till′a. Cinquefoil. Over 500 species of mostly perennial herbs or small shrubs, found in mainly northern temperate and arctic regions.

Description
Stems creeping or erect. Leaves compound. Leaflets 3 or many, hairy. Flowers in numerous small, loose clusters. Calyx of 5 sepals joined at the base. Corolla of 5 petals growing on calyx rim. Stamens numerous.

How to Grow
Most species need full sun and dry, well-drained soil. Easily propagated by division of rootstocks or seeds sown in sandy soil. Divide roots in early spring or early fall. Lift and divide potentillas every 3 years.

atrosanguinea *p. 149*
Ruby Cinquefoil. 12–18 in. (30–45 cm) high. Flowers solitary or in loose clusters, 1 in. (2.5 cm) wide. Himalayas. Plant in average soil. 'Gibson's Scarlet' has single red flowers. Zone 5.

nepalensis *p. 148*
Nepal Cinquefoil. To 2 ft. (60 cm) high. Flowers showy, rose-red, to 1 in. (2.5 cm) wide, long-stalked, in branching clusters. Himalayas. Do not overwater. 'Roxana' has pink, orange, and red-brown flowers. Zone 5.

recta *p. 123*
Sulphur Cinquefoil. Flowering stems to 2 ft. (60 cm) high. Rosette-forming, flowers

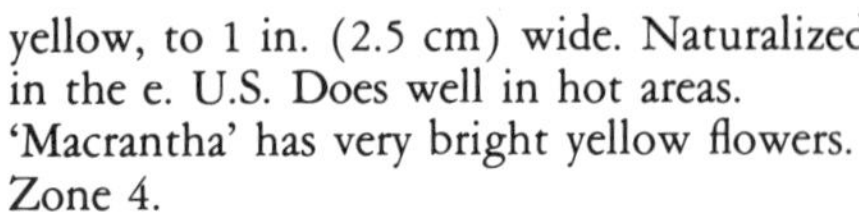

yellow, to 1 in. (2.5 cm) wide. Naturalized in the e. U.S. Does well in hot areas. 'Macrantha' has very bright yellow flowers. Zone 4.

tabernaemontana *p. 119*
Spring Cinquefoil. 3 in. (7.5 cm) high. Rhizomatous; horizontal rooting branches form mats of rosettes. Flowers produced on short stalks, scarcely above level of rosettes, in open, branched groups; yellow, ½ in. (13 mm) wide. Europe. This species can be invasive. Sometimes called *P. crantzii* or *P. verna.* Zone 5.

× ***tonguei*** *p. 124*
Staghorn Cinquefoil. Prostrate, 8–12 in. (20–30 cm) high. Trailing stems with erect tips. Flowers yellow with red center, 1 in. (2.5 cm) wide. Zone 5.

tridentata *p. 236*
Three-toothed Cinquefoil. To 1 ft. (30 cm). Leaflets dark shiny green on upper side. Flowers small, ¼ in. (6 mm) across, white, in loose clusters. E. Northern America. Grow in sandy loam. 'Minima' is 3 in. (7.5 cm) high and has white flowers. Zone 5.

Primula
Primrose family
Primulaceae

Prim′you-la. Over 400 species of low-growing, herbaceous perennials and a few biennials, found mostly in alpine and cool localities.

Description
Stem short, or absent. Leaves crowded, stalked, long and narrow, or roundish or tufted. Flowers on leafless stalks, sometimes with leafy bracts. Calyx of 5 sepals joined halfway, slightly inflated and pale green.

How to Grow
Propagate the species by seed, the named cultivars by division. Easy to grow in moisture-retentive soil in partial shade; many *Primula* will grow in boggy soils. *Primula* thrive in the climate of the Pacific Northwest; they do not like hot, dry summers. Red spider mites may be a problem, particularly in dry areas.

helodoxa *p. 100*
Amber Primrose. 18–36 in. (45–90 cm) high. Yellow flowers, 1 in. (2.5 cm) wide. Yunnan Prov. (China) and Burma. Needs protection, or even a cool greenhouse northward. Thrives in boggy soils. Zone 6.

japonica *p. 179*
Japanese Primrose. Strong-growing, 8–16 in. (20.0–40.5 cm) high. Flowers purple, pink, or white, 1 in. (2.5 cm) wide, glistening, in several whorls on each stalk. Japan. Needs constant moisture and humus-enriched soil. There are many horticultural color forms. Zone 6.

sieboldii *p. 172*
Japanese Star Primrose. To 12 in. (30 cm) high. Flowers in crowded umbels, nearly 2 in. (5 cm) wide, pink or purple, usually with a different colored eye. Japan. Prefers moist sites, but more tolerant of drought than other *Primula* species. Dormant in summer. The Barnhaven strain of English hybrids includes plants with pale or deep pink, purple, or lavender flowers. Zone 5.

veris *p. 113*
Cowslip Primrose. 6–8 in. (15–20 cm) high. Leaves wrinkled, broadly lance-shaped, slightly hairy on underside. Flowers yellow, with orange eye, to ½ in. (13 mm) wide, fragrant, in nodding umbels. Calyx pale green, slightly inflated. Eurasia. Double-flowered forms available. Zones 5–6.

vulgaris *p. 112*
English Primrose. To 6 in. (15 cm) high. Leaves wrinkled, margins crinkled. Flowers numerous or solitary, 1½ in. (4 cm) wide, usually yellow. Europe. Blooms in spring. Needs humus-enriched soil and mulch in hot summer. Often called *P. acaulis.* Blue and double-flowered forms available. Zone 5.

Prunella
Mint family
Labiatae

Pru-nell′a. Seven species of low-growing, hardy herbs, natives of Europe and Asia.

Description
Leaves simple, opposite, veins prominent on underside, toothed. Flowers in dense heads

or spikes. Calyx closes and points upward in dry weather but opens and stands horizontally in damp weather. Stamens 4.

How to Grow
Most species are garden weeds, but can be used for damp and shady places in rock or wild gardens. Easy to propagate from seeds or division, both in early spring.

grandiflora *p. 184*
Self Heal. Hardy perennial, to 12 in. (30 cm) high. Flowers purplish blue, 1 in. (2.5 cm) long. Europe. In cool zones, they thrive in full sun and ordinary soil; but in warmer areas, plants need partial shade and moist, humus-enriched soil. There are several horticultural color forms. 'Rosea' has rose-pink flowers. Zone 5.

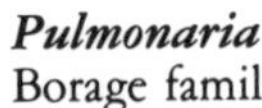

Pulmonaria
Borage family
Boraginaceae

Pul-mo-nay'ri-a. Lungwort. Low-growing perennial herbs comprising about 10 species, natives of Europe.

Description
They have creeping rootstocks. Basal leaves long-stalked, broadly lance-shaped, sometimes mottled. Flowers in terminal, coiled clusters that straighten as the flowers open. Corolla funnel-shaped, sometimes with a hairy throat. Stamens 5.

How to Grow
Pulmonarias make useful spring-flowering border plants. The species below are easy to grow in moist, ordinary garden soil in full to partial shade. Propagate by root division in fall or early spring, or by seeds sown in early spring.

angustifolia *p. 212*
Blue Lungwort; Cowslip Lungwort. 6–12 in. (15–30 cm) high. Flowers blue, ¾–1 in. (19–25 mm) long. A useful border plant. Zone 4.

longifolia *p. 211*
12 in. (30 cm) high. Leaves with white spots. Flowers blue, ¾–1 in. (19–25 mm) long, in dense, terminal heads. Zone 5.

saccharata *p. 210*
Bethlehem Sage. 8–14 in. (20–35 cm) high. Basal leaves mottled, white. Flowers white or reddish purple, ¾–1 in. (19–25 cm) long, in terminal clusters. Prefers full shade. Zone 4.

Ranunculus

Buttercup family
Ranunculaceae

Ra-nun′kew-lus. The buttercups, or crowfoots, comprise a large group of mostly temperate herbs which includes the common Florists' Ranunculus.

Description
Leaves often much cut, lobed, or divided. Flowers mostly yellow, but white or even red in horticultural varieties. Petals and sepals 5 each. Stamens numerous.

How to Grow
The species below is easily grown outdoors in any ordinary garden soil, and is easily propagated by division in spring or fall.

repens *p. 122*
Creeping Buttercup. 1–2 ft. (30–60 cm) high. A creeping, weedy plant with long runners. It roots at the joints and sends up erect, flowering stems. Flowers single, yellow, 1 in. (2.5 cm) wide. Europe, but a common weed in U.S. Cultivar 'Pleniflorus', a double-flowered form, is widely grown. Flowers much-doubled, very profuse, ¾ in. (2 cm) wide. Grow in moist soil in full sun to partial shade. Keep this cultivar in check by pinching off roots at the leaf joints. Also called *R. speciosus.* Zone 4.

Rhexia

Meadowbeauty family
Melastomataceae

Rex′i-a. Meadowbeauty. Pretty little North American perennial herbs; 10 known species, only 2 of any garden interest.

Description
Leaves opposite, prominently 3- to 5-veined. Calyx 4-lobed, bell-shaped at base. Petals 4, oblique, showy. Stamens 8.

How to Grow
The species below are easy to grow in moist, acid to boggy soil in full sun. Do not move them very often. To increase plants, lift clumps in fall or spring, carefully separate, then replant.

mariana *p. 163*
Maryland Meadowbeauty. Slender, 1–2 ft. (30–60 cm) high. Flowers to 1½ in. (4 cm) wide, pale purple, in few-flowered cymes. In pine-barren bogs, e. U.S., west to Ky. Zone 6.

virginica *p. 162*
Deer Grass. 9–18 in. (22.5–45 cm) high, the stem angled. Leaf margins hairy-fringed. Flowers nearly 1½ in. (4 cm) wide, purple, in few-flowered cymes. In sandy bogs along the coast, e. North America. Zone 6.

Rodgersia
Saxifrage family
Saxifragaceae

Rod-jer′si-a. Hardy herbaceous perennials comprising about 5 species, natives of China and Japan.

Description
They have thick, black, spreading rootstocks. Leaves long-stalked, large, bronze-green. Flowers small, numerous, greenish white, in large, showy terminal clusters. Calyx of 5 sepals, usually greenish white. Stamens 10.

How to Grow
Difficult to grow except in moist to wet, humus-enriched soil in full sun. Best along ponds or streams. Also good plants for half-shade borders, when given plenty of space. They benefit from a light covering in winter. Propagate by root division in spring.

aesculifolia *p. 265*
Fingerleaf Rodgersflower. To 4 ft. (1.2 m) high. Leaves palmately compound. Flowers small, creamy white, in conical clusters, 12–18 in. (30–45 cm) long. China. Zones 5–6.

podophylla *p. 101*
Bronzeleaf Rodgersflower. Strong-growing plant, to 5 ft. (1.5 m) high. Flowers yellowish white, ¼ in. (6 mm) wide, in

terminal clusters 1 ft. (30 cm) long. China. Zones 5–6.

Romneya
Poppy family
Papaveraceae

Rom′nee-a. Tender perennial herbs or subshrubs, comprising 2 species from Calif. and Mex.

Description
To 8 ft. (2.4 m) high, with spreading rootstocks and branching stems. Leaves in pairs, stalked, broadly lance-shaped, deeply lobed. Flowers solitary, at ends of branches, white, to 6 in. (15 cm) wide. Stamens numerous.

How to Grow
Beautiful garden plants, but difficult to establish unless grown in pots and then transplanted without disturbing roots. Grow from seeds sown as soon as they are ripe, on a surface of fine, sandy peat in well-drained pans under a jar at 55–60° F. Transplant only when well-rooted. Grow in a sunny, well-drained border with peat and sand added to soil.

coulteri *p. 245*
California Tree Poppy. To 8 ft. (2.4 m) high. Much-branched above. Leaves paperlike. Flowers white, to 6 in. (15 cm) wide, solitary. Calif. and Mexico. Not very hardy in northern zones, even with protection. Zone 7.

Roscoea
Ginger family
Zingiberaceae

Ross-ko′ee-a. About 17 species of perennial herbs with fleshy roots; these plants are half-hardy members of an otherwise tropical family.

Description
Roots fleshy or tuberous, stems erect, leafy, the leaves with clasping and sheathing bases. Flowers orchidlike, tubular, with a hooded upper lip and a pendulous lower lip, solitary or in short spikes.

How to Grow
Best grown in sandy loam with leaf mold additions, in full sun or partial shade. These plants are hardy only in areas with mild winters.

humeana *p. 153*
Hume Roscoea; Ginger. 8–12 in. (20–30 cm) high. Leaves broadly sheathed, veined. Clusters of 2–8 flowers, each violet, 4 in. (10 cm) long. China. Zones 7–8.

Rudbeckia
Daisy family
Compositae

Rood-beck′i-a. Coneflower. Hardy North American annual or biennial herbs, comprising about 25 species.

Description
Leaves usually alternate, veins prominent, margins deeply toothed toward tip. Flowers in terminal or axillary heads, generally yellow, with the disk florets usually brown or black.

How to Grow
Rudbeckias are useful border plants and easy to grow in moist or average well-drained soil in full sun. Propagate by seeds or early spring root division.

fulgida *p. 133*
Orange Coneflower. Stems 2–3 ft. (60–90 cm) high. The var. *fulgida* has daisylike flowerheads, 3 in. (7.5 cm) wide, ray florets bright orange-yellow, central disk florets black. N.J. and Ill. to n. Ala. Var. *speciosa* has flowerheads to 4 in. (10 cm) wide, rays yellow, disk brownish purple. 'Goldsturm', a compact form 2 ft. (60 cm) high with larger flowers, does not come true from seed. Zone 4.

***nitida* 'Herbstsonne'** *p. 133*
4–7 ft. (1.2–2.1 m) high. Very large, single flowers 4 in. (10 cm) wide, with high central cone. Blooms mid- to late summer. Needs staking. Zone 4.

Ruta
Rue family
Rutaceae

Roo′ta. Aromatic perennial herbs or shrubs, all 40 species from Eurasia or the Canary Islands.

Description
Leaves alternate, often bluish-gray. Flowers with 4 sepals and 4 petals, borne in terminal clusters.

How to Grow
Ruta grows best in full sun where soil is light and well-drained. To preserve its bushy shape, prune back to old wood in early spring.

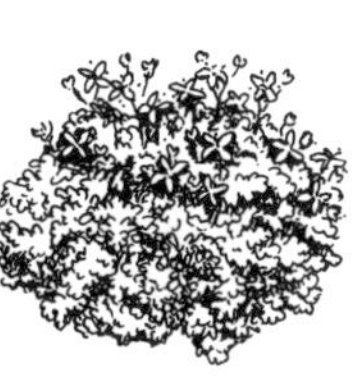

graveolens *p. 99*
Common Rue. An evergreen subshrub or woody herb, 2–3 ft. (90 cm) high. Bruised leaves have a pungent odor. Flowers dull yellow, ½ in. (13 mm) wide, in a loose cyme, concave, fringed on the margin. S. Europe. Requires mulching in severe winters. The moist foliage is an irritant to some. Cultivar 'Jackman's Blue' is 18–24 in. (45–60 cm) high, with intensely blue-green leaves. Zone 5.

Salvia
Mint family
Labiatae

Sal′vi-a. Sage. Annual, biennial, or perennial herbs, subshrubs, or shrubs, comprising about 750 species and distributed throughout the tropical and temperate world. The leaves of some species are used for seasoning.

Description
Leaves in pairs, opposite, sometimes hairy, the margins toothed or deeply cut into segments. Flowers in whorls, growing from the axils of small, leafy bracts and arranged in terminal spikes or racemes. Stamens 4.

How to Grow
All the salvias below are easy to grow in full sun or partial shade, and average to dry, well-drained soil. They are also easy to propagate from seeds, division of rootstocks, or cuttings, all in fall or early spring.

argentea *p. 76*
Silver Sage. To 4 ft. (1.2 m) high, covered with white-woolly hairs. Flowers in 4- to 8-flowered whorls, each to 2¼ in. (5.5 cm) long, whitish-yellow or purplish. Mediterranean region. A short-lived perennial, usually treated as a biennial or annual. Needs full sun. Zone 5.

azurea **var.** ***grandiflora*** *p. 232*
Pitcher's Salvia. 4–5 ft. (1.2–1.5 m) high. Stems hairy, leaves smooth. Flowers 1 in. (2.5 cm) long, blue or white, 6-flowered whorls. Cen. U.S. Prey to white fly. May need mulching in winter. Also sold as *S. pitcheri.* Zone 6.

farinacea *p. 233*
Mealy-Cup Sage. To 3 ft. (90 cm) high, covered with whitish, short hairs, and mealy. Leaves stalked. Flowers ½ in. (13 mm) long in many-whorled racemes, violet-blue. Flower-stalks sometimes bluish. Tex. Good for cutting. Prey to white fly. An excellent annual for northern zones because it reseeds each year. Cultivar 'Catima' is 24 in. (60 cm) high, with deep blue flowers. Zone 8.

officinalis *p. 85*
Garden Sage. To 2 ft. (60 cm) high. Branches and leaves covered with short white hairs. Leaves stalked, wrinkled. Flowers purplish blue or white, 1½ in. (4 cm) long, in many-flowered whorls, in short racemes. Spain. Used for seasoning. It can be clipped to make a low hedge. 'Icterina' is semi-shrubby, with green and yellow variegated foliage. Zone 5.

pratensis *p. 234*
Meadow Clary. To 3 ft. (90 cm) high. Leaves slightly spotted with red. Bracts below the clusters of flowers green. Flowers ½–1 in. (13–25 mm) long, lavender blue. Europe. Zone 6.

× ***superba*** *p. 234*
Violet Sage. Strong-growing, 1½–3 ft. (45–90 cm) high. Bracts purplish. Flowers to ½ in. (13 mm) long, purplish. Produces no pollen, so must be reproduced by division or cuttings. Occasionally prey to white fly. Cultivar 'Mainacht' ('May Night') is 18–24 in. (45–60 cm) high with dark violet-blue flowers. The following are placed under

the umbrella of × *superba: S. memorosa* and *S.* × *sylvestris.* All Zone 5.

Sanguisorba

Rose family
Rosaceae

San-gwi-sor'ba. Burnet. Hardy herbs of north temperate regions, comprising 2 or 3 species.

Description
Leaves alternate, compound. Flowers small, crowded in short spikes at the top of long flowering stalks.

How to Grow
Grown in the border, or for their leaves, which are used for flavoring. Easy to grow in sun or partial shade in moist, organically amended soil. Propagate by seeds sown in early spring or by division of rootstocks in fall or early spring.

canadensis *p. 263*
Great Burnet; American Burnet. Strong-growing, 3–6 ft. (90–180 cm) high. Flowers white, numerous, in spikes 3–6 in. (7.5–15.0 cm) long. E. North America. Grows best in neutral to slightly acid soil rich in peat. Also sold as *Poterium canadense.* Zone 4.

Santolina

Daisy family
Compositae

San-to-ly'na. Evergreen, aromatic subshrubs, most of the 8 species originally from the Mediterranean region.

Description
They have alternate, finely divided leaves, and solitary, globe-shaped, yellow flowerheads, all without ray flowers.

How to Grow
All species grow best in full sun and well-drained soil. In northern climates, they may be treated as annuals, and where winters are cold, they require mulching. Propagate by summer stem cuttings, which root easily in sand.

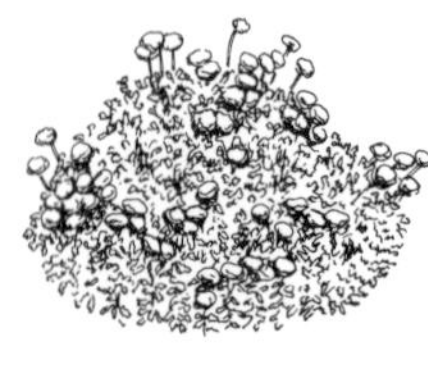

chamaecyparissus *p. 99*
Lavender Cotton. A silvery gray evergreen, 1–2 ft. (30–60 cm) high. Leaves cut into very narrow segments. Flowerheads solitary, ¾ in. (19 cm) wide, yellow, the stalk 6 in. (15 cm) long. S. Europe. Summer. Prune to prevent plants from becoming ragged. Also sold as *S. incana.* Zone 6.

virens *p. 98*
Green Lavender Cotton. Evergreen, 10–18 in. (25–45 cm) high, the foliage smooth and dark green. Leaves very narrow, nearly 2 in. (5 cm) long, the margins toothed. Flowerheads solitary, ½ in. (13 mm) wide, creamy yellow, on stout stalks 6–10 in. (15–25 cm) high. S. Europe. Once called Holy Flax. Zone 6.

Saponaria
Pink family
Caryophyllaceae

Sap-o-nair′i-a. Hardy annual or perennial herbs comprising about 30 species found chiefly in the Mediterranean region.

Description
Leaves simple, opposite, lance-shaped. Flowers showy, in loosely branched clusters, pink or white. Corolla of 5 petals, alternating with the sepals. Stamens 5.

How to Grow
Saponarias are easy to grow in average, well-drained soil in full sun. Good for borders and rock gardens. Easy to propagate from seeds in early spring, division of rootstocks in early spring or fall, or by cuttings. Insert cuttings in a mixture of half sand and half soil and shade from sun until rooted.

ocymoides *p. 155*
Rock Soapwort. Trailing, 4–8 in. (10–20 cm) high. Flowers bright pink, ½ in. (1.3 cm) across, in loose clusters. Calyx purple. Cen. and s. Europe. Plant in sandy soil. There is a white-flowered variety. Zone 4.

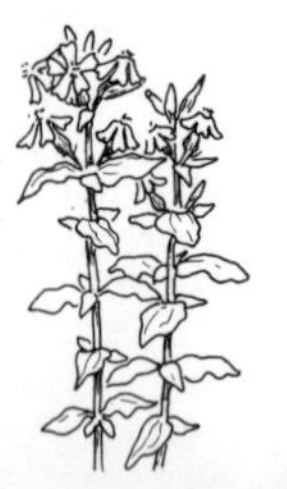

officinalis *p. 180*
Bouncing Bet; Soapwort. 1–3 ft. (30–90 cm) high. Flowers pink or white, 1 in. (2.5 cm) long, in dense clusters. W. Asia. Mostly blooms at night. May be invasive in moist,

fertile soil. Var. *flore-pleno,* with double flowers, is the form usually grown. Both are useful border plants. Zone 4.

Saxifraga

Saxifrage family
Saxifragaceae

Sacks-iff'ra-ga. Saxifrage, Rockfoil. About 300 species of mostly perennial herbs, found chiefly in temperate regions of Europe and America.

Description
Usually low-growing, spreading or creeping; rootstocks spread by offsets or runners. Leaves thick and fleshy or soft and mosslike, sometimes in a rosette, roundish or spoon-shaped to ovalish. Margins often silvery. Flowers pink, white, purple, or yellow, in clusters. Stamens 10 or more.

How to Grow
Saxifragas are useful in rock gardens or borders, since they seldom run over other plants. The foliage changes color with the seasons. Plant in positions shaded from midday sun, or in complete shade, in moist gritty soil with lime. Easy to propagate from seeds in early spring, division of the rootstocks in spring or summer, or by runners and bulblets, the latter found in some species.

stolonifera *p. 240*
Strawberry Geranium. Sends out runners like a strawberry; to 2 ft. (60 cm) long. Leaves hairy, dark green, marked with white on upper side, reddish on underside. Flowers white, ¾ in. (19 mm) across, in loose racemes. E. Asia. Summer. Good evergreen groundcover, and a useful basket or pot plant. Also sold as *S. sarmentosa.* Zone 6.

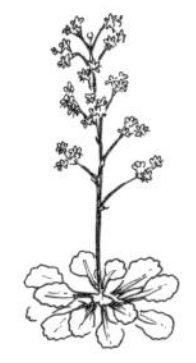

× ***urbium*** *p. 159*
London Pride Saxifrage. To 12 in. (30 cm) high. Flowers pink, 5/16 in. (8 mm) across, borne in an airy cluster. Europe. Best suited to climate like the Pacific Northwest; where summers are hot, plant in a shaded, moist spot. Also sold as *S. umbrosa.* Zone 7.

Scabiosa
Teasel family
Dipsacaceae

Skay′bi-o-sa. Scabious; Pincushion. Hardy annual or perennial herbs comprising about 80 species found mostly in the temperate regions.

Description
Leaves simple, opposite, ovalish or lance-shaped, often lobed or deeply cut. Flowering stalk long. Flowerheads blue, purple, brownish black, reddish brown, pink, cream, or white. Calyx represented by bristles. Stamens 4.

How to Grow
*Scabiosa*s flower for long periods. The species below is easy to grow in full sun in moist, neutral to alkaline, well-drained soil. Propagate in very early spring by seeds or division.

caucasica *p. 200*
Pincushion Flower. To 2½ ft. (75 cm) high. Flowers in flattish heads, blue or white, 2–3 in. (5.0–7.5 cm) across. Caucasus, in the mts. Bears few flowers, so plant together for a good show. 'David Wilkie' has pinkish-purple flowers. Zone 4.

Sedum
Stonecrop family
Crassulaceae

See′dum. Stonecrop. Low-growing, chiefly perennial herbs, comprising about 600 species found through the temperate and colder regions of the northern hemisphere.

Description
Leaves alternate, opposite, or in whorls. Flowers white, yellow, pink, red, or blue, in terminal clusters. Stamens double the number of petals.

How to Grow
Sedums are particularly adapted to the rock garden, but a few species can be used in flower borders. Easy to grow in well-drained, average soil in sun or partial shade. Good drainage is essential, particularly in winter. Propagate by seeds, division, cuttings, or leaves.

aizoon *p. 104*
Aizoon Stonecrop. Strong-growing, 12–18 in. (30–45 cm) high. Rootstocks thick and tuberous. Stems upright. Flowers yellow, to ½ in. (13 mm) across, in terminal branching clusters. Siberia (U.S.S.R.) and Japan. Needs full sun. Sandy, humus-enriched soil is ideal. Zone 4.

'Autumn Joy' *p. 194*
Autumn Joy Sedum. 2 ft. (60 cm) high. Leaves scattered along succulent stems. Flowers ¼–⅜ in. (6–9 mm) across, pink to rusty-red, in clusters that resemble broccoli heads. Tolerant of moist soil. Also sold as 'Indian Chief'. Zone 4.

kamtschaticum *p. 114*
Orange Stonecrop. Erect, 6–12 in. (15–30 cm) high. Flowers orange-yellow, to ¾ in. (19 mm) across. Ne. Asia. Zone 4.

maximum *p. 195*
Great Stonecrop. Tuberous roots and erect stems 1–2 ft. (30–60 cm) high. Leaves egg-shaped. Flowers greenish, ¼ in. (6 mm) across. Late summer. Europe and w. Asia. Cultivar 'Atropurpureum' has reddish-purple foliage and pinkish flowers; other cultivars have variegated leaves. Zone 4.

'Ruby Glow' *p. 151*
Ruby Glow Sedum. 6–8 in. (15–20 cm) high. Leaves fleshy, gray blue. Flowers ¼ in. (6 mm) across, rose crimson, arranged in clusters 2 in. (5 cm) across. Needs full sun. Also sold as 'Rosy Glow'. Zone 4.

sieboldii *p. 154*
October Daphne. A trailing plant, 6–9 in. (15.0–22.5 cm) high. Flowers pink, to ½ in. (13 mm) across. Japan. Late fall. Will not flower in zones with early autumn frosts. Zone 4.

spectabile *p. 195*
Showy Stonecrop. To 2 ft. (60 cm) high. Flowers pink, to ½ in. (13 mm) across. Japan and cen. China. Needs dry soil. Cultivars include 'Brilliant', 18 in. (45 cm) high, with raspberry-red flowers; and 'Meteor', 18 in. (45 cm) high, with deep red flowers. Zone 4.

spurium *p. 150*
Two-row Stonecrop. Creeping evergreen to 6 in. (15 cm) high. Flowers red to pale pink,

to ½ in. (13 mm) across. Caucasus and sw. Asia. Summer. Requires dry soil. Also sold as *S. stoloniferum.* Zone 4.

Shortia
Galax family
Diapensiaceae

Short'i-a. 8 species of low-growing evergreen herbs, natives of the mts. of e. Asia and e. North America.

Description
They have creeping underground stems and basal, roundish or heart-shaped, shining green stalked leaves, the margins wavy. Flowers white, solitary, on leafless stalks to 8 in. (20 cm) high. Corolla bell-shaped. Stamens 10, 5 growing on the petals.

How to Grow
These plants are useful in rock gardens. Grow in cool, moist, well-drained humus-enriched, acid soil, in full or partial shade. In clay loam soils, add peat moss to achieve an acid humus soil. Propagate by early spring division.

galacifolia *p. 152*
Oconee Bells. To 8 in. (20 cm) high. Flowering stalk slender, flowers white, to 1 in. (2.5 cm) across, nodding. Mts. from Va. to Ga. An excellent choice for rock gardens. Difficult to establish, so avoid transplanting. Zone 5.

Sidalcea
Mallow family
Malvaceae

Sy-dall'see-a. False mallow. About 20 species of annual or perennial herbs, natives of w. North America.

Description
Leaves alternate, simple, cut into fingerlike lobes. Flowers purple, pink, or white, in terminal spikes. Stamens in groups united by their filaments.

How to Grow
Sidalceas make good border plants. The species below is easily grown in full sun in

average, well-drained soil with some moisture. Propagate by seeds in early spring, or by spring or fall division.

malviflora *p. 181*
Checkerbloom; Prairie Mallow. Erect, 18–40 in. (45–100 cm) high. Flowers pink, to 1½ in. (4 cm) across, in many-flowered spires that rise above the foliage. Calif. Taller plants need staking. Cultivar 'Loveliness' is 30 in. (75 cm) high, with shell-pink flowers. Also sold as *S.* × *hybrida.* Zone 5.

Silene
Pink family
Caryophyllaceae

Sy-lee′ne. Catchfly; Campion. Tender and hardy annual, biennial, or perennial herbs comprising about 500 species and distributed throughout the world.

Description
Erect, tufted or spreading, the stems or calyx sometimes sticky. Leaves opposite, simple, without teeth. Flowers solitary or in loose-branching clusters, white, pink, or red. Calyx with teethlike lobes. Stamens 10.

How to Grow
Silenes are useful rock garden or border plants. Plant *S. Schafta* in well-drained sandy loam. Easy to grow and propagate from seeds, division, or by cuttings. Cuttings should be inserted in sandy soil in a cold frame and shaded from sun until rooted. Once established, plants should not be moved.

schafta *p. 173*
Moss Campion. To 6 in. (15 cm) high, covered with short soft hairs. Leaves in rosettes. Flowers rose or purple, ¾ in. (2 cm) across, 1–2 flowers on each stalk. Petals notched. Caucasus. Zones 5–6.

Sisyrinchium
Iris family
Iridaceae

Sis-i-rink′i-um. Blue-eyed grass. Low-growing American herbs, comprising about 75 grasslike species.

Description
Leaves erect, long and narrow, parallel-veined, pale green or bluish green. Flowers reddish purple, blue, or yellow, in terminal umbels enclosed in a spathe. Calyx of 3 colored sepals, the corolla of 3 petals, alternating with the sepals, widely open. Stamens 3.

How to Grow
Attractive in flower borders if planted in clumps, and especially good in full sun in damp, well-drained places. Can also be used in wild gardens. Propagate by seeds in early spring or by fall division.

striatum *p. 94*
Argentine Blue-eyed Grass. 12–18 in. (30–45 cm) high. Leaves gray-green, growing in upright clumps, somewhat like irises. Flowers creamy yellow, ¾ in. (2 cm) across, arranged in successive clusters that form a long spike. Chile. Zones 7–8.

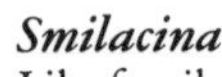

Smilacina
Lily family
Liliaceae

Smy-la-see′na. False Solomon's-Seal. About 25 species of perennial herbs, natives of North America and temperate Asia.

Description
Leaves broadly lance-shaped, with parallel veins. Flowers greenish white, in racemes or terminal branching clusters, sometimes fragrant. Calyx of 3 colored sepals. Corolla of 3 petals alternating with the sepals. Stamens 6 in 2 whorls.

How to Grow
Can be used in hardy borders or wild gardens in shade. Easy to propagate by division.

racemosa *p. 266*
False Solomon's-Seal. To 3 ft. (90 cm) high. Flowers greenish white, in terminal branching clusters 4–6 in. (10–15 cm) long. North America. Plant in slightly acid soil; additions of peat may be necessary. Zone 4.

Solidago
Daisy family
Compositae

Sol-i-day′go. Goldenrod. Coarse, rather weedy herbs. All but a handful of the 130 known species are from the New World, with scattered species in Europe and Asia.

Description
Usually perennial, often branched or arching, with alternate, usually toothed leaves. Flowerheads mostly yellow, the small heads very numerous and crowded in sometimes various clusters, often showy. Best for informal borders.

How to Grow
Goldenrods are very easy to grow in sun or partial shade in moist, well-drained soil. In very rich soil, they may develop more foliage than flowers. Easily divided. Some species spread so fast that they must be watched.

hybrids *p. 117*
Goldenrod. 1–5 ft. (30–150 cm) high. Small flowers are yellow to bright gold, arranged in a dense, panicle-like cluster. Goldenrod spreads quickly in very fertile soil; may self-seed. Variety 'Gold Dwarf' is 12 in. (30 cm) high with yellow flowers. Zone 4.

Stachys
Mint family
Labiatae

Stack′iss. Betony; Woundwort. About 300 species of annual or perennial herbs distributed throughout the world, but chiefly in the temperate zones.

Description
Leaves opposite, ovalish or broadly lance-shaped. Flowers purple, scarlet, yellow, or white, in 2-many-flowered whorls, in terminal spikes. Corolla tubular, opening into 2 lips. Stamens 4.

How to Grow
Useful in flower borders. Easy to grow in average well-drained soil in full sun. Propagate by seeds in early spring or by early spring or fall division.

byzantina *p. 90*
Lamb's-Ears. To 18 in. (45 cm) high, covered with soft, white, woolly hairs. Leaves large. Flowers 1 in. (2.5 cm) across, purple, in densely flowered whorls. Caucasus and Iran. Tolerates dry soil. Cultivar 'Silver Carpet' has unattractive flowers that should be dead-headed; its silver foliage is very ornamental. Also sold as *S. lanata* and *S. olympica.* Zone 5.

macrantha *p. 185*
Big Betony. 12–18 in. (30–45 cm) high. Leaves thick, wrinkled, hairy. Flowers violet-purple, showy, to 1½ in. (4 cm) long, in 20- to 30- flowered whorls on spike that extends above the foliage. Asia Minor. Tolerates partial shade. Cultivar 'Robusta' has rosy-pink flowers. Also sold as *S. grandiflora.* Zone 4.

Stokesia

Daisy family
Compositae

Sto-key′zi-a or stokes′i-a. 1 species, an American hardy perennial herb.

Description

Stems purplish, covered with white matted hairs. Flowerheads 1–4 in. (2.5–10.0 cm) across, solitary or several on a branching stalk; surrounded by several rings of bracts, the outermost with spine-like teeth, the inner sheathing the flowers. Flowers lavender-blue or purplish blue. Ray florets tubular, becoming smaller toward the center.

How to Grow

Easy to grow in sun or partial shade in average, well-drained soil; sandy loam is best. Winter protection is needed where frost is heavy. Propagate by seeds in spring or division of roots in early spring.

laevis *p. 201*
Stokes Aster. To 2 ft. (60 cm) high. Flowers lavender-blue, in heads 2–4 in. (5–10 cm) across. S.C. to La. Also sold as *S. cyanea.* Zones 5–6.

Stylophorum
Poppy family
Papaveraceae

Sty-loff′o-rum. Hardy perennial herbs comprising 3 species, 1 a native of North America and 2 of China.

Description
They have thick rootstocks, yellow sap, and mostly basal leaves, generally deeply cut almost to the midrib into several lobes. Flowers yellow or red. Stamens many.

How to Grow
Generally grown in the wild garden. Often invasive and must be controlled rather than propagated. Does best in moist, rich, well-drained soil and partial shade.

diphyllum *p. 120*
Celandine Poppy. To 18 in. (45 cm) high. Flowers deep yellow, to 2 in. (5 cm) across, in 2- to 5-flowered clusters. W. Pa. to Wis. and Tenn. Transplants easily; divide in fall. Zone 6.

Symphytum
Borage family
Boraginaceae

Sim-fy′tum. Comfrey. About 25 species of hardy perennial herbs, natives of Europe, n. Africa, and w. Asia.

Description
Stem and leaves covered with bristly hairs. Basal leaves large, stem leaves alternate or opposite. Flowers yellowish, blue, white, rose, or purple, in branching clusters. Corolla tubular. Stamens 5.

How to Grow
Easy to grow in sun or partial shade in average well-drained soil. Plant in autumn or spring and propagate by seed or division.

grandiflorum *p. 251*
Ground-cover Comfrey. 8–12 in. (20–30 cm) high. Flowers creamy white, ¾ in. (2 cm) across, tubular, in curved panicles. Caucasus Mts. Easy to control. Cultivars include 'Hidcote Pink', with soft-pink flowers; 'Hidcote Blue', with bluish flowers. Zone 5.

× ***rubrum*** *p. 176*
Comfrey. To 18 in. (45 cm) high. Flowers ½–1 in. (1.3–2.5 cm) long, deep red, tubular, in a curved panicle. Zone 5.

× ***uplandicum*** *p. 227*
Russian Comfrey. 2–3 ft. (60–90 cm) high. Leaves attached to winged stems. Flowers blue, ¾–1 in. (2–2.5 cm) long, arranged in forked clusters in upper leaf axils. Zone 5.

Tanacetum
Daisy family
Compositae

Tan-a-see′tum. Tansy. Rather weedy herbs or subshrubs, all the 50 known species from the north temperate zone. Related to *Chrysanthemum* and *Artemisia.*

Description
The entire or lobed leaves are generally strongly aromatic. Flowerheads yellow.

How to Grow
Plant in sunny or partially shady sites, where soil is well-drained. Easily propagated by division. Transplant in fall or spring.

vulgare **var.** ***crispum*** *p. 98*
Tansy. 2–3 ft. (60–90 cm) high, with alternate, much-dissected leaves. Flowers ⅓ in. (8 mm) wide, yellow, in small, buttonlike heads of disk flowers; heads in a cyme. Europe. Var. *crispum* has more finely divided and crisp leaves. Becomes invasive in moist, fertile soil, and needs frequent division and thinning. Zone 4.

Teucrium
Mint family
Labiatae

Too′kri-um. Germander. Perennial herbs or subshrubs comprising about 300 species, some grown for ornament or fragrance.

Description
Opposite leaves becoming smaller and bractlike near the flower clusters. Flowers in small whorls, arranged mostly in racemes or

spikes. Corolla 2-lipped, the lower lip much larger than the upper. Stamens 4, conspicuously protruding.

How to Grow
The species below is easy to grow in sun or partial shade in average well-drained soil. Propagated by division or seeds.

chamaedrys *p. 189*
Wall Germander. Prostrate subshrub, 1–2 ft. (30–60 cm) high. Flowers red-purple or rose, usually spotted with red and white, ¾ in. (19 mm) long, spikes loose. Europe. A good bedding or edging plant. Prefers full sun. Evergreen, needs protection in northern winters. Zones 5–6.

Thalictrum
Buttercup family
Ranunculaceae

Tha-lick′trum. Meadowrue. A large genus of graceful perennial herbs, most of the 100 species found in the temperate zone.

Description
Basal or alternate leaves twice- or thrice-compound. Flowers small, but handsome because of the large, often branching panicles or racemes. Sepals sometimes colored and petal-like. Stamens numerous and often providing most of the color.

How to Grow
They are easy to grow in moist, well-drained, humus-enriched soil, in sun or partial shade. Divide in spring.

aquilegifolium *p. 194*
Columbine Meadowrue. Branching, 2–3 ft. (60–90 cm) high. Flowers lavender, ½ in. (13 mm) across, male and female on separate plants, male flowers more showy. Eurasia. Needs light shade in hot summers. A handsome plant for borders; also available in white, dark purple, orange, and pink. Zones 5–6.

rochebrunianum *p. 161*
Lavender Mist Meadowrue. 3–5 ft. (90–150 cm) high. Leaves divided into segments suggesting maidenhair fern. Flowers ½ in. (13 mm) across, in a sparse panicle, purple,

sometimes pale purple, or pink-lavender. Japan. Needs staking. Zones 5–6.

speciosissimum *p. 102*
Dusty Meadowrue. Bluish-green, 3–5 ft. (90–150 cm) high. Panicles dense, flowers small, yellow, stamens longer than sepals. S. Europe. Requires staking. Also sold as *T. glaucum.* Zones 5–6.

Thermopsis
Pea family
Leguminosae

Ther-mop′sis. About 20 species of showy-flowered perennial herbs, of North America and Asia.

Description
Leaves alternate, compound, with 3 leaflets. Flowers yellow (in cultivated species), pea-like, in chiefly terminal, erect racemes. Most of them have large leaflike, sometimes clasping, stipules.

How to Grow
Easy to grow in most garden soils, even in relatively infertile ones, but does better in well-drained soil in full sun. Quite drought-resistant. Propagate by spring division or by seeds sown when fresh, since they are slow to germinate.

caroliniana *p. 109*
Carolina Thermopsis. Stout, 3–5 ft. (90–150 cm) high. Leaflets silky-hairy beneath. Flowers yellow, ½–¾ in. (13–19 mm) across, pea-like, in dense racemes 8–10 in. (20–25 cm) long. N.C. to Ga. Also sold as *T. villosa.* Zone 3.

Tradescantia
Spiderwort family
Commelinaceae

Tray-des-kan′ti-a. Spiderwort. Rather weak-stemmed, watery-juiced perennial herbs. About 20 species ranging from e. North America to Argentina.

Description
Leaves long and narrow, or ovalish and stalkless. Flowers whitish, bluish purple, or

even pinkish, and last only one day. Sepals 3, green or colored.

How to Grow
They need well-drained soils and sun or partial shade. Easy to divide in spring; detached joints of stems will usually root in moist, sandy soil.

× ***andersoniana*** *p. 176*
Common Spiderwort. 24–30 in. (60–74 cm) high. Flowers white through pink to blue purple, 1 in. (2.5 cm) wide. Foliage falls over after flowering. Cut foliage back after flowering to produce a neater clump. Cultivars include 'Pauline', with large, pink flowers; and 'Zwaanenberg Blue', with large, blue flowers. Also sold as *T. virginiana.* Zone 5.

hirsuticaulis *p. 216*
To 12 in. (30 cm) high. Leaves covered with stiff hairs. Flowers purple blue, 1 in. (2.5 cm) wide, in terminal umbels. United States. Foliage dies back in summer and reappears in fall. Zone 6.

Tricyrtis
Lily family
Liliaceae

Try-sir′tis. Half-hardy perennial herbs comprising about 12 species, natives of Japan and Taiwan.

Description
Short, thick rootstocks, usually spreading. Leaves alternate, simple, ovalish. Flowers solitary, or in small clusters, large, bell-shaped, whitish or purplish and spotted, starlike when fully open. Calyx of 3 colored sepals. Stamens 6.

How to Grow
The species below needs partial shade and moist, fertile soil that is acid. Propagate by division.

hirta *p. 221*
Toad Lily. To 3 ft. (90 cm) high. Flowers 1 in. (2.5 cm) long, whitish, heavily spotted with purple and black on the inside, in small clusters in axils of leaves. Japan. Flowers are not showy from afar, so choose a site where they can be appreciated. Zone 6.

Trillium
Lily family
Liliaceae

Trill′i-um. Trillium; Wakerobin. Hardy perennial herbs comprising about 30 species, natives of North America and Asia.

Description
Thick, short rootstocks from which arise flowering stalks, bearing scale-like sheathing leaves in a whorl at the base. Leaves ovalish. Flowers pink, white, greenish-white, purplish, or yellow, solitary, short-stalked from the center of the whorl of leaves. Calyx of 3 green sepals. Stamens 6.

How to Grow
Adapted for partially shaded areas of wild gardens, trilliums prefer a deep, rich, moist, acid soil with plenty of humus. Propagate by fall or early spring division.

grandiflorum *p. 249*
Snow Trillium. 12–18 in. (30–45 cm) high. Flowers erect, 2–3 in. (5–7.5 cm) wide, on stalks 3 in. (7.5 cm) long, waxy-white, fading to pink. Quebec to N.C. and Minn. Soil should be consistently moist. Double-flowered forms available. Zone 5.

Trollius
Buttercup family
Ranunculaceae

Trol′i-us. Globeflower. About 20 species of hardy perennial herbs found in damp places throughout the temperate regions of the northern hemisphere.

Description
Rootstocks thick and spreading. Leaves dark or bronzy green, with coarsely toothed lobes. Flowers showy, whitish, orange, yellow, or purple, usually solitary at the ends of the branches. Calyx of 5–15 large, colored, petal-like sepals. Stamens many.

How to Grow
Trollius is easy to grow in cooler regions, and requires moist, boggy soil. Good for sunken gardens and edges of water gardens, although they can grow in flower borders if given similar conditions. Propagate by seeds or division, both in early spring or fall.

europaeus *p. 123*
Common Globeflower. To 2 ft. (60 cm) high. Flowers globular, 1–2 in. (2.5–5.0 cm) across. Sepals and petals lemon-yellow. Europe. Zones 5–6.

ledebourii *p. 106*
Ledebour Globeflower. 2–3 ft. (60–90 cm) high. Flowers orange, 2 in. (5 cm) across. Outer petals characteristically globe-shaped, but inside are narrow, petal-like stamens. Siberia (U.S.S.R.). Cultivar 'Golden Queen' has large, yellow flowers. Zones 5–6.

Uvularia
Lily family
Liliaceae

You-vew-lair′i-a. Bellwort. 5 species of hardy North American perennial herbs.

Description
They have thick creeping rootstocks. Alternate leaves are not stalked, lance-shaped. Flowers bell-shaped or tubular, drooping, solitary, at the ends of the branches. Calyx of 3 colored sepals. Stamens 6.

How to Grow
They are useful plants for borders or wild gardens, and are easy to grow in moist, fertile, slightly acid soil rich in organic matter, and partial to full shade. Propagate by division in fall.

grandiflora *p. 111*
Big Merrybells. To 30 in. (75 cm) high. Flowers yellow, bell-shaped, to 2 in. (5 cm) long, drooping at the ends of the branches. Quebec to Ga. and Okla. Zone 5.

Valeriana
Valerian family
Valerianaceae

Va-leer-i-a′na. About 200 species of perennial herbs, undershrubs, or shrubs, found mostly in the temperate and colder regions of the northern hemisphere and the tropical and warm regions of the southern hemisphere.

Description
Rootstocks thick, spreading, and strong-

scented. Stem leaves lance-shaped. Flowers small, white or rose, in compact roundish clusters at ends of branches. Corolla narrowly tubular. Stamens 3.

How to Grow
Valerianas make good border plants and *V. officinalis* is easy to grow in very moist, well-drained soil in full sun. Propagate by seeds or division in fall or early spring.

officinalis *p. 193*
Common Valerian. 2–4 ft. (60–120 cm) high. Flowers pink, white, or lavender, fragrant, 3/16 in. (5 mm) across. Europe and n. Asia. The roots of this species are used medicinally. Prey to aphids. Zone 5.

Veratrum
Lily family
Liliaceae

Ver-rah′trum. False hellebore. About 45 species of hardy perennial herbs found throughout the northern hemisphere.

Description
Rootstocks thick and highly poisonous. Leaves alternate, clasping the stem, large. Flowers greenish white or purplish, in terminal branching clusters. Calyx of 3 colored sepals. Stamens 6.

How to Grow
Grown in damp, shady borders or wild gardens. Also grown for the extraction of veratrine, a valuable medicine.

viride *p. 79*
American White Hellebore; Indian Poke. 3–7 ft. (90–210 cm) high. Flowers greenish yellow, hairy, to 1 in. (2.5 cm) across, in terminal branching clusters to 2 ft. (60 cm) long. E. North America, and very common in swampy woods. Zones 5–6.

Verbascum
Snapdragon family
Scrophulariaceae

Ver-bas′kum. Mullein. Hardy biennial or perennial herbs, comprising about 250 species found mostly in the Mediterranean region but naturalized throughout the northern hemisphere.

Description
Basal leaves large. Stem leaves smaller. Flowers yellow, tawny red, purple, or white, numerous in showy spikes or racemes. Calyx of 5 sepals. Stamens 5, the filaments covered with showy hairs.

How to Grow
Verbascums are good for large borders or wild gardens. Easy to grow or propagate by seeds in spring, both in light, sandy, well-drained soil in full sun. They do not like wet, cold soil.

chaixii *p. 270*
Chaix Mullein. To 3 ft. (90 cm) high. Flowers ½–1 in. (13–25 mm) wide, yellow with purple hairs on the stamen filaments, in panicles. S. and cen. Europe. Cultivar 'Album' is 3 ft. (90 cm) high, with white flowers and rose stamens. Zone 5.

Verbena
Verbena family
Verbenaceae

Ver-bee'na. Vervain. About 200 species of tender or hardy annual or perennial herbs, mostly natives of America.

Description
Leaves generally opposite. Flowers white, lilac, red, or purple, small, sometimes stalked, in terminal spikes or roundish clusters. Corolla tube long and narrow. Stamens 4.

How to Grow
Verbenas are useful plants for sunny, well-drained borders. Propagate by seeds in early spring. Cuttings taken in early fall assure that a particular color will be retained.

peruviana *p. 151*
3–4 in. (7.5–10 cm) high. Stems prostrate, rooting at the nodes. Flowers bright red, ⅔ in. (16 mm) wide, tubular. S. Brazil to Argentina. Usually grown as an annual. Not hardy in North. Zone 5.

rigida *p. 211*
Vervain. 1–2 ft. (30–60 cm) high. Flowers purplish blue, the dense spikes 1–3 in.

(2.5–7.5 cm) long and 1 in. (2.5 cm) across. Brazil and Argentina. A tender perennial, grown as an annual in northern regions, this plant flowers four months after seeding. Also sold as *V. venosa.* Zone 4.

Veronica
Snapdragon family
Scrophulariaceae

Ver-on′i-ka. Speedwell. A genus of over 250 species of herbs for borders or rock gardens.

Description
Stem leaves usually opposite, upper ones nearly always alternate. Flowers mostly in terminal spikes or racemes. Corolla mostly with a short tube and a spreading, 4- to 5-lobed limb. Stamens 2.

How to Grow
Some are attractive flowering prostrate plants, good for ground cover or edging. All increased by division done after flowering. Most are easy to grow in average well-drained soil, in sun or partial shade.

grandis* var. *holophylla *p. 235*
2–3 ft. (60–90 cm) high. Flowers blue, small, arranged in terminal racemes 6 in. (15 cm) long. Siberia. 'Lavender Charm' has lavender-blue flowers along sturdy spikes. Zone 5.

latifolium *p. 229*
Hungarian Speedwell. 12–18 in. (30–45 cm) high. Flowers blue, ½ in. (13 mm) across, in loose racemes that grow from leaf axils. Cultivar 'Crater Lake Blue' is more compact with bright blue flowers. Zone 4.

spicata *p. 190*
Speedwell. 12–18 in. (30–45 cm) high. Flowers blue, ¼ in. (6 mm) across, on racemes 6 in. (15.0 cm) long. Eurasia. There are many different colored varieties. Zone 4.

virginica *p. 190*
Culver's root; Blackroot. 2–6 ft. (60–180 cm) high. Flowers ⅛ in. (3.2 mm) across, white, in a spike-like raceme 6–8 in. (15–20 cm) long. North America. Cultivar 'Rosea' has pink flowers. Also sold as *Veronicastrum virginicum.* Zone 4.

Viola
Violet family
Violaceae

Vy-o′la. Violet. 500 species of mainly perennial herbs found throughout the temperate regions of the world. This genus includes the violet and the Pansy.

Description
They are low-growing plants, some species producing runners. Leaves basal or growing on the stems. Stem leaves alternate, ovalish. Flowers stalked, solitary, violet, blue, reddish purple, lilac, yellow, or white. Corolla of 5 petals, four arranged in pairs, each pair differing, the lower petal spurred. Stamens 5, with an orange, shield-shaped appendage at the top of each anther.

How to Grow
Most species prefer partial shade and moist, fertile, well-drained soil. They flower best in cooler climates. In winter, mulch. Propagate by seed, by division, or by lifting small plants that grow off runners.

cornuta *p. 172*
Horned Violet. 5–8 in. (12.5–20.0 cm) high. Flowers violet, white, apricot, red, or yellow, 1½ in. (4 cm) across, solitary, stalked, and nodding. Spain and the Pyrenees. Where summers are cool and moist, this species blooms all summer. An organic mulch will keep soil moist. Zone 5.

odorata *p. 204*
Sweet Violet. 6–8 in. (15–20 cm) high, producing long runners. Flowers ¾–1 in. (2–2.5 cm) wide, deep violet or white, sweet-scented, the spur short. Europe, Africa, and Asia. Cultivar 'Royal Robe' has dark purple flowers; 'Alba' is a white form. Cultivar 'Pallida Plena', Neapolitan Violet, has pale lavender double flowers. Var. 'Marie Louise' is also double-flowered with reddish-purple flowers. Zone 5.

striata *p. 248*
Striped Violet. 4–16 in. (10.0–40.5 cm) high. Flowers small, fragrant, ivory-white but veined brown-purple. U.S. Prefers moist, well-drained, and partially shady sites. Zone 5.

Waldsteinia
Rose family
Rosaceae

Wald-sty′ni-a. A small genus of strawberrylike herbs of the rose family, closely related to the strawberry but with dry, hairy fruits.

Description
Plants have creeping rhizomes. Most leaves basal, 3–5 lobed or divided, with toothed or notched tips. Flowers are small, with 5 petals and 5 sepals, and look like yellow strawberry flowers.

How to Grow
Grows easily in both sun and shade, but soil should be well-drained. In hot summers water to keep lush. Propagate by dividing the underground rhizomes.

ternata *p. 121*
Barren Strawberry. 6–12 in. (15–30 cm) high. Evergreen; leaves glossy. Flowers ½ in. (13 mm) across, yellow, borne on a 3- to 8-flowered stem 8 in. (20 cm) long. Central Europe. The flowers are sterile. Zone 4.

Yucca
Agave family
Agavaceae

Yuck′a. About 40 species of chiefly Mexican semidesert plants, a few cultivated in the southern states and West Indies for their striking flower clusters.

Description
Most are stemless, with a basal rosette of tough, leathery leaves. Flowers white (rarely, purple-tinged), waxy, nodding, usually fragrant at night (some blooming only at night), and borne in showy, erect, terminal panicles. Stamens 6.

How to Grow
All do best in well-drained sandy loam, in full sun, and are propagated by seeds or offsets.

filamentosa *p. 92*
Adam's Needle. The most common yucca in cultivation in the East. Practically stemless, the stalk of the flower cluster may be 3–15 ft

(0.9–4.5 m) high; although usually it is 4–5 ft. (1.2–1.5 m) high. Flowers white or cream-white, 2 in. (5 cm) long. Del. to Fla. and Miss. There is also a form with variegated leaves. Zone 5.

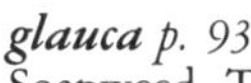

glauca *p. 93*
Soapweed. Trunk short, usually prostrate. Leaves nearly 3 ft. (90 cm) long, white-margined. Flowers greenish white, 2 in. (5 cm) long. N. Mex. northward to Iowa and S. Dak.; one of the hardiest. Zone 5.

Zantedeschia

Arum family
Araceae

Zan-tee-desh′ee-a. Calla lily. A group of tropical herbs, quite different from the genus *Calla.* Calla lilies are popular florists' flowers, widely used for decoration.

Description
They have thick rootstocks and basal, long-stalked leaves that are chiefly arrowhead-shaped or more or less oval heart-shaped. They are grown mostly for the showy, solitary spathes, which are beautifully colored and suggest a large corolla.

How to Grow
North of zone 7, start plants in pots in early spring; keep moist until growth starts, then water moderately. Gradually increase watering so that soil is constantly moist when plant is in full leaf. Plant outside in full sun for flowering in early spring and summer. After flowering, feed weekly with liquid fertilizer. Stop watering in midsummer. North of zone 7, lift rhizome each fall.

aethiopica *p. 248*
Calla Lily. 1–3 ft. (30–90 cm) high. Spathe 5–9 in. (12.5–22.5 cm) long, brilliantly white, surrounding a conspicuous yellow spadix. South Africa. Fragrant. Zone 7.

Appendices

Garden Design

Any garden is the product of its owner, its designer, and the person who maintains it. In real life, most of us play all of these roles at once. A good design must therefore be suited to the site selected by the owner as well as to the time and energy of the person who maintains it.

Whether you start with a new plot of land or a preexisting garden, the first step is to draw a base map. This is a simple sketch that tells you what is on the property and enables you to determine where to place your perennials. The easiest method is to draw an outline of the property using a piece of graph paper. Note the distance between the corners and indicate north with an arrow. Then draw in the major features of the property, including such things as the area occupied by the house, garage, outbuildings, walks, driveway, fences, walls, hedges, and trees.

When you have completed the base map, make a fresh copy if necessary and photocopy it for future use. On a separate piece of paper note sites that offer extra protection and those that receive full sun in the winter. You should also be aware of any area that absorbs heat reflected from the walls and pavement in the summer. Each of these areas is a microclimate that may welcome plants that normally would not thrive in the general conditions of your garden, or might otherwise influence the hardiness of the garden perennials.

Mark any rock outcroppings, high areas, low areas, or spots that appear to have poor drainage. Indicate windy sites, poor views, and areas that receive heavy or light shade. You should also note the materials of which the walks, driveway, walls, and buildings are made; this will help you to choose suitable plants.

Studying the Site

Before you decide where to put your perennial beds, study the space you have and determine the functions you would like each area to serve. Walk around your land, sit in the yard and on the terrace, and look out of the windows of your house to get a sense of how the property should be used. Keeping in mind your life-style, ask yourself the following questions: Where will the trash be placed? Where will the children play? How do guests approach the house? What views do you want to preserve or hide? All of these questions should be addressed relative to existing plantings as well as those you wish to cultivate. Now look at light and shade patterns. Where is there full sun in the morning and afternoon? Where is it sunny all day? Where is there partial shade in the morning, afternoon, and all day? Where is there shade all day? Be sure to observe the shadows cast by the house, fences, walls, trees, and other structures.

How to Use Perennials

The traditional way to grow perennials is in a formal border or flower garden where there is a backdrop such as a wall, hedge, or shrub planting. In such a design the plants are arranged with the tallest in the back and the shortest in the front. Perennials may also be used in island beds, set into the lawn, although these require extra maintenance since the grass must be cut and trimmed on all sides. In these beds, the taller plants are placed in the center and all plants are graded from the tall center to the low edges.

Perennials may also be grouped by specialty use or to suit a specific site. You can have alpine plants in a rock garden, bog plants in a wet area, meadow flowers in a field, or a ground-cover planting under trees or on slopes where grass does not grow or is too difficult to cut. When you choose to use a plant as a ground cover, you must consider not only the color and size of the flowers but the color of the foliage and the size, durability, and overall interest of the plant. Ground covers are usually planted in large masses.

If you have a small area or just a terrace or balcony, you can grow perennials in containers and planters. The problem with these, however, is winter hardiness. In these containers all but the hardiest of perennials will require some form of protection against the winter or need replanting on an annual basis. Insulating the container or moving it to an unheated area out of the wind is usually sufficient. Containers must have adequate drainage and should be large enough to prevent the plants from blowing over in the wind and drying out. Avoid dark colors because they retain excessive heat. Garden containers also work well as accents or in areas where it is impossible to grow perennials in the ground.

Plant Selection

Late winter is a good time to start thinking about new plants for your garden. When the catalogues begin arriving, look through them and make notes on the plants that interest you. Consider the color, height, spread, time of bloom, and special growing requirements of each plant. This information will be helpful in planning the sequence of bloom for your garden. Although the peak bloom will be in May and June, carefully selecting the plants now will give you flowers throughout the growing season. The earliest bloom in the perennial garden comes from bulbs, which can be planted between large clumps of plants and behind plants like irises. The foliage of the perennials hides the dying foliage of the bulbs. The same is true of plants like poppies, which die back in the summer. They should therefore be planted where they will not leave large holes in the border when the foliage dies back. Place them behind plants that do not begin to grow until late in the season (asters or plants with architectural foliage like peonies or iris). Or surround them with annuals.

The easiest way to keep track of what blooms when is by recording the information in your garden journal or on a sheet of paper during each month of the growing season. Write the month at the top of the page and list the plants that bloom that month. If you want to be very methodical, make columns across the page to note

Garden Design

To make a base map, draw an outline of your property on a piece of graph paper, then draw in the house, any outbuildings, driveways, fences, trees and bushes, and any preexisting flower beds. Indicate the northern point of a compass with an arrow. Make several copies of your base map and store the original in a safe place.

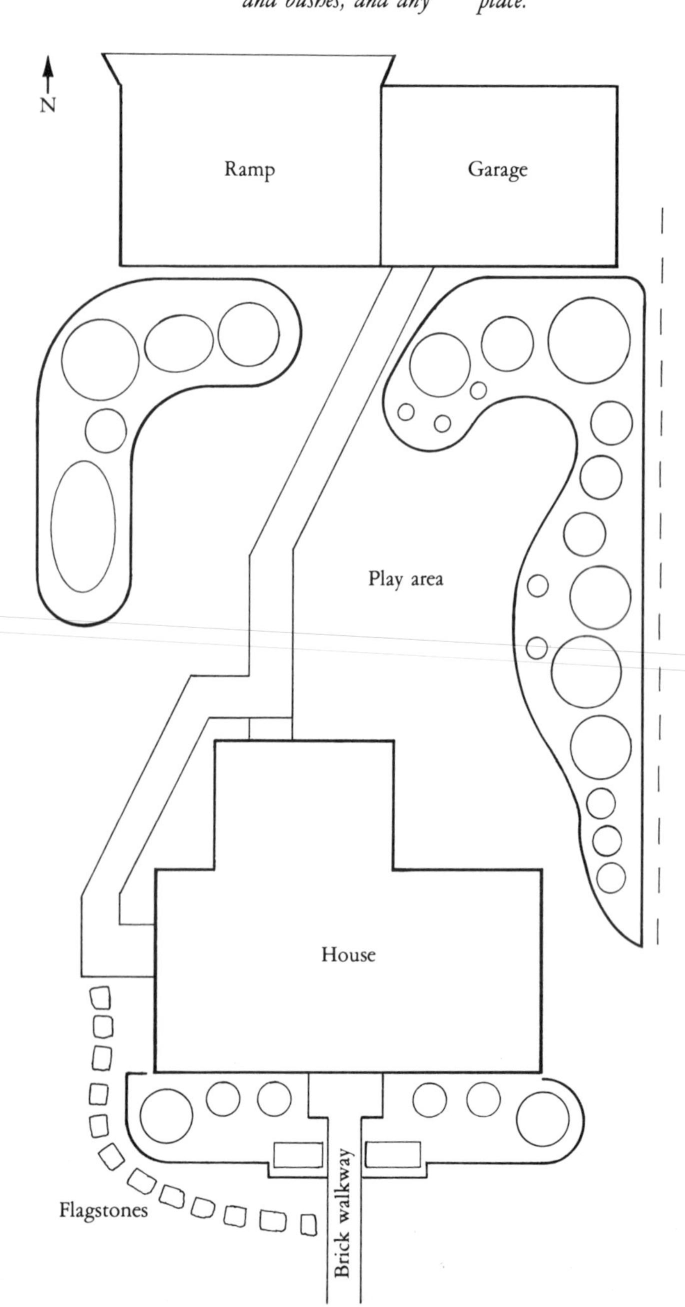

On a clean copy of your base map, indicate which areas receive strong sun, which are cast in shade, and which have partial sun. Indicate, too, windy spots, protected spots, views that you want to hide, areas that are poorly drained, and those that are elevated. Use this information to select suitable plants for your garden.

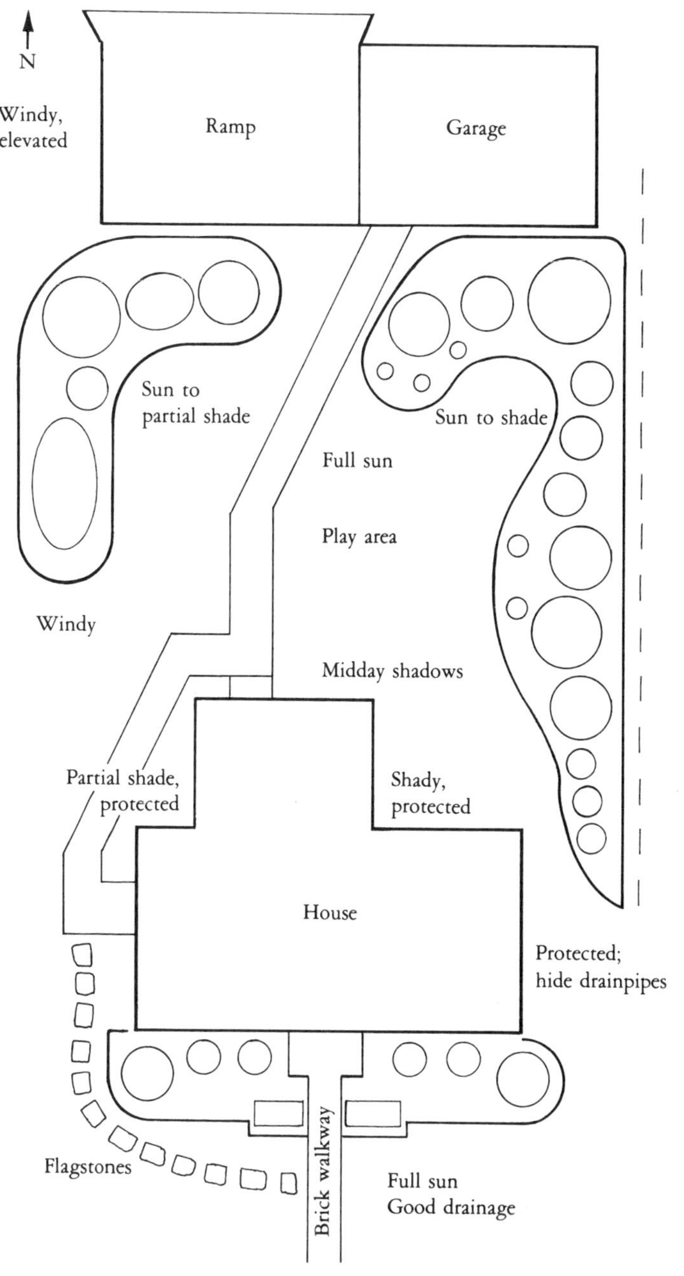

such features as color, height, and spread. These sheets will then form a blueprint for arranging the plants in the garden.

Color

The choice of color combinations is essentially a personal one, but there are some basic facts that can help you decide what colors to use in the garden. Perennials, which bloom at different times throughout the growing season, allow you to vary the color scheme. It can be yellow and red in the spring fading to blue, pink, and white in the summer and ending with deep reds, bronzes, and yellow-golds in the fall.

Colors are grouped in two basic categories, the warm colors and the cool colors. Warm colors are reds, oranges, and yellows. They are also known as advancing colors because they draw the eye and make the object seem closer than it really is. The cool colors are blue, violet, and green. They are known as receding colors because they make the objects appear farther away. Careful use of these groups can make a small space seem larger or a larger space closer. Colors that offer great contrast, such as red and green or blue and orange, can add drama to a garden. Colors that are closely related, such as blue and violet or red and orange, are more harmonious. Pastels tend to be more subtle, and white can offset harsh contrasts. If you plan to use large masses of brilliant colors and you do not want a lot of drama, separate the colors with green foliage, silvery foliage, or white flowers. These will soften the dramatic effect. Sun and shadow also affect color. Shadow darkens tones; sun intensifies them.

Putting It Together

Once you have completed your base map, listed the plants of your choice, and decided on the colors you like, it can all be put together. Make sure you have a good mix of flower shapes and foliage. In the perennial garden, foliage offers interest and acts as a background for the flowers. Since foliage usually lasts longer than flowers, you will want to give this feature of your design careful consideration. Place the names of the selected plants on the base map in their appropriate location. Based on the number of square feet designated for that plant, and the recommended spacing, calculate how many plants you need and place your orders.

The greatest challenge, and delight, to the gardener is time. A garden changes with time—the time of day during which you view the garden, the season of the year, or the chronological age of the garden. Time is the compound element that challenges the gardener in the execution of his or her design. And one of the most satisfying things about gardening with perennials is that you can dig them up and move them around, changing the garden to accommodate new plants or ideas. If a low-maintenance garden interests you, simply leave the original planting alone. But if you love to make changes, perennials are more than willing to cooperate.

Cut Flowers

One of the most satisfying by-products of a flourishing perennial garden is having a supply of beautifully fresh, seasonally changing flowers to cut for the house. You don't have to study flower arranging or follow formal rules of design in order to create lovely bouquets, but there are certain tools and tricks that will make the process easier and the end result more successful.

Cut your flowers in the cool of the day, either early in the morning or late in the afternoon, not in the heat of midday. Use a sharp knife or a pair of floral scissors.

Take a pail of slightly warm water to the garden with you and put the flowers into the water as you cut them. Flowers that never get a chance to wilt when they are first cut will last much longer in an arrangement. There are a couple of exceptions to this rule. Poppies and other flowers with thick sap must have their stems seared with a flame before they are put into water. The stems of lilacs and other woody plants should be smashed with a hammer after cutting; this is done to expose as much stem area as possible to the water. Keep your pail of flowers in a cool room away from direct sunlight until you are ready to arrange them. At that time, strip off any foliage that would otherwise be under water feeding the bacteria that prey on cut flowers. If you change the water and recut the stems every day or so, you will get maximum life from your arrangement. If your flowers reach perfection on Tuesday and you want them for a Saturday party, cut them just before they open fully and put them into water in the refrigerator. Put them into fresh water after you bring them out.

Containers and Supplies

Anything that holds water can be used for flowers—a teacup, a French mustard jar, a wine carafe, a pitcher, or a bottle—but the right vase will enhance any arrangement. Silver and crystal are formal. Copper and brass suit the fall tones of bronze, yellow, and deep red, but they are usually unattractive set next to spring pastels. Clear glass is always appropriate, but it won't work if you want to hide the stems or a stem holder. Ceramic vases are generally the most versatile and are always suitable and easy to use. Remember that the best containers are the simplest, those that attract little attention and at the same time add to the overall appearance of the arrangement.

The narrower the opening at the neck of the vase, the easier the flowers are to arrange. If you use a widemouthed container, you will need some type of holder to anchor the flowers. Pin holders work best for low bowls. The pins anchor the stems, and where there are enough foliage and flowers, the anchor is hidden. Another easy holder is florist's Oasis, a soft, water-absorbent foam that can make anyone a pro. But be sure the Oasis is soaking wet and heavy before you use it. If you can't fit it tightly into the bowl by cutting it to shape, you may have to put two strips of tape across the top to keep

Cut Flowers

When you arrange flowers, the vase you use is almost as important as the flowers you select. Low, rounded vases are a good choice for large, rounded arrangements.

Simple crockery containers are ideal for daisies and other casual flowers.

Cylindrical glass containers set off the handsome profile of exotic, lily-like flowers, while both crystal and silver vases are perfect for elegant, sophisticated arrangements.

a very heavy arrangement anchored. Long, narrow-necked vases rarely require anchoring material.

Types of Arrangements

Great arrangements do not have to be large masses of bold foliage or flowers. A single flower in a bud vase, or a few field flowers in a jar on the kitchen table can be charming and effective. In general, the height of an arrangement should be in proportion to the size of the container and the space in which it is placed. A good rule of thumb is to make the arrangement two and a half times the height of the container. This, of course, depends upon the width and the type of container. If you're using a bud vase, the arrangement may be lower; if it's a low ceramic bowl, a higher arrangement is in order.

Arrangements are generally vertical, horizontal, circular, or triangular in shape. Vertical arrangements, as exemplified by *ikebana,* the Japanese style of flower arranging, are simple and modernistic and often used in modern, stark, or narrow spaces. Horizontal arrangements are quieter and less dramatic. They are good for viewing from above and, together with circular arrangements, are ideal as centerpieces. Circular arrangements, which are seen from all sides, are best as centerpieces or on small tables where they can be viewed from above. The most widely used arrangement is triangular, which can be adapted to most settings. One-sided triangular arrangements—symmetrical or asymmetrical—are used for mantles, entranceways, or dining tables.

Regardless of the shape or style, arrangements should not be too frail or too bulky for their location or contain flowers that are too heavy for delicate containers. It's a good idea to put the arrangement where you'd like to have it before you add the last flowers. If you haven't picked enough, you can always pick a few more.

Designing with Flowers

Good designs are patterns of lines, masses, and open spaces. Leave spaces between the flowers to avoid a two-dimensional look. The stems should angle to a central point to create a flow. Imagine the arrangement is a hand-held bouquet. Could you tie a ribbon at the base of the stems and hold the arrangement in your hand unchanged? If not, the stem angle is wrong and the arrangement may be too flat.

Color also sets the mood for the arrangement. The hot colors—reds, yellows, and oranges—draw the eye and make the flowers look closer; while the cool ones—blues, violets, and greens—make the arrangement recede. For a more dramatic effect, try the shocking contrast of blue and orange; for animation, orange, green, and violet; for harmony, use pastels.

The easiest way to learn is to do. Look at magazines, florists' windows, and the homes of friends, then experiment. Above all, enjoy working with flowers.

Calendar

There is no such thing as a totally maintenance-free garden, but once established, perennials are among the most carefree of plants. Still, if you want to keep them in peak condition, there are certain tasks that must be performed. Think of these as guidelines rather than as hard-and-fast rules; your own enthusiasm for gardening and an understanding of local environmental conditions will help to determine how conscientious you need to be.

This calendar is arranged according to the months of the year and is divided into four sections: the North, the Northwest, the South, and the Southwest.

Use common sense when you determine the area in which you live. If your garden is in Virginia, it lies in what we refer to as the South. If the winter has been very harsh, however, refer to the information given for the North as you plan your gardening activities.

Don't be too rigid planning your monthly gardening tasks either. If you live in the North and the winter has been exceptionally mild, you may be able to step up your gardening activities by as much as six weeks.

Remember, the dates of the first and last frosts in your region are always the best indicators of when winter actually begins and spring ends.

North

Here the North encompasses a large area of the country: the states of the Northeast, south through Maryland, north to the Ohio River, and west to the Rockies.

January

As winter swirls outside, new garden catalogues will begin to arrive, and gardeners, eager for spring, can now review last year's notes and plan which seeds and plants to purchase for the coming season. Keep in mind how much space is available for starting seeds; plants may be more practical. Check your winter mulch, adding additional amounts if necessary. Old Christmas tree branches help to prevent loose mulches from being scattered by the wind.

February

On mild days, prune deciduous background shrubs, but be careful not to step on the crowns of perennials while you work. If any plants have heaved from the ground as a result of alternate freezing and thawing, carefully press them back into the soil and add extra protective mulch. Sharpen and repair your garden tools and order new ones if necessary. Make sure you have adequate peat pots and growing medium for starting seeds. Look for early-blooming bulbs like *Galanthus* (snowdrops) and *Eranthus* (winter aconite), and early plants like *Helleborus* (Christmas rose).

March
As your seed packages begin to arrive, mark them with the date they are to be sown and store them in a cool area. Indoors, sow those that are to be moved outdoors after the last frost. Plants should be unpacked immediately and checked for damage, disease, or other problems. If you can't plant them right away, keep them damp, but not wet, and store them in a cool place until you can get them into the ground. Discard coarse mulches like straw and Christmas tree branches when the weather begins to warm and the wind has died down. Remove the mulch from perennials that are beginning to grow and add it to the compost pile. Fertilize perennials if the ground has thawed. If any perennials that are beginning to grow need transplanting, this is the time to start doing it. Cut ornamental grasses to the ground at the end of the month.

April
Remove all winter debris and remaining mulches and add them to the compost pile. If necessary, continue to transplant perennials, beginning with those that flower first. Make sure the beds are well prepared before the perennials are transplanted. Begin staking plants that need support as they start to grow. Watch for early signs of disease or insect problems. Seeds started last month may be ready for thinning or transplanting, either to cold frames or the garden.

May
Sow seeds of perennials outdoors, making sure the seedbed contains adequate organic matter. Perennial and biennial seeds can be sown from now through September to produce stout plants for next year's flowering. Fertilize peonies early this month with a complete fertilizer and disbud the stems, allowing only the top bud to remain. Make sure flowering peony stems are staked to keep the flowers from falling to the ground when it rains.

June
This is the month to enjoy the flowers that now reward your effort and care. Remove the spent blossoms and the foliage of early-blooming perennials and bulbs that have turned yellow. Transplant young perennials to the garden from pots, seedbeds, and frames. Pinch chrysanthemums and similar plants to encourage side branch development. Watch for slugs.

July
Watering and weeding are major concerns; mulch will facilitate both. Soak the garden, remove the weeds, and then mulch to retain moisture and reduce weed-seed germination. Sow delphinium seeds for next year's bloom. Dig and divide bearded irises. Watch for sudden storms that can break off improperly staked perennials. Chrysanthemums should be given their final pinch.

August
Perennials that have finished blooming can be cut back, but leave some foliage. Cut any flowers or grasses you want to dry. Complete plans for fall planting and order spring-flowering bulbs.

September
Prepare beds for fall planting, working organic matter into the soil. Divide and transplant early-blooming perennials. If they are big enough, transplant seedlings to their permanent location.

October
Clean up garden litter and add it to the compost pile. To kill perennial weeds, cultivate all areas from which frost-killed foliage was removed. Clean and bind all stakes into bundles for use next year.

November
Finish the garden cleanup. Collect materials for winter mulching, but don't add them to the beds until the ground has frozen. Tools and equipment should be winterized. Clean and check them before they are put into storage. Make sure the supports of all vines are strong enough to avoid physical injury from winter winds.

December
Most of the work for the year is finished. If weather permits, do a final garden cleanup. Plan to mulch with evergreen branches at the end of the month. Leave the brown foliage of ornamental grasses for winter interest.

Northwest
The Northwest extends from the Rocky Mountain states west to the Pacific.

January
The garden catalogues have arrived and it is not too early to send in your first seed orders. Check your seed-starting supplies and equipment. Review last year's garden notes and transcribe significant dates and reminders to yourself into a new journal.

February
Start seeds indoors. When the danger of frost has passed, plant bulbs like lilies outdoors.

March
Planting of perennials should begin this month. Remove the seed heads of early-blooming bulbs, but leave the foliage to ripen. Sow seeds of slower growing perennials.

April
Fertilize perennials before new growth begins. Sow seeds of late-blooming perennials, take cuttings of chrysanthemums, and plant tender bulbs, such as gladioli, that are used as fillers.

May
All pinching of perennials to encourage branching should be done this month. Seeds of perennials and biennials for bloom next year can be sown through August. Remove yellowed foliage of spring-flowering bulbs; the bulbs can be lifted and stored for replanting in the fall. Remove dead flowerheads of early bloomers.

June
Remove spent flowers from early bloomers and stake and mulch late bloomers. Watch for pest problems.

July
Divide and replant early-blooming perennials like primroses. Stake tall late bloomers like asters. You can continue to plant chrysanthemums until the middle of the month.

August
Dig and replant irises, Shasta daisies, poppies, and other spring-flowering perennials. Plant fall-blooming bulbs.

September
Begin fall cleanup. Add leaves and plant rubbish to the compost pile. Dig up and transplant perennials like peonies. Plant fall-blooming bulbs and lilies as well as seedlings of flowers like foxgloves, primroses, and Canterbury bells.

October
Mulch fall-planted perennials. If the weather is still mild you can continue to plant. Plant spring-blooming bulbs.

November
Cut back the tops of dormant perennials. Leave the tops of those that are green. In milder areas the remaining perennials can be transplanted. Mulch new plantings.

December
Do a general garden cleanup. Protect late-planted material with a mulch. Prepare plans for seed orders. Plant the last of the spring-flowering bulbs.

South

Here, the South includes all states from Virginia south to the Gulf of Mexico and west to the Louisiana/Texas border.

January

In warmer areas, it is time to plant the early lily bulbs. Soil can be prepared for later planting.

February

Transplant perennials before the new growth is too advanced. Begin a fertilization program. Sow seeds of late varieties.

March

Most perennials can be dug up and divided this month. Mulch plants that are beginning to grow, keeping the mulch off the crown. You can begin to set out young seedlings.

April

Seedlings can be transplanted from the frames to the garden. Set out plants like chrysanthemums and pinch back the tops to induce branching. Watch for the development of disease and insect problems, and keep the weeds under control.

May

Protect young plants set out earlier from strong sun and wind. Mulch plants to conserve moisture. Take cuttings of chrysanthemums and start new plants for bloom next year. Seeds can be sown from now until July.

June

Finish mulching. Watch for diseases that flourish as humidity rises. Crabgrass control should begin now; most of it can be removed from the flower beds by hand. Water thoroughly as needed.

July

Cuttings can be taken this month. Transplant bearded irises. Disbud chrysanthemums and stake late-flowering plants. Continue to remove spent flowers.

August

Fertilize fall-blooming plants and give chrysanthemums their final pinch. Divide and transplant day lilies, Shasta daisies, and other perennials when they finish blooming.

September

Divide and transplant perennials that flower in early summer. Fertilize chrysanthemums for the last time when the buds begin to show. Prepare all garden areas for fall planting.

October
Divide remaining perennials. Plant spring-flowering bulbs and remove any perennial weeds from the beds. Check the seedlings that were transplanted.

November
Clean up plants that have died back. Clean all tools and check them for repairs. Sow seeds of plants like *Gaillardia* and early perennials. Mulch newly planted perennials.

December
This is the last cleanup of the season. Remove the dead foliage of dormant plants. Check the mulch on all plantings.

Southwest
The Southwest extends from Texas through Arizona, New Mexico, and all of California.

January
Plant perennials this month and divide and transplant early bloomers.

February
This is the month for planting. Soak all newly planted perennials to ensure that the soil is kept moist.

March
Fertilize perennials. Plant lily bulbs outside. Mulch growing plants and keep them watered.

April
Pinch plants and continue to fertilize perennials. Plant chrysanthemums. Delphiniums and other plants in the cold frame can be set out.

May
Start chrysanthemums from cuttings to increase the number of plants that bloom in the fall. Pinch plants in the garden. Irrigate all plants, and when the soil is thoroughly moist, mulch to conserve moisture. Stake large perennials that will bloom later in the season.

June
Water conservation is very important. Check all mulch and add more if necessary. Stake late-blooming plants. Protect young plants from extreme heat.

July
Spring flowering bulbs can be dug up and stored for replanting in the fall. Remove the yellowed foliage of those that are to remain in the garden. Sow seeds of columbines and primroses, and divide the bearded irises. Give plants a dose of liquid fertilizer.

August
Prepare orders for fall planting of perennials from seeds and bulbs. Cut back leggy plants to encourage new growth.

September
Order spring bulbs for planting in October. Keep all areas watered. Plant seedlings of early-season perennials.

October
Plant late-flowering spring bulbs like tulips and narcissus. Plant seedlings to add winter color.

November
Remove all plant litter and add it to the compost pile. Transplant remaining perennials, cutting back the tops. Mulch new plantings.

December
Be prepared for unusual frosts: Protect tender perennials. Plant early-blooming perennials and clean up plants that are dormant.

Garden Diary

Keeping track of seed orders, weather conditions, and what bloomed where in last year's garden doesn't have to involve a lot of paper work, but a few carefully thought-out notes are invaluable. The easiest way to keep your notes is to record them in a garden diary or journal.

Getting Started

A notebook, loose-leaf or bound, or anything similar can serve as a journal. Many gardeners prefer to keep their records in a loose-leaf binder that lies flat when it is opened. Good journal notes include not only the tasks you performed, the weather, and the day the seeds arrived, but your feelings about the garden. Did you like the color of the new astilbe? Did the fragrance of the old-fashioned lavender in the potpourri last? Were the delphiniums as tall as you would have liked? A journal is a personal account of your garden.

You can add entries every day, once a week, or whenever you have something to record. They need not be fancy or rigid in format, but they should be neat so you can read them at a later date. It also helps to be consistent in the type of entries you make. You then have a basis of comparison from one year to the next.

Plant and Seed Orders

Record plant and seed orders. If you have a plant that is of special interest to you or a friend, you can then find out where you obtained it. The copy will also serve as a checklist against the actual plants or seeds received. It is a method of ensuring that plants received are the same as those ordered.

Mapping Your Garden

Another important document is a base map of the garden. It will help you to locate where you originally planted the red sedum that has somehow walked across the garden. Instructions for drawing a base map are on page 422.

Whenever you move a plant, take note of it in case the label gets lost or misplaced. In these days of multitudinous cultivars, labels are a necessity, at least until you learn the name and location of each plant by heart and can recall them from year to year. The best type is a 3-inch wooden label. Using an indelible pen or lead pencil, write the name of the plant on the label in full. Place the label in the center of the planting where it can be seen but isn't too obvious. Check periodically to be sure it hasn't been dug up.

Once you have used your journal, it will be easier for you to design your own format. Be sure it is neat and, above all, that the entries are dated. These records will serve not only as a history of your garden, but as a history of you the gardener.

Typical Entries

Weather	Note such unusual features as late or early frosts, heavy rain and wind, or hailstorms, plus high and low temperatures, humidity levels, and the date of each rainfall.
Propagation records	Record when seeds were planted, what cuttings were taken and how many rooted, how long it took, the method you used to root them, when you divided peonies or other plants.
Flower records	Note the new varieties that you plant and describe how they perform. Would you plant them again? Recommend them to a friend?
Pests and diseases	Which pests and diseases plagued your garden and how did you treat them? What was used, how much, and when?
Soil improvement	Log all the soil improvements you make and record the results of any soil tests.
Fertilizers	Which did you use, how much, and when?
Colors	What colors did you like? Which would you change and where? Make a note to move that pink aster away from the yellow mums.
Bloom duration	How long did a plant stay in flower? When did flowers first appear and when were they all spent?
Accomplishments	What did you grow that was "impossible," new, or exciting?
Advice	What did fellow gardeners suggest that you do? What worked and what didn't?
Personal events	Record personal experiences. How your son helped you weed and pulled out all the *Heleniums* because he thought they were dandelions.
Books and articles	Keep a record of gardening articles that you may want to refer to again. Note as well any new books that have appeared that you want to read.

Pests & Diseases

Because plant pests and diseases are a fact of life for a gardener, it is helpful to become familiar with common pests and diseases in your area and to learn how to control them.

Symptoms of Plant Problems
Because the same general symptoms are associated with many diseases and pests, some experience is needed to determine their causes.

Diseases
Both fungi and bacteria are responsible for a variety of diseases ranging from leafspots and wilts to root rot, but bacterial diseases usually make the affected plant tissues appear wetter than fungi do. Diseases caused by viruses and mycoplasma, often transmitted by aphids and leafhoppers, display such symptoms as mottled yellow or deformed leaves and stunted growth.

Insect Pests
Numerous insects attack plants. Sap-sucking insects—including aphids, leafhoppers, and scale insects—suck plant juices. The affected plant becomes yellow, stunted, and misshapen. Aphids and scale insects produce honeydew, a sticky substance that attracts ants and sooty mold fungus growth. Other pests with rasping-sucking mouthparts, such as thrips and spider mites, scrape plant tissue and then suck the juices that well up in the injured areas.
Leaf-chewers, namely beetles and caterpillars, consume plant leaves, whole or in part. Leafminers make tunnels within the leaves, creating brown trails and causing leaf tissue to dry. In contrast, borers tunnel into shoots and stems, and their young larvae consume plant tissue, weakening the plant. Some insects, such as various grubs and maggots, feed on roots, weakening or killing the plant.

Nematodes
Microscopic roundworms called nematodes are other pests that attack roots and cause stunting and poor plant growth. Some nematodes produce galls on roots and others produce them on leaves.

Environmental Stresses
Some types of plant illness result from environment-related stress, such as severe wind, drought, flooding, or extreme cold. Other problems are caused by salt toxicity, rodents, birds, nutritional deficiencies or excesses, pesticides, or damage from lawnmowers. Many of these injuries are avoidable if you take proper precautions.

Controlling Plant Problems
Always buy healthy disease- and insect-free plants, and select resistant varieties when available. Check leaves and stems for dead areas or

off-color and stunted tissue. Later, when you plant your flowers, be sure to prepare the soil properly.

Routine Preventives

By cultivating the soil routinely you will expose insects and disease-causing organisms to the sun and thus lessen their chances of surviving in your garden. In the fall be sure to destroy infested or diseased plants, remove dead leaves and flowers, and clean up plant debris. Do not add diseased or infested material to the compost pile. Spray plants with water from time to time to dislodge insect pests and remove suffocating dust. Pick off the larger insects by hand. To discourage fungal leafspots and blights, always water plants in the morning and allow the leaves to dry off before nightfall. For the same reason, provide adequate air circulation around leaves and stems by spacing plants properly.

Weeds provide a home for insects and diseases, so pull them up or use herbicides. But do not apply herbicides, including "weed-and-feed" lawn preparations, too close to flower beds. Herbicide injury may cause elongated, straplike, or downward-cupping leaves. Spray weed-killers when there is little air movement, but not on a very hot, dry day.

Insecticides and Fungicides

To protect plant tissue from injury due to insects and diseases, a number of insecticides and fungicides are available. However, few products control diseases due to bacteria, viruses, and mycoplasma. Pesticides are usually either "protectant" or "systemic" in nature. Protectants protect uninfected foliage from insects or disease organisms, while systemics move through the plant and provide some therapeutic or eradicant action as well as protection. Botanical insecticides such as pyrethrum and rotenone have a shorter residual effect on pests, but are considered less toxic and generally safer for the user and the environment than inorganic chemical insecticides. Biological control through the use of organisms like *Bacillus thuringiensis* (a bacterium toxic to moth and butterfly larvae) is effective and safe.

Recommended pesticides may vary to some extent from region to region. Consult your local Cooperative Extension Service or plant professional regarding the appropriate material to use. Always check the pesticide label to be sure that it is registered for use on the pest and plant with which you are dealing. Follow the label concerning safety precautions, dosage, and frequency of application.

Recognizing Pests and Diseases

Learning to recognize the insects and diseases that plague garden plants is a first step toward controlling them. The chart on the following pages describes the most common pests and diseases that attack perennials, the damage they cause, and control measures.

Pest

Aphids

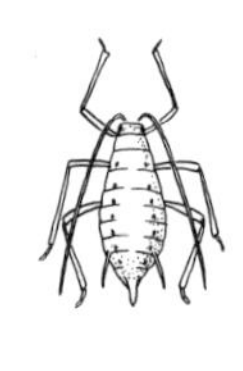

Leaf-feeding Beetles

Leaf-feeding Caterpillars

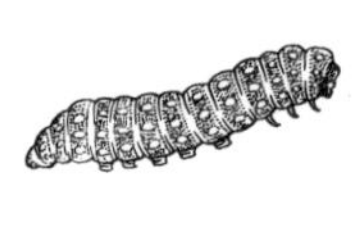

Leafhoppers

Leafminers

Description	*Damage*	*Controls*
Tiny green, brown, or reddish, pear-shaped, soft-bodied insects in clusters on buds, shoots, and undersides of leaves.	Suck plant juices, causing stunted or deformed blooms and leaves. Some transmit plant viruses. Secretions attract ants.	Spray with strong stream of water, insecticidal soap, sabadilla, neem extract, or rotenone/pyrethrin. Encourage beneficial insects, such as lacewings and parasitic wasps.
Hard-shelled, oval to oblong insects on leaves, stems, and flowers.	Chew plant parts leaving holes. Larvae of some feed on roots.	Handpick and destroy. Spray with sabadilla, rotenone, or rotenone/pyrethrin mix.
Soft-bodied, wormlike crawling insects with several pairs of legs. May be smooth, hairy, or spiny. Adults are moths or butterflies.	Consume part or all of leaves. Flowers and shoots may also be eaten.	Handpick and destroy. Spray with *Bacillus thuringiensis,* neem extract, or rotenone/pyrethrin.
Small, greenish, wedge-shaped, soft-bodied insects on undersides of leaves. Quickly hop when disturbed.	Suck plant juices, causing discolored leaves and plants. Some transmit plant virus and mycoplasma diseases.	Spray with sabadilla, horticultural oil, insecticidal soap, or pyrethrum. Dust with diatomaceous earth. Trap with yellow sticky traps.
Small pale larvae of flies or beetles. Feed between leaf surfaces.	Leaves show yellow, then brown, oval or meandering papery blotches. Leaves may drop.	Remove badly infested leaves. Often kept in check by natural enemies. Spray with horticultural oil or neem extract.

Pest

Nematodes

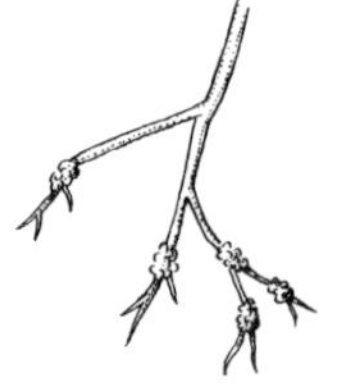

Plant Bugs

Scale

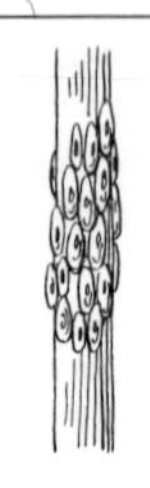

Slugs and Snails

Spider Mites

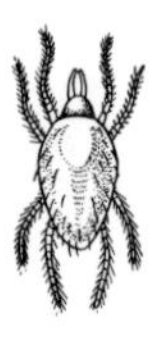

Description	Damage	Controls
Microscopic roundworms, usually associated with roots. Cause various diseases.	Stunted, off-color plants that do not respond to water or fertilizer. Minute galls may be present on roots.	Remove and destroy badly infested plants. Plant nematode-resistant stock. Treat soil with plenty of organic matter, Clandosan, beneficial nematodes, or neem extract.
Oblong, flattened, greenish-yellow insects, ¼–⅓ inch long. Some with black stripes. Wings held flat over abdomen.	Suck plant juices, causing spots on leaves. Some deform roots and shoots.	Spray with sabadilla, insecticidal soap, or rotenone/pyrethrin.
Small, waxy, soft or hard-bodied stationary insects on shoots and leaves. May be red, white, brown, black, or gray.	Suck plant juices, causing stunted, off-color plants. May cover large portion of cane.	Prune off badly infested plant parts. Spray with insecticidal soap or horticultural oil. Release lacewings.
Gray, slimy, soft-bodied mollusks with or without a hard outer shell. Leave slime trails on leaves; found in damp places.	Feed at night, rasping holes in leaves.	Handpick. Eliminate hiding places. Protect plants with copper-band barrier. Trap with "Slug Saloon" or "Snailer" and nontoxic, grain-based bait.
Tiny golden, red, or brown arachnids on undersides of leaves. Profuse fine webs seen with heavy infestations.	Scrape leaves and suck plant juices. Leaves become pale and dry. Plant may be stunted.	Spray with strong jet of water, insecticidal soap, horticultural oil, or sulfur. Release predatory mites.

Pest or Disease

Spittlebugs

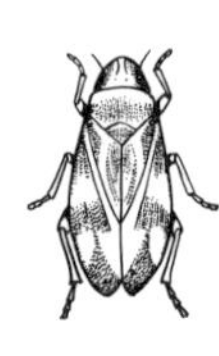
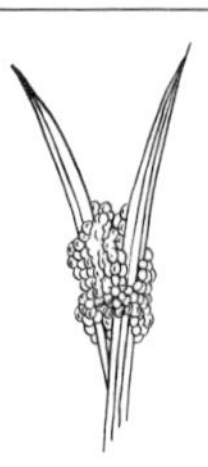

Stalk Borers

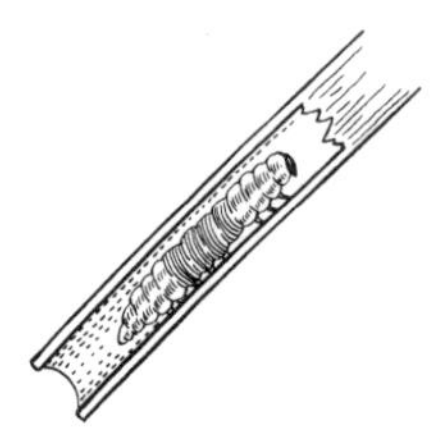

Thrips

Whiteflies

Damping-off

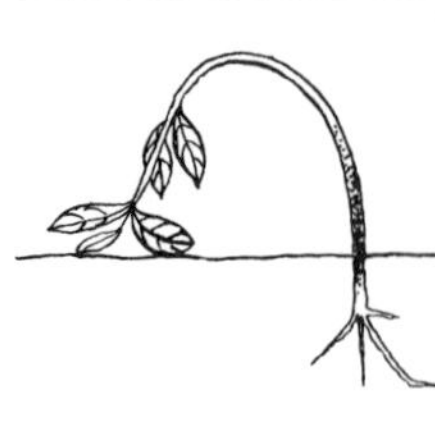

Description	Damage	Controls
Brown, green, or gray, ¼ inch long, robust sucking insects. Young covered with frothy spittle mass.	Suck plant juices. Can stunt and weaken plants, but often causes little but cosmetic harm.	If damage occurs, spray with insecticidal soap.
Cream and brown or purple, striped caterpillars found on or inside stems of herbaceous plants.	Burrow inside stems, plant wilts and dies.	Remove badly infested plants. Slit stems and kill borers or inject beneficial nematodes.
Very small, slender, brown, yellow, or black insects with narrow fringed wings. Rasping-sucking mouthparts.	Scrape and suck plant tissue. Cause browning, white flecking, and gumminess. Sometimes deform flowers, buds, and leaves.	Remove infested flowers and buds. Spray with insecticidal soap, horticultural oil, neem, or rotenone/pyrethrin.
Tiny flies with white, powdery wings. Fly up in great numbers when disturbed. Secrete honeydew.	Suck plant juices. Plants look yellow, sickly, and stunted.	Spray with insecticidal soap, horticultural oil, neem, or rotenone/pyrethrin. Catch with yellow sticky traps. Release whitefly parasite.
Soil-borne fungal disease that attacks seeds and seedlings.	Rotting of seeds and seedlings, resulting in poor stands. Stems may become black, dry, and hard.	Start seed in sterile perlite or vermiculite. Keep soil temperatures at optimum for rapid germination. Don't overwater. Provide good air circulation for seedlings.

Disease

Leaf Spots

Powdery Mildew

Rust

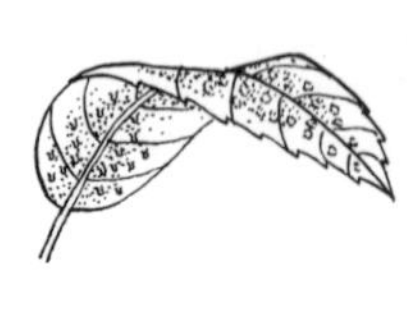

Viruses

Wilts

Description	Damage	Controls
Spots on leaves or flowers caused by fungi encouraged by humid or wet weather.	Tan, brown, or black spots on leaves or flowers. If serious, leaves may drop from plant.	Pick off damaged leaves. Spray with sulfur, Bordeaux mixture, or copper.
White, powdery fungal disease on aerial plant parts.	Reddish spots and powdery fungal growth. Leaves may be distorted and drop. Stems, buds, and flowers are also affected.	Remove and destroy badly infected leaves. Wash weekly with heavy stream of water. Spray with sulfur or Bordeaux mixture.
Fungal disease leaving orange powdery spots called pustules, usually on undersides of leaves.	Leaves and stems may be attacked. Infected leaves may drop.	Increase air circulation. Water at soil line or early in day. Discard fallen debris. Remove and destroy infected canes and leaves. Spray with sulfur.
Various diseases, including mosaics, that cause off-color, stunted plants. May be transmitted by aphids.	Crinkled, mottled, deformed leaves, stunted plants, poor growth.	Remove and destroy infected plants. Control the insect vector (usually aphids or leafhoppers), if present. Buy only healthy plants.
Soil-borne fungal diseases that cause wilting, stunting, and eventual death of plants.	Leaves turn yellow and entire plant may wilt and die. Roots may rot.	Remove and destroy infected plants. Sterilize pruners before reuse. Practice crop rotation. Use resistant varieties.

Buying Plants

Where do gardeners find the many and varied perennials that fill their gardens? They start some plants from seeds or cuttings that friends and neighbors have given them. Most perennials, however, particularly the newest cultivars, come either from local garden centers and specialty nurseries or by mail order.

Ordering Through the Mail

Many mail-order nurseries advertise their catalogues in the classified section of garden magazines. Plants may be available for either spring or autumn shipping. Nurseries frequently dig up plants for early spring delivery the previous autumn, then store them in refrigerators over the winter. This is necessary because field-grown plants cannot be dug when the ground is frozen. Perennials shipped in autumn are freshly dug and packed just as they begin to go dormant. Consequently they can make the transfer into your garden with less shock then plants that have been held out of the ground for long periods of time. Some plants, such as Oriental poppies, lilies (except in the coldest climates), and peonies, are traditionally planted in autumn. Some nurseries, however, do not have a full selection of other perennials available at that time.

Whether you order for spring or fall delivery, be sure to send your order in early to get the best selection, since uncommon perennials are frequently in short supply. Study the catalogues in advance to become familiar with the suppliers' policy on terms of sale, shipping dates, and plant guarantees. It is helpful to specify a shipping date that coordinates with the best planting time in your area, especially if the mail-order source is located in another section of the country. At present, delivery by United Parcel Service seems to be more reliable than the U.S. Postal Service. The cost may be higher, but plants arrive faster and in better condition.

Do not expect too much initially from mail-order perennials. You are basically buying rootstock, and the plants you receive won't look like the glowing pictures in the catalogue. Give them some time and proper care, however, and they will soon catch up with established plants in your garden.

It is important for fellow gardeners that you report to the supplier any plants that are unsatisfactory. Most nurserymen are honest and anxious to protect their reputations. Write a letter specifically describing the problem (plant dead, dried out, or unusually small) and indicate whether you want a refund or replacement. The catalogue should state the firm's policy on refunds.

Shopping at Local Nurseries

Some local retail garden centers or specialty nurseries offer catalogues, too. Try to get one before you visit the nursery, so you can determine what choices will be available. In spring you will find the best selections, but visit your garden center in summer or early fall as well to see plants at their mature height or in flower.

Look for plants that appear healthy and well cared for, with no evidence of insects or diseases present. Insect-ridden or diseased plants will not perform well, and they can also introduce problems to the healthy plants in your garden. Look for plants with deep green foliage and dense, compact growth. Attractive growth sells itself, but choose perennials with multistemmed bases instead of ones that have just a few long stalks with single flowers at the tips. When you are not sure what a mature plant will look like or the kind of sun, soil, and water it requires, ask for help. Every nursery should have a knowledgeable staff, whether it is the largest garden center in your area or a "mom and pop" operation selling plants off a back porch. If the salesperson does not answer your questions, or at least offer to find an answer, look elsewhere for your plants.

Planting
The perfect planting day is cool, cloudy, and calm. Since such days rarely seem to match the gardener's schedule, at least avoid planting on a windy day or during a heat wave. When planting perennials that have been potted in a peat-lite mix, combine part of the mix with garden soil to ease root transition from the lighter medium to the heavier one. If mail-order plants appear desiccated when they arrive, soak them in a one-quarter strength soluble fertilizer solution for an hour before planting or potting up. Water plants thoroughly after you have planted them. Unless an inch of rain falls in a week, continue to water them every three or four days until they are established.

Mail-order Nurseries versus Garden Centers
Is it preferable to buy plants from a local garden center or from a mail-order nursery? Before you decide, consider the advantages of each.

When you buy plants locally, you can see what you are getting and choose the plants individually. Plants are likely to be larger than those bought through the mail, and they will make an instant show in the garden. Since plants in garden centers are usually sold in pots, they may be held in a shady spot until it suits your schedule to plant them.

Mail-order sources frequently offer a wider selection of plants. These plants, however, are usually shipped bare root, have been out of the ground for longer periods of time, and demand immediate attention upon their arrival.

Price alone is not a reliable criterion for choosing one plant source over another, since cost is not always an indication of plant size or quality. The cost of a plant also reflects, to some extent, its availability and ease of propagation.

Whether you buy plants from a local garden center or from a mail order nursery, beware of extravagant claims for plant performance. If it sounds too good to be true, it probably is.

Nurseries

Bluebird Nursery Inc.
515 Linden Street, Clarkson, NE 68629

Bluestone Perennials Inc.
7211 Middle Ridge Road, Madison, OH 44057

Busse Gardens
635 E. 7th Street, Route 2, Box 13, Cokato, MN 55321

Caprice Farm Nursery
15425 S.W. Pleasant Hill Road, Sherwood, OR 97140

Carroll Gardens
P.O. Box 310, 444 East Main Street, Westminster, MD 21157

Crownsville Nursery
1241 Generals Highway, Crownsville, MD 21032

Garden Place
6780 Heisley Road, P.O. Box 388, Mentor, OH 44061

Hauser's Superior View Farm
Route 1, Box 199, Bayfield, WI 54814

Holbrook Farm & Nursery
Route 2, Box 223B, 5025, Fletcher, NC 28732

Chas. Klehm & Son Nursery
2E Algonquin Road, Arlington Heights, IL 60005

Lamb Nurseries
E. 101 Sharp Avenue, Spokane, WA 99202

Milaeger's Gardens
4848 Douglas Avenue, Racine, WI 53402

Park Seed Co., Inc.
Greenwood, SC 29647

Powell's Gardens
Route 2, Box 86, Highway 70, Princeton, NC 27569

Prairie Nursery
P.O. Box 365, Westfield, WI 53964

Stokes Seeds Inc.
Box 548, Buffalo, NY 14240

Sweet Springs Perennial Growers
2065 Ferndale Road, Arroyo Grande, CA 93420

Thompson & Morgan
P.O. Box 1308, Jackson, NJ 08527

Tranquil Lake Nursery
45 River Street, Rehoboth, MA 02769

Andre Viette Farm & Nursery
Route 1, Box 16, Fisherville, VA 22939

Wayside Gardens
Hodges, SC 29695

White Flower Farm
Litchfield, CT 06759

Gilbert H. Wild & Son Inc.
HPB-84, 1112 Joplin Street, Sarcoxie, MO 64862

Woodlanders Inc.
1128 Colleton Avenue, Aiken, SC 29801

Glossary

Achene
A small, dry, seedlike fruit with a thin wall that does not split open.

Acid soil
Soil with a pH value of 6 or lower.

Acute
Pointed.

Aggregate fruit
A fused cluster of several fruits, each one formed from an individual ovary, but all derived from a single flower.

Alkaline soil
Soil with a pH value of more than 7.

Alternate
Arranged singly along a twig or shoot, and not in whorls or opposite pairs.

Annual
A plant whose entire life span, from sprouting to flowering and producing seeds, is encompassed in a single growing season. Annuals survive cold or dry seasons as dormant seeds. See also Biennial and Perennial.

Anther
The terminal part of a stamen, containing pollen in one or more pollen sacs.

Areole
A raised or sunken spot on the stem of a cactus, usually bearing spines.

Axil
The angle formed by a leafstalk and the stem from which it grows.

Axis
The central stalk of a compound leaf or flower cluster.

Basal leaf
A leaf at the base of a stem.

Beard
A fringelike growth on a petal, as in many irises and some orchids.

Berry
A fleshy fruit, with one to many seeds, developed from a single ovary.

Biennial
A plant whose life span extends to two growing seasons, sprouting in the first growing season and then flowering, producing seed, and dying in the second. See also Annual and Perennial.

Bisexual
A flower with both stamens and pistils present.

Blade
The broad, flat part of a leaf.

Bract
A modified and often scalelike leaf, usually located at the base of a flower, a fruit, or a cluster of flowers or fruits.

Bristle
A stiff, short hair on a stem or leaf.

Bud
A young and undeveloped leaf, flower, or shoot, usually covered tightly with scales.

Bulb
A short underground stem, the swollen portion consisting mostly of fleshy, food-storing scale leaves.

Bulblet
A small bulb produced at the periphery of a larger bulb.

Bulbil
A small bulblike structure, usually borne among the flowers or in the axil of a leaf, but never at ground level like a true bulb.

Calyx
Collectively, the sepals of a flower.

Capsule
A dry fruit containing more than one cell, splitting along more than one groove.

Clasping
Surrounding or partly surrounding the stem, as in the base of the leaves of certain plants.

Claw
The narrowed basal portion of a petal in certain plants.

Cleft leaf
A leaf divided at least halfway to the midrib. See also Lobed leaf and Dissected leaf.

Clone
A group of plants all originating by vegetative propagation from a single plant, and therefore genetically identical to it and to one another.

Compound leaf
A leaf made up of two or more leaflets.

Corm
A solid underground stem, resembling a bulb but lacking scales; often with a membranous coat.

Corolla
Collectively, the petals of a flower.

Corona
A crownlike structure on some corollas, as in daffodils and the Milkweed family.

Corymb
A flower cluster with a flat top, in which the individual pedicels emerge from the axis at different points, rather than at the same point as in an umbel, and blooming from the edges toward the center.

Creeping
Prostrate or trailing over the ground or over other plants.

Crest
A ridge or appendage on petals, flower clusters, or leaves.

Cross-pollination
The transfer of pollen from one plant to another.

Crown
That part of a plant between the roots and the stem, usually at soil level.

Cultivar
An unvarying plant variety, maintained by vegetative propagation or by inbred seed.

Cutting
A piece of plant without roots; set in a rooting medium, it develops roots, and is then potted as a new plant.

Cyme
A branching flower cluster that blooms from the center toward the edges, and in which the tip of the axis always bears a flower.

Dead-heading
Removing blooms that are spent.

Deciduous
Dropping its leaves; not evergreen.

Disbudding
The pinching off of selected buds to benefit those left to grow.

Disk flower
The small tubular flowers in the central part of a floral head, as in most members of the Daisy family. Also called a disk floret.

Dissected leaf
A deeply cut leaf, the clefts not reaching the midrib; same as a divided leaf. See also Cleft leaf and Lobed leaf.

Division
Propagation by division of crowns or tubers into segments that can be induced to send out roots.

Double-flowered
Having more than the usual number of petals, usually arranged in extra rows.

Drooping
Pendent or hanging, as in the branches and shoots of a weeping willow.

Evergreen
Retaining leaves for most or all of an annual cycle.

Everlasting
A plant whose flowers can be prepared for dried arrangements.

Fall
One of the sepals of an iris flower, usually drooping. See also Standard.

Fertile
Bearing both stamens and pistils, and therefore able to produce seed.

Filament
The threadlike lower portion of a stamen, bearing the anther.

Floret
One of many very small flowers in a dense flower cluster, especially in the flower heads of the daisy family.

Fruit
The mature, fully developed ovary of a flower, containing one or more seeds.

Genus
A group of closely related species; plural, genera.

Germinate
To sprout.

Glaucous
Covered with a waxy bloom or fine pale powder that rubs off easily.

Herb
A plant without a permanent, woody stem, usually dying back during cold weather.

Herbaceous perennial
An herb that dies back each fall, but sends out new shoots and flowers for several successive years.

Horticulture
The cultivation of plants for ornament or food.

Humus
Partly or wholly decomposed vegetable matter; an important constituent of garden soil.

Hybrid
A plant resulting from a cross between two parent plants belonging to different species, subspecies, or genera.

Inferior ovary
An ovary positioned below the sepals, petals, and stamens, which seem to grow from its top.

Inflorescence
A flower cluster.

Invasive
Aggressively spreading away from cultivation.

Irregular flower
A flower with petals that are not uniform in shape but usually grouped to form upper and lower "lips"; generally bilaterally symmetrical.

Lanceolate
Shaped like a lance; several times longer than wide, pointed at the tip and broadest near the base.

Lateral bud
A bud borne in the axil of a leaf or branch; not terminal.

Layering
A method of propagation in which a stem is induced to send out roots by surrounding it with soil.

Leaf axil
The angle between the petiole of a leaf and the stem to which it is attached.

Leaflet
One of the subdivisions of a compound leaf.

Leaf margin
The edge of a leaf.

Linear
Long, narrow, and parallel-sided.

Loam
A humus-rich soil containing up to 25 percent clay, up to 50 percent silt, and less than 50 percent sand.

Lobe
A segment of a cleft leaf or petal.

Lobed leaf
A leaf whose margin is shallowly divided. See also Cleft leaf and Dissected leaf.

Midrib
The primary rib or mid-vein of a leaf or leaflet.

Mulch
A protective covering spread over the soil around the base of plants to retard evaporation, control temperature, or enrich the soil.

Multiple fruit
A fused cluster of several fruits, each one derived from a separate flower.

Naturalized
Established as a part of the flora in an area other than the place of origin.

Neutral soil
Soil that is neither acid nor alkaline, having a pH value of 7.

Node
The place on the stem where leaves or branches are attached.

Offset
A short, lateral shoot arising near the base of a plant, readily producing new roots, and useful in propagation.

Opposite
Arranged along a twig or shoot in pairs, with one on each side, and not alternate or in whorls.

Ovary
The swollen base of a pistil, within which seeds develop.

Ovate
Oval, with the broader end at the base.

Palmate
Having veins or leaflets arranged like the fingers on a hand, arising from a single point. See also Pinnate.

Panicle
An open flower cluster, blooming from bottom to top, and never terminating in a flower.

Pappus
A bristle, scale, or crown on seedlike fruits.

Peat moss
Partly decomposed moss, rich in nutrients and with a high water retention, used as a component of garden soil.

Pedicel
The stalk of an individual flower.

Perennial
A plant whose life span extends over several growing seasons and that produces seeds in several growing seasons, rather than only one. See also Annual and Biennial.

Perianth
The calyx and corolla or, in flowers without two distinct series of outer parts (sepals and petals), the outer whorl.

Petal
One of a series of flower parts lying within the sepals and next to the stamens and pistils, often large and brightly colored.

Petiole
The stalk of a leaf.

pH
A symbol for the hydrogen ion content of the soil, and thus a means of expressing the acidity or alkalinity of the soil.

Pinnate
With leaflets arranged in two rows along an axis; pinnately compound.

Pistil
The female reproductive organ of a flower, consisting of an ovary, style, and stigma.

Pod
A dry, one-celled fruit, splitting along natural grooved lines, with thicker walls than a capsule.

Pollen
Minute grains containing the male germ cells and released by the stamens.

Propagate
To produce new plants, either by vegetative means involving the rooting of pieces of a plant, or by sowing seeds.

Prostrate
Lying on the ground; creeping.

Raceme
A long flower cluster on which individual flowers each bloom on small stalks from a common, larger, central stalk.

Radial flower
A flower with the symmetry of a wheel; often called regular.

Ray flower
A flower at the edge of a flowerhead of the Daisy family, usually bearing a conspicuous, straplike ray.

Regular flower
With petals and sepals arranged around the center, like the spokes of a wheel; always radially symmetrical.

Rhizomatous
Having rhizomes.

Rhizome
A horizontal underground stem, distinguished from a root by the presence of nodes, and often enlarged by food storage.

Rootstock
The swollen, more or less elongate stem of a perennial herb.

Rosette
A crowded cluster of leaves; usually basal, circular, and at ground level.

Runner
A prostrate shoot, rooting at its nodes.

Seed
A fertilized, ripened ovule, almost always covered with a protective coating and contained in a fruit.

Sepal
One of the outermost series of flower parts, arranged in a ring outside the petals, and usually green and leaflike.

Sessile
Without a petiole.

Sheathing base
A tubular covering around the base of a stem or around the lower part of an internode above the node; found in grasses.

Simple leaf
A leaf with an undivided blade; not compound or composed of leaflets.

Solitary
Borne singly or alone; not in clusters.

Spadix
A dense spike of tiny flowers, usually enclosed in a spathe, as in members of the Arum family.

Spathe
A bract or pair of bracts, often large, enclosing the flowers, as in members of the Arum family.

Species
A population of plants or animals whose members are at least potentially able to breed with each other, but which is reproductively isolated from other populations.

Spike
An elongated flower cluster; individual flowers lack stalks.

Spine
A strong, sharp, usually woody projection from the stem or branches of a plant, not usually from a bud.

Spur
A tubular elongation in the petals or sepals of certain flowers, usually containing nectar.

Stamen
The male reproductive organ of a flower, consisting of a filament and a pollen-containing anther.

Standard
The upper petal or banner of a pea flower. An iris petal, usually erect. See also Fall.

Sterile
Lacking stamens or pistils, and therefore not capable of producing seeds.

Stipule
A small appendage, often leaflike, on either side of the base of some petioles.

Style
The elongated part of a pistil between the stigma and the ovary.

Subshrub
A partly woody plant.

Subspecies
A naturally occurring geographical variant of a species.

Succulent
A plant with thick, fleshy leaves or stems that contain abundant water-storage tissue. Cacti and stonecrops are examples.

Superior ovary
An ovary in the center of a flower, with the sepals, petals, and stamens attached near its base.

Tap root
The main, central root of a plant.

Terminal bud
A bud borne at the tip of a stem or shoot, rather than in the axil of a leaf. See also Lateral bud.

Terminal raceme
A raceme borne at the tip of the main stem of a plant.

Terminal spike
A spike borne at the tip of the main stem of a plant.

Throat
The opening between the bases of the corolla lobes of a flower, leading into the corolla tube.

Toothed
Having the margin shallowly divided into small, toothlike segments.

Tuber
A swollen, mostly underground stem that bears buds and serves as a storage site for food.

Tufted
Growing in dense clumps, cushions, or tufts.

Two-lipped
Having two lips, as in certain irregular flowers.

Umbel
A flower cluster in which the individual flower stalks grow from the same point, like the ribs of an umbrella.

Unisexual flower
A flower bearing only stamens or pistils and not both.

Variegated
Marked, striped, or blotched with some color other than green.

Variety
A population of plants that differ consistently from the typical form of the species, either occurring naturally or produced in cultivation.

Vegetative propagation
Propagation by means other than seed.

Whorl
A group of three or more leaves or shoots, all emerging from a stem at a single node.

Whorled
Arranged along a twig or shoot in groups of three or more at each node.

Wing
A thin, flat extension found at the margins of a seed or leafstalk or along the stem; the lateral petal of a pea flower.

Photo Credits

Ruth Allen
A well-known nature photographer, Ruth Allen studied taxonomy at the University of Pennsylvania. Recently her work appeared in the Audubon Society Nature Guides.
132B, 162A

Thomas E. Eltzroth
The co-author of *How to Grow a Thriving Vegetable Garden* and a dedicated home gardener, Thomas E. Eltzroth is also a professor of horticulture at San Luis Obispo in California.
230A

Derek Fell
A widely published garden writer, Derek Fell also has a large collection of plant photographs. His publications include *Annuals,* an HP Book; his photographic work appears in numerous illustrated articles on gardening.
109B, 143A, 197A, 235B

Pamela J. Harper
Serving as a consultant on this book, Pamela J. Harper has an outstanding library of photographs of plants and gardens numbering some 80,000 slides. She is also a well-known horticultural writer and lecturer. More than half of the pictures included in this guide and the cover photograph are credited to Mrs. Harper.
76A, 76B, 77A, 77B, 80A, 80B, 81A, 81B, 82A, 82B, 83B, 86A, 87A, 87B, 88B, 89A, 90B, 92A, 93B, 95A, 95B, 96A, 96B, 97A, 97B, 98B, 100A, 100B, 101A, 102A, 103A, 103B, 104B, 106B, 107A, 107B, 108A, 108B, 109A, 110A, 110B, 111A, 111B, 112B, 113A, 113B, 114A, 114B, 115A, 115B, 116B, 117A, 118A, 119A, 119B, 120B, 121A, 124A, 124B, 125A, 127A, 128A, 128B, 129A, 129B, 131A, 131B, 132A, 133A, 133B, 134B, 135B, 136A, 137B, 138A, 139B, 140B, 141B, 142A, 143B, 144B, 145B, 147A, 148B, 149A, 149B, 150B, 151A, 151B, 153A, 153B, 154A, 155A, 155B, 156B, 158A, 158B, 159A, 159B, 160A, 160B, 161A, 162B, 163A, 163B, 164B, 165A, 166B, 167A, 168B, 169A, 170A, 171A, 171B, 172B, 173A, 174B, 175A, 175B, 176A, 177A, 177B, 178A, 179A, 179B, 180B, 182A, 182B, 183A, 183B, 184B, 186A, 187A, 190A, 191A, 191B, 192A, 192B, 193B, 195A, 195B, 196A, 196B, 197B, 200A, 201A, 201B, 202B, 203B, 204A, 204B, 205A, 205B, 206A, 207A, 207B, 208A, 208B, 209A, 209B, 210B, 211A, 212A, 212B, 214A, 214B, 215A, 215B, 216A, 217A, 217B, 219B, 220A, 220B, 221A, 221B, 222A, 222B, 223A, 223B, 224B, 225A, 225B, 226A, 226B, 227B, 228A, 228B, 229A, 230B, 231A, 231B, 232A, 233A, 233B, 234B, 235A, 236B, 237A, 237B, 238B, 239A, 239B, 240B, 241A, 241B, 242A, 242B, 243A, 243B, 244A, 244B, 245A, 245B, 246B, 247A, 247B, 248A, 249A, 250A, 250B, 251A, 251B, 252A, 252B, 253A, 254A, 255A, 256A, 257B, 258A, 258B, 259B, 260A, 260B, 261A, 262A, 262B, 263A, 263B, 264B, 265A, 265B, 266A, 267A, 267B, 268A, 268B, 269A, 270A, 270B, 271A, 271B, COVER

The letter after each page number refers to the position of the color plates. A *represents the picture at the top and* B *the picture at the bottom. Some pictures are also in the Color Key. Photographs reproduced with permission.*

Walter H. Hodge
A leading botanist, Walter H. Hodge has photographed plants and animals throughout the world and has written some 200 papers on horticulture and natural history. He is the author of *The Audubon Society Book of Wildflowers.*
259A, 261B

Sonja Bullaty and Angelo Lomeo
A celebrated husband-and-wife team, Sonja Bullaty and Angelo Lomeo have contributed picture essays to leading publications, such as LIFE and *Horizon,* and to various books, including *The Audubon Society Field Guide to North American Trees* (two volumes) and to the Time-Life Gardening series.
125B, 190B

John A. Lynch
A photographer for 12 years, John Lynch specializes in gardening, wildflowers, and New England landscapes. His work has appeared in *Horticulture* magazine and *Flower and Garden,* among others. He contributes photographs regularly to the New York Times gardening section.
152A, 248B, 249B, 264A

Joy Spurr
A nature photographer for over 30 years, Joy Spurr manages a photographic agency in Seattle, Washington, that features natural history subjects. Her photographs have been published in numerous publications, including the Audubon Society Nature Guides and *Pacific Horticulture.* She also teaches photo workshops and writes photoessays for *Pacific Northwest* magazine.
106A, 116A, 139A, 145A, 193A, 224A, 240A, 253B

Steven M. Still
Editor of the perennial descriptions in this guide, Steven M. Still teaches at Ohio State University in Columbus and is the Executive Secretary of the Perennial Plant Association. He is a prolific photographer.
78A, 78B, 79A, 79B, 83A, 84A, 84B, 85A, 85B, 86B, 88A, 89B, 90A, 91A, 91B, 92B, 93A, 94A, 94B, 98A, 99A, 99B, 101B, 102B, 104A, 105A, 105B, 112A, 117B, 118B, 120A, 121B, 122A, 122B, 123A, 123B, 126A, 126B, 127B, 130A, 130B, 134A, 135A, 136B, 137A, 138B, 140A, 141A, 142B, 144A, 146A, 146B, 147B, 148A, 150A, 152B, 154B, 156A, 157A, 157B, 161B, 164A, 165B, 166A, 167B, 168A, 169B, 170B, 172A, 173B, 174A, 176B, 178B, 180A, 181A, 181B, 184A, 185A, 185B, 186B, 187B, 188A, 188B, 189A, 189B, 194A, 194B, 198A, 198B, 199A, 199B, 200B, 201B, 202A, 203A, 206B, 210A, 211B, 213A, 213B, 216B, 218A, 218B, 219A, 227A, 229B, 232B, 234A, 236A, 238A, 246A, 254B, 255B, 256B, 257A, 266B, 269B

Index

Numbers in boldface type refer to pages on which color plates appear.

Titles available in the Taylor's Guide series:

Taylor's Guide to Annuals
Taylor's Guide to Perennials
Taylor's Guide to Roses, Revised Edition
Taylor's Guide to Bulbs
Taylor's Guide to Ground Covers
Taylor's Guide to Houseplants
Taylor's Guide to Vegetables
Taylor's Guide to Shrubs
Taylor's Guide to Trees
Taylor's Guide to Garden Design
Taylor's Guide to Water-Saving Gardening
Taylor's Guide to Gardening Techniques
Taylor's Guide to Gardening in the South
Taylor's Guide to Gardening in the Southwest
Taylor's Guide to Natural Gardening
Taylor's Guide to Specialty Nurseries
Taylor's Guide to Shade Gardening
Taylor's Guide to Herbs
Taylor's Guide to Container Gardening
Taylor's Guide to Heirloom Vegetables
Taylor's Guide to Fruits and Berries
Taylor's Guide to Orchids
Taylor's Guide to Seashore Gardening
Taylor's Master Guide to Gardening

At your bookstore or by calling 1-800-225-3362

Chanticleer Staff

Prepared and produced by Chanticleer Press, Inc.

Founding Publisher: Paul Steiner
Publisher: Andrew Stewart

Staff for this book:

Editor-in-Chief: Gudrun Buettner
Executive Editor: Susan Costello
Managing Editor: Jane Opper
Series Editor: Mary Beth Brewer
Assistant Editors: David Allen, Leslie Ann Marchal
Production Manager: Helga Lose, Gina Stead
Art Director: Carol Nehring
Art Associate: Ayn Svoboda
Picture Library: Edward Douglas
Natural History Editor: John Farrand, Jr.
Drawings: Robin A. Jess, Sarah Pletts, Aija Sears, Alan D. Singer
Zone Map: Paul Singer
Design: Massimo Vignelli